ON WING
AND
WILD WATER

*The books that describe
Mike Tomkies' twenty wilderness
years in the Scottish Highlands:*

BETWEEN EARTH AND PARADISE
(now revised and reissued)
A LAST WILD PLACE
WILDCAT HAVEN
OUT OF THE WILD
GOLDEN EAGLE YEARS
(now revised and reissued)
ON WING AND WILD WATER
MOOBLI
LAST WILD YEARS

★

IN SPAIN'S SECRET WILDERNESS

ON WING
AND
WILD WATER

Mike Tomkies

JONATHAN CAPE
LONDON

First published 1987
This paperback edition published 1994
Text and photographs copyright © 1987 Mike Tomkies
Jonathan Cape, 20 Vauxhall Bridge Road, London SW1V 2SA

A CIP catalogue record for the book
is available from The British Library

ISBN 0-224-03683-1

Printed and bound in Great Britain by
Mackays of Chatham PLC, Chatham, Kent

Contents

This story begins where my book *Golden Eagle Years* ended.

PART ONE

1 · The Eagles in Winter

Around the mountain ramparts above the cottage, the storms howled, desisted, and struck again. Dwarf trees, which had fought hard to cling their roots to starvation rock fissures, shook their crowns in petty and impotent rage against the imminence of final uprooted death. Hailstones smashed off a remaining withered leaf here and there, and in the lulls of the storm swirls of mist eddied down to the lone human living primitively below, hiding the higher world from his eyes. Wild creatures were suffering up there. Down one gully a shivering red-deer hind limped brokenly on Sheraton-thin legs between the grey granite boulders, seeking shelter in the patch of conifer trees below. The wood, warm to her quavering gaze, would eventually become her shroud.

I had not seen any of my nearest golden eagle family since Christmas Day, and that was five weeks ago. As the winter doled out more than its usual share of rain, shrieking gales and blizzards, I worried about how the bird kings were faring. Despite the harsh weather, red-deer carrion, on which eagles largely depend for winter food in the western Highlands, had been scarce that season. So far I had found only one stag calf dying in the woods around my remote home, ten days earlier. Hoping it would help feed the eagles, I had hauled it up the steep tussocky slopes to a grassy plateau at 300 feet.

Today was not the fairest of days. The south-west winds carried wispy skeins of mist and occasional light drizzle showers, yet it was reasonably mild for the time of year, and so I decided on a long trek

7

above the eagles' 1,200-foot eyrie, to try and catch sight of any of the mighty birds. Calling Moobli, the gentle giant Alsatian who for seven years had helped me track Highland wildlife, I slung the camera pack over my shoulders and began to weave my way slowly upwards.

We soon reached the deer carcass. With disappointment I saw that it had not been touched by crows, ravens or foxes, never mind eagles. Where had the great raptors gone? Had they perhaps migrated to the gentler slopes of west Argyll, where rabbits flourished and sheep and deer carrion were more common than in our area?

On we hiked up over the dark tawny hills with their numberless crests and ridges, labouring in and out of steep gullies and burn ravines, until we came to a sharp drop at about 1,600 feet. As we veered down to the south-west Moobli began prancing, scenting high, a sure sign of some animal ahead. Sure enough, there below us in a grassy dell stood a small herd of five red-deer hinds and two calves. They were grazing a small patch of short grasses, the bright greens of which contrasted strangely with the long damp white molinia bents which lay draped like rotting straw over their acres of tussocks. I had taken enough pictures of hinds over the years so I carried on down, scaring them away.

We were now half a mile from the eyrie itself and two small glens above it. Two hundred feet lower we came to the edge of a long sharp cliff veering away to the north-west. I saw the tips of some dark twigs of a small rowan tree growing from the rockface half-way along. I wondered if I might find a new eyrie site there. I hoped I would not find a dead eaglet. It is not uncommon for young eagles to die in their first winter if they have not learnt to forage and hunt properly. The ground now fell away steeply, almost sheer, and it was so slippery on the short wet turf that I had to watch carefully where I was putting my feet.

Suddenly I heard a loud swishing noise. I looked up to see that the rowan tree, which grew out at right-angles to the cliff, was whipping up and down as if it was alive. In the same instant I caught sight of a small dark eagle winging weakly away into the void.

It was Apollo, without a doubt. I could see the white patches of the immature eagle in his wings. He looked bedraggled and in poor shape. He appeared truncated, with just two or three feathers left in his tail, a sure sign of starvation. He flapped feebly like a heron, his head and body bobbing up and down between the wing strokes as he glided unstably to the south-east and then turned, as if coming back. I took my pack off and grabbed the camera, but he turned again and vanished behind a ridge to the east.

He won't last much longer if he doesn't find any carrion, I thought. I wished then I had possessed the foresight to backpack one of the stag calf's haunches over the hills. But how was I to know? Until then I had believed all the eagle literature I had read, which held that eaglets leave their parents and cut out of the territory in which they are reared in late autumn, or at the very latest by December.

I climbed up to the rowan, which proved to be an ideal eagle perch or roosting site as it was protected by rock on three sides. There were two white splashes below the tree, showing that Apollo must have been eating *something* fairly recently. I was sure he had been perching on the trunk of the rowan and watching the deer, doubtless hoping that one of the calves would drop.

I felt sorry for poor Apollo. I had a special reason for wanting him to survive, for I had watched him growing up and flying from the nest since he had hatched from the egg.

For seven years I had tried to follow the fortunes of his mother, a massive dark veteran female who had mysteriously appeared over my head on many a trek, as if she were curious about the solitary human who had moved into the lonely cottage on her territory. I had been struck with awe at my very first sight of her, when she had tried to land on the tall spruce that dominates the woods around my home one windy day in March. Her wings spanned at least seven feet, and when I witnessed the majesty of her flight, the way in which she was able to 'jet glide' on the very edge of the wind at great speeds without the need of a single wing-beat, I had felt her to be truly nature's dark angel of death. She moved serenely, mistress of the aerial chase, and I named her Atalanta, after the fleet mythical Greek goddess of the Calydonian Hunt.

Atalanta inspired in me a relentless fascination with golden eagles, and over the years, both alone and through the help of fine young keeper friends, I studied six pairs of eagles at their nests, and located twenty-seven eyries in an area of three hundred square miles. This work, under licence from the Nature Conservancy Council, which required me to make detailed reports on the birds' breeding success, was arduous.

It seemed almost a personal reward when last year Atalanta successfully raised twin eagles in Eyrie 27. By then she had acquired a new mate, a dapper chunky young male who could not have been more than four years old for he still had white plumage at the base of his wings. I named him Melanion, after the mythical Greek youth who married Atalanta after beating her in a foot race by throwing down golden apples which she paused to pick up. To rear twin chicks is rare in the eagles' world for usually the weaker, smaller chick is bullied by the larger or else perishes in the competition for food. Watching from a hide as the two grew up amicably together, not once squabbling, had been a fine experience.

The smaller chick liked to warm himself in every patch of sun on the nest, so I named him Apollo, after the Greek god of the sun. The bigger female chick seemed to seek the shade so I called her Diana, after the goddess who drove the moon chariot. I attributed the extra-ordinary success of this nest to young Melanion as much as to Atalanta's competence as a mother, for he had brought in an exceptional amount of prey. Once I saw him come in with two young curlews, one in each set of talons, and set them three feet apart on the long nest ledge, as if to ensure the chicks would not fight over the food.

After witnessing the eaglets' first flights on July 5, and finding them still being attended by their parents almost a week later, I became worried as summer turned to autumn and I did not see either of them. Then, on October 26, while hiking with Moobli along the boggy shore of the loch which stretches below my cottage, I looked up to behold a superb sight. Above me, Atalanta was sailing airily along, closely followed by Melanion. Then the eaglets came to join them. The four huge birds began soaring round each other, the immature white wing patches of Diana and Apollo blazing like metallic fires in the afternoon sunshine. Glad as I was to know both eaglets were surviving well, I was even more surprised some moments later when two more eagles, adult male and female, headed in from the north and for a while there were six eagles circling amicably round each other. It was the third time I had known this multiple flying of eagles in autumn, and it had seemed a sure indication that the birds' territorial instincts lessen after the nesting season.

I wondered what the explanation could be, for all the eagle books I had read held the birds to be fiercely territorial. In the years I had studied them through all the seasons, however, I had sometimes seen eagles flying over another pair's territory, and never had I witnessed them being molested or driven off by the resident pair. Indeed, I had come to regard eagles as highly sagacious birds. Did they possess ways of communicating with each other, even to the point of agreeing over territories? Perhaps the adults in such multiple autumn flyings are related to each other. Nevertheless, it was with this extraordinary sighting that I ended my book, *Golden Eagle Years*.

On treks during the following winter I kept a sharp lookout for the eagles but did not see one again until November 21. On that mild but windy and misty day, filled with driving drizzle, a female black-cap (rare in the area) landed on my bird table. I went outside to see if it had a mate, and there spotted Atalanta heading over from the east. She soared above the small west wood, shook her wings like a giant tern, as if trying to dislodge the rain drops from her long wing feathers, then fell rapidly towards the shore beyond the wood with her huge talons extended. The estate deer stalkers had made one of their infrequent boat trips up the loch to cull hinds that morning and I wondered if they had left a gralloch (the gut contents) or a hind's head on the shore. I stalked carefully through the wood but by the time I reached the shore Atalanta had gone. There was no sign of any deer remains.

After heavy snowfalls I took Moobli for a trek on the last day of the month. It was bitterly cold. Although the sun had risen above the southern hills around midday, it was still low in the sky and its bright beams did nothing to warm me. We toiled up the steepest gully, where all the water pools were frozen over. My left foot went through the ice and was soaked. I swiftly wrung out my double socks, but the foot hurt with cold for the rest of the trek. We were heading over the top, slippery hard crusted snow making steep descents dangerous, when I noticed many hooded crows and ravens on the highest hill a mile up to the north-east. There was something white and flocculent lying on a heathery ridge. Just then Atalanta, followed by Melanion, flew over the peak from the north and began to circle as I took photos.

As we crouched behind a large rock, I saw the eaglet Diana fly over from the north-east, circle the crows and land on a ridge a quarter-mile to the east of them. I knew it was Diana not only because of her large size but from the distinctive squashed oval shape of her creamy wing patches. Just then another dark cross-like shape wafted over from the west. It was Apollo, again distinguishable because he was smaller, as were his wing patches which were shaped in a rough parallelogram. We waited in the freezing cold, hoping the eagles would go to what looked like a sheep carcass, but presently they all took off and vanished over the peaks to the north.

We hiked up over the snow, skirting the deep drifts, and found the carcass of an old ewe. It had been opened up at the shoulder. From Moobli's scenting behaviour and his cocking a leg on tufts, I knew it was the work of a fox. I soon found large fox prints, a full 2¼ inches long, in the snow beyond the threshed-about area. If the eagles needed the ewe meat they would soon return, so we left quickly. On the way home I checked an eyrie in a short but sheer rockface, the first I had ever found and the closest to the cottage. To my surprise, a long hank of the sheep's wool lay draped over the nest, which also had a few new sticks added to it. If it was good to know both eaglets were still alive, it was even better to anticipate that Atalanta and Melanion might use this eyrie in the spring. We had no sooner reached home than Melanion came right over the cottage, banked and headed straight back to the north. Perhaps he had come to ensure that we had departed.

I left the area alone for a while, then hiked up to the peaks under a dark sky amid hail showers on Christmas Day. There was nothing left of the ewe carcass but scattered wool, the skull and part of the spine. As we stood looking at it, Diana came overhead and glided to land on a ridge to the north-west.

Atrocious weather set in after that, giving me on December 30 the worst boat trip of my entire life. It took an hour and a half in a howling gale, banging up and down in crashing waves, to reach the small bay six miles away where I parked my Land-Rover in a pine wood. The Unilever fish farm which had been set up in the bay the year before, with assurances that only a few experimental tanks were to be established, now displayed so many tanks that I was forced to go broadside to the waves and the boat shipped a lot of water. The wooden runways on which I hauled the boat out of the water on a trolley had begun to rot. The next storm smashed them up. After a forty-four-mile drive to the nearest town, I discovered the price of timber had risen so high that I could afford only enough to make one long new one.

As the days passed under leaden skies, I felt I was living in a sombre tomb. The five hours of daylight at this time of year were so dismal that often I had to light the paraffin lamp at midday in order to see at my desk near the window. I seriously began to question in this, my fifteenth year of living in the wilds, the wisdom of carrying on. Although my wildlife books had attracted excellent reviews, I was still barely earning a living from them. In real terms I was making far less than I had fifteen years earlier as a journalist in Hollywood. Did my nature books have much real effect anyway? My work seemed to be largely ignored by learned journals and the academic world.

Other things were going wrong too. A long-promised contract for a book had not materialised, although I had almost finished the year and a half's slog writing it. Moobli had developed an arthritic growth in a rear leg and had begun to limp on treks. If the condition did not improve it boded ill for his future. During the last two eagle seasons I had experienced pains in my knees when carrying heavy packs over the mountains, and a doctor had informed me I had osteo-arthritis.

Apart from loneliness, which again had begun to bite into my spirit just when I thought I had it beaten, the way of life was becoming a burden. Whereas most mountain-trekking men operated from a comfortable home base, mine was extremely harsh and demanding. In severe winter weather, I often had to wheelbarrow water from the burn fifty yards away, after breaking the ice when the pipe that usually brought it froze solid. Just to keep going I had to maintain boats, engine and cottage, cultivate my garden for vegetables, carry and chop wood to keep warm, scythe hay, cage young trees, write a score of letters every week to readers of my books, file cuttings, type my lengthy diaries and new books, make my own meals, wash and mend clothes, battle with the loch in storms to fetch mail and supplies – all before I even set foot on the Hill, which was the *main* work. Well, I chose this way of life, so quit grumbling!

One thing above all else held me to my Highland fastness – the lure of the eagles.

2 · A Matter of Life and Death

It was because I had not seen any of the birds for five weeks that I set out with Moobli on that early February day to check the area round the eyrie in which they had been raised. I wanted to find out whether the eagles were still on the territory, and if so how they were faring. It was then that I saw Apollo winging weakly away from the lone rowan tree on the long rockface.

I decided to work my way down over the two small glens to check Eyrie 27 itself. Perhaps we would find Diana nearby. As this was the time of year when eagles were courting, and for a month had been refurbishing old eyries with new twigs and branches, I would not go close to the nest. Instead, I headed round behind the eyrie cliff, then towards the west where I could have a clear view of the nest ledge from over two hundred yards. It was not likely that Atalanta would use the eyrie again this year, for in the years of studying six nesting pairs I had only once known eagles use the same nest two seasons in succession. Just in case she did use it again, however, I had made a superb new hide site by persuading a visiting friend the previous autumn to help me dig out with a crowbar a suitable hole among huge sunken boulders. This was a task I could not have accomplished alone.

We were heading along a broad ledge well behind the eyrie cliff when something made me look up at the crest above us. Atalanta was winging towards the spot where Apollo had been perched with some prey in her talons. Suddenly she turned into the south-west

14

wind, disappearing and reappearing in the misty rain, then flew slowly behind a ridge. I ran up an almost sheer slab of rock to see her coming down, her wings tucked back and the huge grapnel talons of one foot extended for landing. I stalked her carefully through the heather and had just spied her perched on a large rock when she took off again. I saw that her talons were now empty. She spread her death-angel wings and was across the wide corrie below the eyrie in seconds. As often, she did not just flap and fly – she felt the tensions in the slight winds, decided where to go, set her wings back and suddenly began to move fast and smoothly as if powered by light itself. Soon she was just a dark dot against the slopes of the largest mountain south of the loch, the one I called Eagle Rock mountain. Again she had gone over the territory of another pair of eagles. I went over to the rock and found a headless grouse from which all the main wing feathers had been plucked.

If it was surprising to find Apollo still on the eyrie ground in February, it was even more astonishing that Atalanta had been intending to feed him. Clearly she had realised he was in poor shape and had been bringing the grouse to him. Again it went against all the books. She had turned after seeing Apollo was not on the rowan-tree perch, had dropped the grouse, and had then headed away to the south-west, no doubt after seeing us. I was sorry to have accidentally interrupted her mission, but knowing eagles can locate their young on the ground, never mind in the air, from a distance of two miles, I hoped she would find him again and feed him the grouse. With so many tail feathers missing, I doubted Apollo's ability to hunt for himself, and felt sadly that his days were numbered.

Quickly, I checked the eyrie and saw it had been slightly built up with a few fresh heather sprigs. This meant little as eagles usually titivate several nests before deciding which one to use. With the fine new hide site, it would be wonderful if Atalanta and Melanion bred in it again this season.

Calling Moobli, who had begun to limp again, I hastily cleared away from the area. We tramped back over the hills to Wildernesse, the name I had given to the old stone cottage that stood like a well-rooted oak below a gorge in the Inverness-shire mountains, my home for the past eight years. As Moobli flumped down on his bed I realised I had only felt a few knee twinges during the whole seven-mile mountain trek, though I had not also been carrying a hide as well as the camera gear.

Four days later, having seen nothing of the eagles in the vicinity, I hiked up to the deer-calf carcass. It had been almost totally demolished by foxes, and by badgers too, judging by some nearby dung pits and the way skin had been flensed back neatly from the bones. There was nothing much left now for the eagles.

I started searching the woods for any other deer that had died. Suddenly Moobli got a scent in the strong north-easterly wind and began prancing excitedly. Thinking he might put up a fox for me to photograph, and knowing that with his limp he could not catch it, I gave him the command to go on. He shot off at a speed I no longer thought him capable of to the north and vanished through the trees. I looked for him up to the 300-foot level and finally found his paw scrapes in the earth near the pool which fed our water pipe. It had been raining heavily and the burn was a raging torrent. Surely he could not have crossed it?

It was an hour before he returned, his muzzle bloody, his gut full, his flanks wet. I told him off and slapped him for his rare lapse, then urged him to take me to whatever he had eaten from. He took me to the burn and stared across into the clearing on the far side. Obviously he *had* crossed it. I went back into the cottage for metal-spiked wellingtons which would not slip on the rocks, and the trousers of a rain suit which would prevent water slapping over the tops of the boots. Somehow I managed to ford the swollen torrent. Moobli hurled himself across, and took me below some rock escarpments.

'Good boy, find the deer. Find the deer,' I urged him.

Soon we came upon a huge old hind which had been wounded in a rear hip, perhaps by a glancing bullet from a poor shot. The gut had been penetrated and half the upper front leg had gone, clearly Moobli's work. I had been right to tell him off.

Four more times I forded the raging waters, luckily without falling over. I collected my skinning knife and a rope, removed the rear haunches as meat for Moobli and carried them back to hang in the woodshed. Then I went back again, put the rope round the hind's neck and started dragging the carcass uphill to a broad deer crossing higher up the burn where the flow of the waters would be less. Even without her haunches she was the heaviest old hind I had ever handled, and by the time I got the remains the quarter of a mile up to the deer crossing I had run out of steam.

Next day I completed the haul. I heaved the carcass across the burn and through the deep tussocks another quarter-mile to near the remains of the old calf carcass, though in a more open spot. Even heaving the body a mere foot at a time through the tussocks made the rope burn my hands. Finally I had it in place. Would Atalanta or Melanion find it and bring Apollo, if he could fly that far, to feed from it?

During the next week a large fox opened up the hind carcass and rolled out the stomach and intestines, partly filled with half-digested heather and grasses, as if to ensure they would not taint the meat. The fox only came at night. Judging from Moobli's sniffing out of its scent posts, it prowled round the edges of the Wildernesse woods, never coming nearer than to make a furtive urination on a mossy rock near the burn in the east wood. Perhaps it considered the rest of the wood as Moobli's territory. A large female buzzard also came down in the poor dawn light, pecking the flesh away neatly beneath the flaps of skin. Of the eagles, however, there was no sign.

Nightly snow showers were followed by days of driving gales and rain, so it was like living in a marsh with a constant running tap overhead and mud everywhere. On my next supply trip I learned that the fish farm was going to expand, and that meant even more tanks in the once pristine bay where I parked my boat. I also heard that two men who had bought an isolated cottage opposite the fish farm were starting an adventure and sailing school. Another house, half a mile nearer to me than the fish farm, had been visited by the Minister for Defence, who was interested in turning it into a military training centre.

For eight years, summer and winter, I had ploughed the thirteen-mile return journey up and down the loch, and I was tired of this tedious and often dangerous chore. It was time to make a change. After some negotiations, the Forestry Commission allowed me, for a reasonable fee, to park my Land-Rover opposite my home on a track which was shortly to be made into a gravel road. It took a whole day to move the boats and to drive the Land-Rover to the new site. There was now only a two-mile return journey by boat across the loch, but I would have to drive over a 1,000-foot pass, often buried under deep snow in winter, for a return distance of fifty miles to pick up mail. Still, it was easier than having to row the length of the loch or to lead a pack animal on foot there and back, as would have been necessary in so remote a spot in the old days.

On February 15 I started trekking up to Eyrie 1, but long before I reached it a fine drizzle began to fall. Being soaked on a trek was normal enough, so I carried on. The nest ledge showed no new signs of occupation. Not a fresh twig or eagle feather was to be seen, so it was not even being used as a roosting site. I wandered up towards the highest peak to the north-east. After half a mile I saw Melanion and eaglet Diana hunting together above the peak, soaring round in easy circles, their heads occasionally turned side-ways as they glared down at a small herd of hinds and calves below. Hoping they would now find the remains of the hind I had hauled up the hillside, I abruptly turned for home, making a wide semi-circle away from the hind.

A week later, with the sun breaking through small gaps in the clouds, I cut the one remaining foreleg off the hind, put it in my backpack, and trekked with Moobli over the steep hills towards the place where we had last seen Apollo and Atalanta. Above 600 feet snow lay on all the ledges, shelves and small eyebrows of land. We found the five-toed tracks of a brave vole that had ventured from its burrow to nibble sparse new grass shoots.

Apollo's rowan-tree perch in the cleft of the long cliff looked deserted, with no white droppings to be seen. As we cut south-west down to Eyrie 27, Melanion came winging over it from the west. He flapped hard upwards, closed his wings and went into a nosedive for about thirty yards, pulled up out of it, flapped higher, nosedived again and then went into a 'jet glide' right across the loch and over Eagle Rock mountain. Like Atalanta on our last visit to the area, he crossed right over the territory of the eagle pair that nested there.

I was heartened by seeing his undulating courtship display right above last year's nesting eyrie. My spirits rose even higher when we found a new 'kill rock' or perching post just behind the eyrie cliff. These 'posts' are used by eagles to pluck and dismember prey before feeding and, in the nesting season, before taking food to the eaglets. This one was a large square rock, and the feathers and bones of a hooded crow and a ptarmigan lay all over it.

We headed west before going down to check the nest ledge, but took a more northerly route than usual round a high knoll. I noticed a high crag about a quarter-mile to the north-west. As I could not recall seeing it before, I thought I would take a closer look. It was dangerous climbing up to the daunting V-shaped crag because all the runty ridges on the nearly sheer ground were filled with ice and snow and it was hard to keep my footing. For once, Moobli could not follow and had to make a wide shallow detour to catch me up. I climbed nearer, and was just thinking the crag could be a good site for another eyrie when through the binoculars my eyes made it out. Here was Eyrie 28.

Yet again I felt the sharp thrill of discovery. For so large a bird the eagle can be extremely elusive. Indeed, I knew many village folk who had lived all their lives in eagle country without ever seeing one. Even the nests, which on rock ledges can be six feet across and two or three feet deep, are hard to see. The woven stick piles become so weathered they merge almost perfectly with any surrounding vegetation and the colours of the lichened granite cliffs.

This nest, which also faced due south like Eyrie 27, had been built up so high there was little more than a foot between the top of it and the overhanging rock. I doubted if the eagles could use it again until the gales blew some of the thick sticks away. There was nowhere to build a hide that would enable me to look down on to the nest, which was buttressed at the front by a small thick bent rowan tree, and also partly hidden by the walls of a V-shaped fissure. Even when an eaglet would be full-grown and standing at the front of the nest, I would not be able to photograph more than its chest and head, never mind see exactly what prey had been brought in.

Climbing back down, with Apollo still on my mind, I checked Eyrie 27 – no new building – then searched the steep ground below the cliff. Although I found no dead eaglet, nor any signs of one when I scanned the whole face with binoculars, I felt sure Apollo had perished. What I did see was a number of eagle breast feathers festooning a small leafless birch growing out of the rockface. At least one of the eagles seemed to be using the cliff as a roost and preening site.

I had just gratefully dropped the hind foreleg below the cliff when Moobli, who was limping again, nosed out a dead deer calf. It had many deep wounds on its neck and I felt sure it had been scavenged by the eagles. They had no real need of my foreleg after all. We went to check a fox den in a tangled cairn of rocks sixty yards south-east of the eyrie. Judging from the scattered bits of deer carrion and Moobli's frequent whines as he hobbled over the great rocks, there was a fox in it too.

At the foot of the eagles' glen on the way back I saw an eagle sitting on the edge of a heathery precipice. I crawled to a big rock just in time to take a picture as the huge bird sailed away. It was Diana, still on her parents' territory.

In early March I hiked with Moobli along the lochside ridges until opposite the eyries, then emerged on to the crest to sit in a natural armchair in the rocks below a leafless rowan. Normally eagles lay their usual two eggs (sometimes one, rarely three) between mid-March and mid-April, so if either of these nests were to be used this year they should now be well built up. I could see no signs of new activity. We climbed up to the hide site. I was staring through the binoculars, seeing that only a large tuft of tussock grasses had been dropped on Eyrie 27, when Melanion came soaring over the cliff in the bitter east winds. I made the 'keeyoo' whistle, similar to an eaglet's call, that I often made when seeing either of this pair. He turned his head to look down at us, did not circle round as he sometimes did, and took off to the south. He made two tremendous 'golden ball' dives, hurtling down like a plummet with his wings closed, opening them again to swoop up and repeat the process. Then he set his wings sideways to the wind, went into a fast glide and vanished over the ridge four miles away in just over two minutes. He must have been travelling at around 100 miles per hour.

After a further climb I found that Eyrie 28 had lost a few sticks in the gales, but nothing new had been added. I recalled then that I had not seen Atalanta for many weeks. I had always regarded her as a veteran, even old, bird.

Ten days later, boating part of the way to make the trek shorter for Moobli, I checked the eyries again. They remained in the same condition and we saw none of the eagles. I began to wonder if Atalanta was dead.

In late March I had to drive south to sign the contract for my first eagle book and to discuss which photos were to be included. At the same time I took Moobli to a leading vet. The diagnosis was dire, for spinal nerve degeneration had set in. Even with the supply of pills which the vet gave me, Moobli would never again recover his former mobility. I drove home in a despondent frame of mind, a mood that did not lift when more treks revealed that the eyries of two other eagle pairs were also unoccupied. Then suddenly everything was cast aside by an incident with another kind of rare bird which urgently needed help.

3 · Swan Song

I was working at my desk one day in early April when I heard odd faint '*hoop*' calls, given singly every few seconds. I looked out to see a lone whooper swan drifting in the water near one of the bays on the opposite side of the loch. I had seen this swan for two days now, always in the same area, and had idly wondered why it did not fly somewhere else.

As I watched, it climbed out of the water, walked slowly up the shingle of the beach, then flumped down on its stomach, abruptly facing a wall of granite. It stayed there all day, occasionally reaching back with its long neck to preen its wings and tail feathers, still emitting the odd mournful '*hoop*' note. Was there something wrong with it?

Whooper swans, which have patterns of black and pale fiery yellow on their wedge-shaped beaks and carry their heads more erectly than mute swans, had long been for me the great white angels of the loch. Having wintered here, this bird should by now have been with others of its kind on the whoopers' 500-mile non-stop flight to Iceland, where they take advantage of the short fine season so far north to rear their young. They ceased to breed in Britain in the eighteenth century, but in recent years a rare pair or two have nested in the Highlands, though not to my knowledge on my loch.

In the deserted lakes of the vast tundra, the pen incubates the three to five creamy-white to bluish eggs, which hatch exceptionally quickly for their size – sometimes in less than thirty-five days, up to nine days sooner than those of the golden eagle. The cygnets can fly when they are just over eight weeks old. Then all the birds concentrate on feeding, building stamina and strength for the great southerly flight back to their winter dormitories in Britain and Ireland, where about two thousand of them stay on the Scottish lochs.

Many a time in late October or early November have I been enthralled while in my boat to see a flock winging in from the far north. Sometimes they pass so low overhead I can hear their great wings whistling like wind harps and the music of their voices as they communicate with each other with melodic '*ungh*' and '*angha*' calls. Often they look tired, and well they might after their long non-stop journey maintaining speeds of around fifty miles an hour. One by one they widely extend their dark webbed feet, like the landing gear of planes, and with winnowing feathery back strokes of their wings, sloosh down into the brassy bright surface of the loch. Instantly each bird stretches its long neck and beak deep into the water – how good it must feel to take a drink and to rest at last after so heroic a flight, after their long night's journey into day.

Every autumn as the whoopers come winging in, sometimes shining like silver ghosts in the dawn light before the sun rises beyond the hills, there is a sense of continuity, of permanence, about the joy I feel at seeing the great white angels of the loch back again.

Whoopers are not strictly 'colony' birds, though they form loosely organised small feeding flocks in winter because they know there is safety in numbers when they feed on water plants, insects, and graze on marshy waterside pastures. If one bird spots a pair of predatory foxes, or a frisky dog, its sudden calling or flying up warns the others, and the scattering of the flock makes it harder for a single victim to be concentrated upon and taken. They also 'talk' to each other when grazing, making soft, short '*owoo*' and '*whooau*' sounds, and each swan spaces itself from its fellows so it has plenty of room to look around, feed and fly up without collision should there be an alarm.

Having now seen this swan all on its own for more than two days, I began to feel sure it was ill. Whoopers are not mature enough to breed until they are four years old and, as they can live for more than twenty years, many spend their last years without breeding. Perhaps this bird was just too old to make the long northerly flight back to the tundra. I did not think it could be poisoned from picking

22

up fishermen's lead shots in its gizzard. In recent years lead has killed many mute swans on the rivers and reservoirs farther south. Extremely little shot was used in the kind of salmon and sea-trout fishing that took place on this loch; and any lead that was lost would surely end up in waters too deep for a swan to reach it on the bottom. Yet this bird would not have cut out from its fellows for so long if it had been in good shape. Maybe, like an aged Eskimo who could no longer keep up with his or her family in the old days of the nomadic hunting trails, it had cut out to die.

In the dusk at 7.30 p.m. it was on its feet, standing at the edge of the beach and drinking. It lowered its beak into the water and then held its head up, but it seemed to be finding it difficult to swallow. It was hard to see precisely from almost a mile away. The whooper then stumbled back up to the wall of rock and stretched its neck downwards several times before flopping down again. It was still disinclined to swim and I was sure it had not eaten for several days. In the near dark it gave out the occasional '*hoop*' call, but most of the time it lay with its head and neck back under its wing feathers. I felt the poor swan was dying like most wild creatures die – alone, unloved, unwanted, deserted by its own kind. Cold on the stones, cold on the hill, cold in the forest, the slow coldness of death seeping up into its bones. Not raging at the dying of its day but taking, accepting; in a strange way, understanding its fate.

After a cold night, the next day dawned in a cloudless sky. I looked out to see the swan standing on the shore. It turned and walked weakly to below an alder tree where again it flopped down. I had no doubt now that I should try to help it. I made a loose-knotted lasso from a length of supple plaited rope and then waited until the sun had risen above the mountains. I hauled the boat out over its wooden runway, put in the petrol tank, lasso and a sack in which to put the swan if I caught it, and pulled on a pair of thick gloves. I had often read that an angry swan can break a human arm with a blow from its strong wings, but had always believed this to be a myth. At least it would have to be a somewhat feeble arm. Even so, I donned two sweaters under my largest jacket. Then I called Moobli into the boat, thinking I might need his help to round up the big bird over land.

As we set off, I saw that the swan was now in the water and paddling slowly along towards the west, still giving the odd '*hoop*' call as it went. Maybe it had just been taking a long rest after all.

Now I had the boat in the water, I decided to approach closely. If the bird took off normally, I could safely assume it was going to be all right.

As we came near the swan indeed tried to fly but just succeeded in hunching itself through the water with churning movements of its wings, the way I had once seen a bald eagle do in Canada after getting its talons into a salmon. It seemed unable to get its wings clear of the surface and to beat them with enough power to rise into the air. Clearly the swan was very weak.

I had the deuce of a job to catch it. As soon as I got close, the swan put on a spurt and twisted suddenly away at right-angles to the boat as I swept past. It could turn far more sharply than I could, and the boat's momentum made it impossible to stop in time. So round I had to go again. The bird now seemed every bit as big as a mute swan. I whirled the lasso round my head in the way a film cowboy had once taught me to do in Hollywood, but with the first throw it missed completely. On the second, the rope came down on the swan's back and dropped off again. I was about to give up the hopeless task, but then decided to have one more try.

This time the lasso snagged round the swan's left shoulder, behind the long, sharp, forward-pointing elbow of its wing. As it tried to swim away, so the rope tightened on the joint, and round the bird came. I pulled it in towards the stern of the boat, its long neck behind the engine, seized the base of the neck with my right hand, lifted the swan aboard and held its wings fast with my left arm. It was over.

To my surprise it did not struggle, apart from one weak attempt to jump out of the boat; there was no need to try and put it into the sack. On the way home I just held the swan gently round the neck with my left hand while operating the boat engine with my right. It had huge gryphon-black three-toed webbed feet which pointed inwards in a pigeon-toed way. I carried it up to the cottage under my right arm and set it down in the large kitchen. Again it did not struggle, or even try to peck, though its head and yellow and black beak were near my face. I raced out again with a rake, boated to the next bay and hauled up all the water plants I could. These I put into two large bowls of water near the swan. I also cut tender kale leaves from my garden and set these down too. Leaving the bird to settle, I took Moobli for a trek up to the peak overlooking the great glen below Guardian mountain.

As we set off I saw two dippers, Britain's smallest diving birds, in what seemed a courtship chase from the nearest islet, where common gulls had a small breeding colony. The foremost dipper, probably the female, kept landing in the water and performing somersaults before going on again, with the male tumbling in behind her each time. I checked Eyrie 1, only to find recent gales had blown away most of the old nest. There was no trace of new building. As I stood there a female kestrel glided by, fanning her long coppery wings briefly, her bright tail glinting in the sunlight. I took the sheerest route up to the peak while Moobli made a longer and more gentle detour. Suddenly I felt sharp pains in the middle of my chest, my legs felt weak, trembly, and I had to sit down. Maybe the old heart's giving out, I thought as I rested. So what? I'd sooner go here than in some hospital ward. Just then I heard a brief scuffing as a hind which had been lying down shot to her feet and went down the slope in a series of four-footed jumps like a chamois. One doesn't often see that.

When we got back I found the whooper had touched none of the food. Now, when I went near, it stood up menacingly, hissing through open beak, and held its wings open as if ready to strike out with one or the other. Well, I would have to feed it somehow. I made some bread and milk and boiled two eggs which I cut up into small pieces. Then I took hold of its neck so that I could get some of the food into its beak.

The swan did not appreciate this performance one bit and several times smashed me on the arm with a wing. It did not strike out with the whole wing but beat the elbow joint downwards with a hard smashing blow which bruised my arm. I noticed this elbow had two large bones sticking out, about an inch apart, both covered with tiny scaly feathers. It was these joints which gave such a nasty knock on the downward smash, though the blows were not hard enough to break a man's arm. Even so, the pain lasted a long time afterwards, and of course this swan was not fully fit.

I opened its beak and, looking down the gullet, saw that the windpipe was in front of the food pipe and that it was protected from food going down it by a four-muscled valve. As soon as any milk or food touched the flesh in front of it, the valve snapped shut. The swan seemed unable to swallow the food that at first I just left in its beak. In the end I had to poke the food a fair way down the gullet with the end of my smoothest bluntest toothbrush. Only then did the food go down. It took half an hour to get most of the bread and milk and eggs down the bird.

I left the swan alone for a couple of hours, then carried it out into the afternoon sunshine, set it down on the grass and sat down with Moobli a few yards away. The whooper did not try to fly or even walk away but stood looking at us, as if calmly wondering how it had ended up in so peculiar a predicament. After a while it began preening its tail feathers with its beak, and I thought then that it would be all right. Towards dusk I fed it once more, and this time it actually appeared to be trying to co-operate. At least it did not hit me with its wings again. Thinking it would recover better in its normal outdoor environment than in the artificial confines of a human kitchen, and to protect it from any marauding fox, I carried it out to the enclosures where I had once reared wildcats. There I set down the bowls of water plants, kale, a fresh supply of bread and milk and chopped-up boiled eggs.

In the morning some of the water plants and bread and milk had gone and the swan was standing up looking through the netting at the loch. I left the enclosure door wide open so that it was free to go if it chose, and if it could. All day it remained there, however, and ate no more food. Towards evening I tried to feed it again, but it simply lay there with its long neck and head extended over the grasses. When I gently lifted its head, I heard an extraordinary sound.

The swan was making it, a high, dying, humming, mewing sound, through its half-closed beak. It was a weird, high-pitched, almost singing noise which to me held the very epitome of sadness. I had read that when a swan is dying it makes a soft wailing lament, the 'swansong' in fact, but I had always believed this to be a myth. Now I knew, with a sense of dejection, that this was indeed the sound that I was hearing. I tried to coax some more food into the beak, but the swan would not eat. If it was near its end, should I carry it down to die more naturally on the loch shore? No, I decided, for a fox could well find it and add brutality to its dying moments. Instead, I moved it gently to the most comfortable grasses and shut the enclosure door.

In the morning the swan was dead, stretched out as if sleeping peacefully on the sward. One dark eye remained open, as if it had died gazing at the sky through which it had doubtless travelled many thousands of miles.

I carried the now cold bird into the cottage, marvelling at the beauty of the snow-white plumage. It measured 4 ft 4 ins from beak to tip of tail and, despite being starved, weighed 13¾ lbs. Its wings spanned seven feet exactly, about the same as those of a female eagle. I was surprised to find it had thirty tail feathers, even more than the great eagle, which usually has only twelve. Wishing to find out what had caused its death, I sent the remains to the Wildlife Analysis Unit at Eastcraigs in Edinburgh, and in due course back came the report:

> It was in poor condition and was affected with nephritis (inflammation of the kidneys) and visceral gout. The kidneys were enlarged and pale with urates in their substance, and urates were deposited on the surface of the heart. There was no obstruction of the respiratory tract and faulty heart action caused by urates on its surface could have been responsible for the symptoms shown . . . Inflammation of the kidneys in birds is a common cause of death but the reasons for the breakdown in kidney function are often difficult to determine. Various adverse environmental factors probably contribute.

I queried the nephritis and asked if they had been able to estimate the swan's age. Dr J. W. Macdonald, who had performed the post mortem at the Ministry of Agriculture, Fisheries and Food veterinary laboratory at Lasswade, wrote back to me saying that the kidneys were the organs most susceptible to any acute stress, such as chilling or water shortage.

> Possible adverse environmental factors include excessive heat, excessive cold or wild fluctuations of temperature, strong winds, lack of food or water, bullying or overcrowding. The latter would not be a problem in Argyll but these are possible factors responsible for death when infectious diseases are ruled out. I am afraid I could not age the bird.

Certainly there had been wild fluctuations recently in the weather, with sub-zero frosty nights being replaced by warm sunny days, and alternating with south-westerly gales filled with driving rain. It seemed this had been enough to cause kidney malfunction in what I felt sure was a fairly old swan.

4 · *Ancient Survivors Return*

A long spell of sunny weather followed the death of the swan, and I used the fine days, when the sun was not yet too hot, to carry on with eagle treks. As I set out with Moobli on April 10, eaglet Diana came soaring over us and I took four photos of her. She sailed in slow anti-clockwise circles, occasionally looking down at us and the cottage, then rose higher and went into a fast glide to the west. When we returned in the afternoon I saw her again, floating east-wards over unused Eyrie 1. As she went past a rockface lined with dwarf trees, a pair of kestrels launched themselves from it and began to mob her.

Flapping wildly, they managed to catch her up and started swooping round her, looking as tiny as swallows, mere shining, diving lights flashing in the sunshine around her massive form. She seemed to take no notice, and sailed serenely on until she vanished over a far ridge. The falcons then gave up. Two days later I hiked up to the rockface and found the kestrels' nesting ledge, but it was in an impossible spot for good observations or photographs.

On May 25, my fifty-fourth birthday, I decided to take a last look at Eyries 27 and 28. Boating to a convenient bay, I set off on the hard hike with Moobli. As we neared Eyrie 27 we paused to check an old fox den in some huge boulders, but it was empty. I stood up again and felt suddenly faint. Everything around me had a blackish tinge, my heart appeared to stop beating and I could hardly breathe. I felt terrible, and thought I was going to die. As a surge of panic went through me, the one thing I was sure of was that I did not *want* to die. Then came the rueful thought that if I did, at least this would be a good place to go, here below the finest eyrie of all, which had given me the finest observations and pictures so far. I stood still for a while as the blackness cleared from my vision. Moobli sat looking at me with anxious query.

'Come on, old timer,' I said. 'If you can keep going, I'm sure I can.'

We set off again, moving far more slowly and easily than usual, and eventually reached the eyrie face. Taking my time, I scrambled up. There were some eagle's incubating feathers on the ledge and a new pellet of regurgitated fur and bones, but there was no fresh vegetation. I was sure Atalanta had not laid eggs there this year. One of the eagles was using it just as an occasional roost. We climbed on up and found a new clump of sword rush on Eyrie 28 but no other sign of use.

I was feeling fine now. We tramped right over the peak to search the northern faces of that mountain range, but apart from a new roosting site containing a few feathers and white splashes below an umbrella canopy of rock, we found no evidence of new eyries.

Suddenly there was a swishing noise above. I looked up to see Melanion flap upwards and then go into his territorial 'ball of gold' dive, level out and glide down to the west. I tried to storm back over the tops to see where he went, but there was just too much terrain in between us and he had gone. I sat down for a rest and to eat my lunch above some sheer dark cliffs which overlooked a yawning glen. I had just tossed the last scraps to Moobli when I saw a huge brown bird sailing towards us from the west, its great wings held out in a shallow V.

As I grabbed my camera from the pack, another dark brown bird, which I thought was a big female buzzard, appeared as if from nowhere and struck into the first bird which turned half-way upside down before righting itself again. I saw then that the second bird was Melanion and either he had made a symbolic food pass to the first bird, clearly a female eagle, or had actually attacked it. He turned off, and the larger bird headed towards us.

It was Diana, the two white ovals on her huge wings showing clearly. As she circled right over our heads, I managed to take three wonderful pictures, the best I had ever taken of a flying eagle. I could see her feet and black talons bunched beneath her tail, her golden eyes and beak, everything, before she vanished over the tops to the east. I was still not sure if Melanion had actually meant to drive her away, but as she was still on her parents' territory at this extraordinarily late date, right in the middle of what should have been their breeding season, it seemed a distinct possibility.

On the last mile, as we headed home, Moobli's weak rear leg collapsed completely, and he had to hop along on three legs as best he could. Fortunately the way was all downhill, but I knew then that his trekking days were virtually over.

Two days later I set off alone to check a distant eagle nest, Eyrie 18. Moobli gazed at me sadly as I left him and trudged off at the start of a really hard hike which I had come to call the 'killer trek', and which involved negotiating three deep glens and a total of 12,000 feet of steep elevations, both up and down. Within two hours I was on the high tops overlooking the deepest of the glens, on the far side of which lay the most northerly of my eyries. I still had to descend almost 2,000 feet and then climb another 1,000 feet up to it. All round me golden plovers sounded their mournful '*klee*' notes from the tops of rocks, while below a large herd of hinds and yearlings ran this way and that on the turfy ridges of the steep slopes. They were somehow aware of danger but could not get any scent. One hind walked with her long ears so far forward they looked like antennae. The sky had clouded over. As I began the almost sheer descent, I was hit by so heavy a shower I was forced to shelter under a looming rock.

Eventually I reached the dark buttress which contained the nest. The thick, stunted rowan tree in a rocky recess thirty yards south of the nest was still being used as a roosting site. Preened eagle feathers fluttered from its twigs; two pellets lay below it and there were white splashes everywhere. To my surprise and disappointment, after climbing to the north of the eyrie so as to look down into it, the nest contained only one fresh sprig of heather. I was sure it was not in use, for if it had been I would have seen an eagle by now.

For a long time I had been wondering if this nest was indeed one of Atalanta's, though it seemed too far away from her other eyries. Three years earlier I had found a well-fledged eaglet in it, but had not seen either of the adults at that time. If it was one of hers, I was baffled by the apparent fact that she was not breeding this season.

Disheartened, I scrambled back down to the river. I had just started the hard, almost sheer climb out of the glen, when I saw an eagle resembling Melanion heading east over the crests far above. After a half-mile it flew back to the west again, then turned to the south-west and disappeared from sight. I wondered then if this pair had another eyrie somewhere on the south side of the glen. Any attempt to look for it that day, however, was unthinkable. The sky had turned black and oily, and torrential rain began to fall. The climb out was hell! At times I was hanging on to the slippery steep slopes with both hands and the toes of my wet boots, unable to go farther as the hissing rain drenched me to the skin. Down I had to go again, and again, seeking other routes. Eventually, chest heaving like an old horse escaped from the knacker's yard, I hauled myself over the top.

As I traversed the remaining four miles of glens towards home, sploshing in and out of cold black peat pools, slipping often as I negotiated the rocky ravines of burns, I felt a mere speck in a mighty landscape. Lightning flashed among the dark granite crags, thunder banged its awesome tympani around the peaks, and the rain fell mercilessly, laced with the icy cold of winter. Despite my exertions, I shivered for most of the way. I had seldom been so glad to see Wildernesse, a tiny, white, green-roofed dot, appear below me on the final descent. Moobli's joy at my return was certainly matched by mine.

I should explain here that golden eagles, as well as black-throated divers and peregrines, are among more than eighty protected species of birds on Schedule 1. It is an offence to possess, take, sell or kill any of these birds. It is also an offence to disturb any such bird while it is building a nest or is in, on or near a nest containing eggs or young, or to disturb its dependent young. Before 1976 the maximum penalty for such an offence stood as low as £25. Conservationists continued to press and the penalty was gradually raised until, under the Wildlife and Countryside Act of 1981, it stands today at £2,000. Yet we need precise knowledge of birds like eagles – their diet, nesting, breeding and hunting success, their relationship to stock farming, and many other factors that affect their lives – if we are to apply appropriate conservation measures. In order to facilitate the gathering of information, the Nature Conservancy Council issues a few qualified individuals each year with special examination and photographic licences which allow one legally to observe the birds closely at the nest for scientific, educational and conservation purposes.

Although I had applied for my usual licences to work with eagles and monitor their breeding success, this year's renewals had not yet arrived. There had been rumours that the Nature Conservancy Council was planning to launch a full-scale survey of golden eagles, including the two pairs in the Lake District, and I wondered if that was why the licences were delayed. Perhaps they did not wish me to do the work this year, or wanted eagle areas left completely alone.

As the weeks passed, however, it slowly became clear that in any case, licences or not, I would be able to do little work with eagles in this season. More treks revealed that the forest immediately below the two main eyries of Pair Two had recently been felled, and the two other eyries I knew for the pair were not occupied. A visit to one of my keeper friends, Greg Hunter, who had helped me in my first season to photograph eagles on his huge estate many miles to the west, revealed that Pair Three were not breeding either this year. This was probably due to a hill fire which had got out of control in their territory, destroying much vegetation over an area of 2,000 acres. Yet Greg had received his own licences and was intending to photograph Pair Four himself. While he would have helped me again if I had asked, I felt I now had enough pictures of eagles to forgo the seventy-mile return drives that would be involved, especially with the highly increased cost of petrol. Nor did I feel it right for me to muscle in on, or cramp, his own work. The main nest of Pair Five, which I had already worked for two seasons, had lost five feet off its top and, along with two other eyries of this pair, was now not being used. The pair probably had another eyrie, but my new parking situation meant a sixty-mile return drive just to start searching their terrain. Pair Six were breeding, but the eyrie was in an inaccessible 1,600-foot cliff, impossible to photograph. In any case, I was more interested in the two nearest pairs that I had been watching all year round. These would not take up too much time while I was racing to finish my first eagle book, for I needed the money due on its delivery to the publishers. To make matters worse, the ballrace of my 640mm telephoto lens broke down in early June. Until I could have it expertly repaired on my next trip south, I could only operate it by jamming it slightly with oiled cloth, and it was of little use with fast-moving birds like eagles.

On June 5 a marine biologist I knew called John, who worked at a White Fish Authority fish farm on the coast, came up to me in the store at the end of the loch, his face animated, his voice filled with excitement.

'Mike! Just the man I want to see. I was walking along the sea-shore the other afternoon when I saw an oyster-catcher flying along. It was calling loudly and moving fast. Suddenly a big sort of hawk came down out of the sky at great speed and hit into it. There was a puff of feathers, then the oyster-catcher fell to the ground, dead. The hawk flew off, perhaps because I was near, but I left quickly so it could get back to its meal. What could it be – a goshawk, pere-grine falcon? It was a good deal bigger than a kestrel.'

He described the bird as having bluey-black upper parts, with dark bars across a creamy chest. We tried to reason it out. I doubted that even a 14-inch female kestrel could strike down a hefty fast-flying 17-inch oyster-catcher in flight. The kestrel has coppery-rufous upper parts anyway. Goshawks had been increasing in Britain in recent years, either deliberately released or escaping from captivity; by 1980 the Royal Society for the Protection of Birds had established that there were some 60 pairs in 13 different areas. The 21-inch goshawk was quite capable of striking down an oyster-catcher but, again, the goshawk has dark-brownish upper parts. To me it sounded more like the work of a peregrine falcon, probably a female, which is 19 inches long. At any rate, I envied John this sighting.

Later, as I boated home, I saw an even rarer bird in action. The magnificent black-throated diver was winging westwards over the loch's surface with a fish in its bill. These 27-inch-long divers, with their superb summer plumage of greys, blacks, purples, and sym-metrical griddles, bars and circles of white, are perhaps the most spectacular of our water birds. They are rarer even than the golden eagle, numbering only some 150 pairs in all Britain, and are mainly confined to the larger lochs of the Highlands and Islands.

These divers are truly ancient survivors from the Palaeocene era of thirty-five million years ago, just after the dinosaurs became extinct and the early toothed birds evolved into two main types – those with well-developed wings such as we know today, and almost wingless water birds which had well-developed legs for swimming. In a sense divers, with their short wings and powerful rear-situated legs for diving after fish, represent a missing link. Because they nest only a few feet from the shoreline, their eggs can be washed away when rainstorms cause loch levels to rise, when levels change due to the use of waters for hydro-electricity, or just from the wash of power boats. Being wary of humans, they are easily put off their nests by unknowing fishermen or trippers in boats, causing the eggs to chill. In north America, where they are known as 'loons', their population has dwindled by more than 50 per cent in the last fifty years, and Loon Preservation Committees have been set up to warn lakeside residents and boat-owners to stay away from the nest sanctuaries, and to go slow when passing near them. The Cree Indians named the bird *mookwa*, or spirit of the northern waters, and believed its weird wailing call represented the anguish of a dead warrior denied entry to heaven.

For seven years I followed the fortunes of my nearest pair, which nested twice on the nearest islet, and in that time reared seven young to the flying stage. This year again I applied for a licence to photograph them, but because they were not nesting on the same islet, and because of all my other work and the fact that the licences had not come, I had so far not searched other distant islets for their nest.

Almost a month later, when I was in the store again, a young man who had once helped me work with eagles said he was sure he had seen a peregrine falcon flying near a certain cliff not far from the sea. I drove down to take a look. The cliff was a huge, dark, forbidding rampart that reared completely sheer above a small public road. It was over 700 feet high and filled with small ledges and rocky overhangs. Dwarf oaks, birches, ash trees and rowans sprouted from any niche where their roots could take hold.

On the other side of the single-track road, and opposite the cliff, rose a steep rounded hill, about 150 feet high, which was covered with long heather. Its top made a good vantage point, and years before I had used it to locate two ravens' nests on one of the craggy buttresses of the cliff. I climbed up and trained the binoculars. The ravens' nests were still there, both under sheltering overhanging rocks, with one at ten o'clock and five yards above the other. The lower nest had white splashes below it and had certainly been used that year, but ravens are early nesters and any young which had been raised there would be flying by now.

For over three hours I kept a good watch all along the great cliff in cloudy but fair light. Not a peregrine did I see. The odd thing was that I saw no ravens either, yet there were nearly always ravens flying in the vicinity of that cliff when they had nested there, even in summer. Well, I thought, maybe my young friend had only seen a kestrel after all.

On July 11 I visited Greg Hunter and we had a rare night out together in a luxurious restaurant and bar which had once been a castle. Naturally, I told Greg my eagle woes and that my licences had not arrived anyway. He said his licences had only recently arrived, but he too had failed with eagles this season. Busy with estate work, he had intended to start photography late in the season, but when he had checked the larch-tree eyrie of Pair Four in late June he had found the single eaglet dead in the nest.

Several of our acquaintances came into the bar that night, one of them another young man who had helped me with Pair Five in a previous year. When he heard our news, he said, 'You lads should have checked with me a few weeks back. I accidentally found a new eyrie for that pair while gathering sheep. It had a fat healthy eaglet in it too!'

He described the rough location of the new eyrie, above a small dark lochan, less than a mile from the pair's two main eyries.

After a rather festive night, I gladly accepted Greg's kind offer of a bed at his home. Next morning, as we exchanged friendly banter and ate a hearty breakfast, I found I had so enjoyed the rare human company and heady talk that I was loath to return home immediately to isolation. As it was also a Sunday, Greg had the day off. We decided to go on a trek and try to find the new eyrie. We assembled our cameras ready for action and prepared to set off in our separate vehicles.

'If I see anything I'll stop,' Greg said.

We had gone only half a mile above a wide bay on a sea loch when Greg suddenly pulled his van up behind a small cliff and leaped out with his camera.

'Otter!' he hissed as I stopped behind him and leaped out with mine. 'Watch it all the time and don't move until it dives.'

I had spent many hours immersed in deep heather above that bay over the past few years, believing its rolling kelp beds and rocky islets to be an ideal place for otters, but had never seen one. This morning I had barely given the place a cursory glance as we had driven along. But there, some fifty yards out, was the black dot of an otter's head, making a wide V in the calm surface as it weaved along. Then it dived.

Immediately Greg, who is 6 ft 3 ins tall and well built, went off like a rocket, at a speedy gallop I didn't know he had in him, and I felt the long unused sprint muscles in my thighs pull painfully as I tried to catch up. He was using exactly the same technique for stalking a swimming otter that I did for diving ducks, and which I thought I had invented – wait till they dive, run like hell to get nearer, then freeze motionless as they resurface.

We gained the screen of some roadside crags before the otter came up again. Then we worked our way through leg-breaking rocky gullies and thick tangling bracken and heather down the steep escarpment to the shore. A few yards ahead, right on the edge of the sea, was a huge rounded rock, thirty feet long and five feet high, a perfect natural hide. We crawled on our stomachs and slowly edged our cameras over it.

The otter was swimming nonchalantly along, pausing now and then to peer into the sky and show its creamy throat, hanging motionless in the water like a seal. The whole sea was alive with sprats, shimmering like sequins as they twisted sideways in the sunshine. Black-headed gulls wafted above the surface, then dived in after them with short plunges of just their heads and shoulders, like amateur ospreys, missing more fish than they caught.

At first, the otter seemed unconcerned, just rolling and gambolling in the watery paradise. Then his head twisted sharply from side to side and he dived, his thick poker-like tail flopping over comically, the last of him to disappear. He came up ten yards farther along with a sprat in his mouth, and swam to a rock covered with seaweed.

Without hurry the otter clambered out, pinned the sprat down below a webbed forepaw, then shook his white-whiskered head with a curiously slow sideways motion to clear water from his hair and ears, and scented the air before munching up the sprat in seconds.

He stayed on the rock for a few minutes, enjoying the heat of the sun as I clicked away, then slid back into the water. He resurfaced two minutes later, climbed to another rock crevice, nosed under the seaweed and came out with a medium-sized crab in his mouth. One of the crab's pincers seemed to have a tight grip on his neck. The otter blithely ignored this and cheerfully crunched up the crab, its hard shell apparently giving no trouble to his sharp teeth.

We watched him for half an hour, casually swimming along, rolling in beds of kelp as if enjoying the caresses of the soft weeds against his body. Then, as otters have an uncanny ability to do, he slid below the surface and disappeared. I noticed Greg had taken only one photograph and asked him why.

'Oh, I have closer stuff on otters than that!' he replied. He liked to put one down, did Greg.

We drove off to find the eyrie with lighter hearts. Like many experiences in the wild, it had been all the more wonderful for having been entirely unexpected. Parking Greg's van off a main road, we both continued in my four-wheel drive Land-Rover over a bumpy, muddy track until we reached the cover of a small wood. We climbed up the steep hill to over 1,000 feet, Greg leading the way, his great young legs stumping like pistons, so that I had a hard task to keep up. Finally, we sat on a rock and scanned the cliff faces above the small lochan. No eyries. A quarter of a mile ahead a steep ridge rose up to divide the faces into two sections. I said I thought the eyrie would be in the far faces, beyond the ridge. Greg agreed it probably was. We hiked down, past the lochan, and up to the top of the ridge. We located Eyrie 29 on a small ledge, which could have been overlooked from a hide, on a steep rocky slope forty yards away. It had certainly been used for breeding, for there were the remains and bones of prey on the nest and many white splashes beneath it. Only once in this area of the west Highlands had I known an eaglet to stay in the nest beyond mid-July, and even then it had first flown at the usual time and afterwards returned. We were too late, but it was good to know about the site.

On the way home I found the new eagle, black-throated diver and peregrine licences from the Nature Conservancy Council awaiting collection at the post office. If they arrived after any eaglets would normally have flown from their nests, they were also far too late for me to work with the divers, whose chicks take to the water by the end of June. Yet my suspicions that the N.C.C. wanted to prevent my work with eagles this year seemed unfounded. The letter accompanying the licences said the infuriating delay had been caused by severe staffing difficulties during that year's Civil Service strike. Well, I could still go and check the peregrines, for if any young had hatched this year they would still be flying around the falcons' cliff near the sea.

It was all too easy, in my lonely outpost, to suppose that rumours of a proposed government golden eagle survey had some connection with the long wait for licence renewal. Greg had been visited by a leading scientist from the N.C.C. looking for a good study area, and my old friend Dick Balharry, who was the Council's Chief Warden for the north-east region of Scotland, eventually confirmed the launch of an eagle survey. The news made me hope all the more that my years of work with eagles, undertaken entirely at my own expense, would not be just brushed aside. Dick had been in favour of it at the outset, and I felt due some proper recognition, in the sense that at least I should be helped financially to continue monitoring all the eyries I knew. A year earlier I had mapped out for the Royal Society for the Protection of Birds the sites of the twenty-seven eagle eyries I knew in my area – all but three unknown to them – on the understanding that the sites would not be divulged to anyone else, or even visited without my being consulted. I did this so that if anything happened to me on the hills some other suitable person could carry on the work.

I wrote to the scientist who had visited Greg, inquiring whether some sort of contract might be available for someone who knew all the eyries, the lie of the land, and had as much experience with eagles as I had. At first, there was no reply. I also wrote to the N.C.C. in Edinburgh and was invited to call in for a talk with leading officials towards the end of July.

When I went to check the peregrines' sea cliff, I again met the marine biologist who told me that an expert local amateur ornithologist had definitely seen three fledgelings. He had watched them calling to their parents and flying short distances among the small crags of the cliff. I spent three hours on the hill opposite the nesting face, but again I saw no falcons. On my way home I called on Greg Hunter, knowing he also was aware of the falcons. To my surprise, he told me that he and Roger Broad, assistant Highland officer of the R.S.P.B., had actually ringed the nestlings a few weeks earlier. At least it was good to have the breeding success of these rare birds thus confirmed.

My visit to the N.C.C. officials in Edinburgh was arranged to coincide with a trip south to visit my publisher and to have my camera lens repaired. I was greeted cordially and told of their battles to secure land for nature reserves. We discussed many aspects of conservation, especially the problems that rare and spectacular species like eagles face, such as direct persecution, poisoning, innocent disturbance, loss of habitat and the theft of eggs and chicks. I said I thought much more could be done to protect wildcats, pine martens, otters and eagles, and urged more contact with people who actually lived in wild areas, for the fate of such species often depended on the activities and attitudes of these folk. It was my experience that few landowners, farmers, shepherds, keepers or crofters knew anything of the Nature Conservancy Council's work and needed to be weaned away from mistaken ideas about predation. This work was surely every bit as important as their sometimes rather abstruse scientific surveys.

I then asked if there was a contract being offered for a field worker on the eagle survey and, if so, whether I could apply for it. They told me that the post of field worker had already been filled – by Dr Jeff Watson (son of bird artist Donald Watson), who had gained a PhD at Aberdeen University for his paper on the Seychelles kestrel. I wondered what the Seychelles kestrel had to do with eagles in Scotland, and how this stripling would perform on the Hill.

I hid my disappointment, offered any help I could give, and drove away over the border into England.

5 · *Barn Owls in the Roof*

I camped for the night in a small pine wood not far from Wigton. With Moobli sprawled on his bed across the front seats and our suppers cooking away on the truck's little camp stove, I reached for a small box of files. Since my first four wildlife books had been published, I had received many letters from readers telling me of their own wildlife experiences. Whenever I was on a rare trip south it had become my habit to call in and see one or two of these folk. Now I extracted from the files a particularly intriguing letter. It was from Lyn Gitsham, who lived with her two sons in a remote farmhouse not far from Doncaster. While most people usually wrote to me about their experiences with blue tits, blackbirds, hedgehogs and the like, Lyn had written to me about her barn owls.

Don't laugh, she had said, but some barn owls have made a nest in the chimney stack on the old house here. The trouble was she couldn't see it, though the owls were easy to see when they flew to an old barn at night.

As I read the letter again, I thought it unlikely the owls would nest there. Possibly she had just spotted one flying into a temporary roost. Nevertheless, I resolved to visit Lyn and try to see the owls for myself. I fed Moobli under the starry sky outside before settling down to my own stew. My mind went back to my only encounter with a wild barn owl in the north-west Highlands, where they are rare.

It had occurred on a calm, misty day in late April six years earlier.

Moobli and I were returning from a long trek through the lochside woods east of our home and I was trying to locate nests of hooded crows, sparrowhawks or buzzards before the foliage grew thick. We zig-zagged up and down the steep, rocky, wooded slopes. We had crossed a shelf pool in a tumbling burn, unable to avoid being splashed without labouring round a fallen oak which lay across a rockfall, when Moobli scented something higher up and led me behind a large boulder. There lay the wing of a barn owl. Its orange-brown feathers were unmistakable.

I followed a trail of feathers upward until I came to a primary wing feather that had been driven through some moss below the arching root of a fallen tree. Clearly something had killed the owl, and I tried to reconstruct what had happened. On the root some overlaying moss had been ripped off. Below the root, and others near it, was a natural chamber in the leaf-covered earth.

None of the feathers had been clipped, as happens when a fox kills and eats a bird. I was sure this was the work of a wildcat. Possibly the owl had been displaced from its home in a barn, had been looking for a new one, such as in a hollow tree, and had perched for a rest on the mossy root. Its killer had probably seen its ghostly whitish form land and had stalked it, coming at it from below, via the natural chamber. A wildcat whacks out with one or both sets of claws, often stunning its victim, pulls it back into the mouth for the killing bite, then makes several raking slashes to complete the work. This wildcat had probably lashed out but the owl, having strong legs, must have leaped, lost the first feathers, then fluttered, half-tumbling downwards, losing a feather here and there as the cat chased after it.

Four yards below were a mass of head and chest feathers. The wildcat had probably caught up with it there, attacking as usual the head and throat area, whereas a stoat would go for the big veins under the wings. These feathers had the unmistakable black and white 'eyes' of the barn owl on their fawn ends. Severe injury had been inflicted at that spot, but clearly the owl had had enough strength left to struggle down again, because it was five yards farther on that the wing had been torn off.

By then the owl was doubtless dead, and the wildcat had carried it farther down, the feathers becoming fewer and fewer until they ended in a pile, which included the other wing, not far from a small pool in the burn. Here it seemed the wildcat had eaten its meal.

41

I looked about. There were two trails to the pool, which was sheltered on three sides by flat rocks, an ideal watering place for a furtive animal. I found a bank with vole holes in it and saw two frogs hopping away from our sudden appearance. It seemed a regular hunting place for a wildcat.

In a muddy spot I found one four-toed print, rounder than a fox's and without the claw marks which a fox often leaves in mud. The final clue was a cluster of scratch marks about two feet up on the bark of a small birch tree. It seemed the cat had eaten its fill, had taken a drink at the pool, and then on its way home had stretched up on the tree to sharpen its claws.

It was a sad piece of detective work, but there was no point in being sentimental. The owl had been unsure of the new terrain and one predator had been killed by a more powerful predator. In the kingdoms of the wild there is no mercy, nor any conscious cruelty. Survival is paramount. Predators evolved with fangs and claws to fulfil their natural roles.

As I now finished my supper in the truck, I reflected that I had not seen barn owls in the wild since I was a youth learning about nature in the woods and fields of Sussex. It would be good if I could now see Lyn's owls, even better if I could photograph them in flight.

Next day I telephoned Lyn, arranged to meet her at a roadside café, and bowled on down to south Yorkshire. She invited me for afternoon tea at the farm and I gladly accepted. Lyn was a strong handsome Yorkshire farm lass with a natural Irene Papas sort of dignity, who drove tractors, lugged bales and pulled her full weight in helping her two brothers run the farm. She took us for a walk round the farmlands and I photographed a flying kestrel. As we strolled across the fields, I asked her to show me the old ruin where the owls were nesting.

'It's not out here,' Lyn replied to my surprise. 'They're in the centre chimney of our own house! And they perch near us – last night the three young came out on to the roof and looked down at us while their parents fed them.'

We went back to the house and Lyn indicated the stack. I could hardly believe it. Barn owls have been declining in numbers for forty years, first due to gamekeeper persecution, then to pesticides in their prey in the 1960s, as well as to the modernisation of old farm buildings, the loss of rough land to agriculture, and to accidents on motorways where they hunt the uncut banks and are hit by vehicles.

Yet here, apparently, a pair had chosen to raise a brood in the chimney of a busy farmhouse where many children played and callers were frequent. I asked Lyn if I could get nearer the stack and keep watch, for clearly these owls were not too bothered by human presence.

It so happened that Lyn had some portable scaffolding which had just been taken down after work was completed on the house. Within minutes her sons, David and Wayne, and two of their schoolpals, had the scaffolding up again five yards from the house. A plywood platform was roped on twenty feet up, and sacking was tied round the top square of the poles as a hide. The youngsters were stationed at strategic spots in bushes and trees round the house, to give a quiet whistle to alert me whenever they spotted an owl nearby.

Well before sundown I saw the white-dished face and dark eyes of an adult barn owl peer round the side of the stack. Then it was away on slender wings, more slender and pointed than a tawny owl's. It flew, gliding frequently like a fulmar, to the roof of a Dutch barn nearby, landed, and from this spy post, bent down comically like a parrot, watching the ground below intently. In mere seconds it saw something, dropped like a stone into the grasses, then came flying in with a large woodmouse in its beak. It flew towards the stack, stuck out its long feathered shanks and yellowish toes and talons and landed in the stack.

Immediately the youngsters inside made odd chittering hissing calls, '*sheeer, sheerrree*', as they competed for the food. Then out came the adult again, followed seconds later by its mate, and both flew round the house, occasionally making eerie '*shreeesh*' calls, not loud, but weird and ghostly in effect. Both landed on the barn roof again, but seeing nothing they took off to float over a marshy area near a small mere.

Suddenly, out popped a fully fledged youngster and landed on the apex of the roof. Then came another, and a third, the first two shuffling sideways to my left with amusing careful steps to make way for the third. All had different faces: one longer beaked, slim and gloomy, one squarer faced with an oddly solemn philosophical look, and the third with a rounder, shorter mask, which set its head back on its shoulders, half-closed its eyes and made it look as if it was smiling blissfully at the thought of the meal ahead.

Then back came both parents, one with a mouse, one with a

short-tailed vole, and what a commotion the youngsters made as they shuffled their wings, hissed and squeaked and looked in danger of tumbling from the roof as two of them received and gulped down their prey. Now the parents flew round the roof, gliding close to the owlets, landing near them, clearly inducing them to fly too. And one by one they did, each following a parent down to the marsh until all was again silence.

As I thanked Lyn and the kids for their help, they told me the youngsters had been flying for nearly two weeks. Each dawn they returned to roost during the day in the chimney stack, clearly trusting the humans in whose home they had chosen to live, paying 'rent' by killing many crop-devouring mice and voles.

In 1932 a survey of barn owls concluded there were 12,500 pairs in England and Wales, plus another 1,500 pairs in all Ireland. Between 1983 and 1985 a new survey was conducted by the Hawk Trust and the British Trust for Ornithology. Colin Shawyer, of the Hawk Trust, tells me there are still estimated to be 1,500 pairs in Ireland, but numbers have dwindled to 6,000 pairs in England and Wales, with a further 1,000 pairs in Scotland.

A pair of barn owls can take 3,000 small rodents in a year, including young rats. For years, some European farmers have built owl doors high in their barns and fixed tea chests on to beams as nest sites. Recently British farmers have taken to doing the same. Encouraging these fascinating farmers' friends certainly makes sense, and I hope more landowners follow suit.

In London I dashed around to complete all my business, and at the R.S.P.C.A. clinic in Putney I was given a course of injections to administer which would help alleviate Moobli's condition.

I hurried back to the Highlands because I had agreed to do a BBC Radio Scotland 'Wildwatch' programme (repeated later in Radio 4's 'Living World' series) with interviewer Chris Lowell. I took him to the road that ran by the peregrine cliffs, for I still cherished a faint hope of seeing one of the falcons myself. I made what I hoped were cogent pleas for the conservation of rare species like wildcat, pine marten, otter and eagle, and showed him otter prints in the river mud, an otter's holt, an occupied wildcat lair and a badger sett. We had an action-packed few hours, for we also saw the usual small birds, including a tribe of bullfinches, a heron, a red squirrel, a roe doe giving suck to her fawn, flying buzzards, ravens and gulls. We were gazing at a fox track in a marshy area, and searching for wildcat prints too, when Chris nudged my arm.

'What's that bird up there, Mike?'

I followed his gaze. You could have knocked me down with a rush stem. There it was at last.

'A young peregrine,' I said.

'Isn't it superb?'

It was high above us, perched on a jutting crag, and as it looked down the dark 'moustaches' on each side of its hooked blue-black beak lent a sombre look to its face. Although it was a dull day, we could see its plumage was new-looking, and on its fluffed-out creamy chest feathers the rich dark bars showed up clearly. As we watched, it opened and fanned its long, barred wings gently, as if still being careful about feeling the currents of the slight wind.

Among the mail I picked up on the day of the programme was a reply from the leading Nature Conservancy Council scientist to whom I had written before the trip south. It said that the N.C.C. was setting up a golden eagle and land-use study to find out whether recent changes – for example, in extensive afforestation and improved sheep husbandry – were having any effect on the breeding performance and population of golden eagles in Scotland. My letter offering help was being passed to the N.C.C. scientist supervising the survey and it would be up to him or the field worker, Jeff Watson, to make contact with me.

On the afternoon of our return to Wildernesse I wandered round the east wood in a calm misty drizzle and saw a ghostly whitish form sitting out on the loch beyond the weed beds, not far from the gulls' islet. It was one of the rare black-throated divers. I raced to the cottage for the telephoto lens (which had now been repaired) and hurried back to stalk it over the burn, keeping out of its sight behind some alders, then wriggling on my belly through the wet grasses. The little black biting midges were at their devilish worst, and I had to keep wiping my face to relieve the ticklish agony of their tiny, thrusting, sucking daggers. The bird dived often, but awkwardly, and even when it saw me it did not move away. It seemed so tame that I wondered if there was something wrong with it. I kept a sharp lookout and saw the pair several times before they left the loch as usual in early September to winter on the sea, but not once did I see a chick with them. They had not succeeded in raising any young that season.

On August 29 I had more news of the peregrines. I was in the distant store when I met the new keeper and ghillie of the estate on the far eastern march of which I lived. His name was Duncan, and he had a formidable reputation as a first-class salmon fisherman. He had been fishing the river with two clients the previous week, about half a mile south of the cliff, when the three young peregrines had flown above the opposite bank.

'They had beautiful fresh new plumage, so they looked bigger than peregrines normally do,' he said. 'Two of them began chasing a young mallard, shrieking and fighting over it as they all flew along. Then the duck fell into the river, dying. The nearest fisherman tried to drop his fly over the mallard, so we could haul it back and let the birds have it, but he missed and it floated on down the river, with the young falcons in pursuit. It vanished round a bend, so we don't know if the peregrines finally got it or not.'

I repressed a sigh of frustration. What a sequence of pictures that incident could have made, though it was good to know the young peregrines were surviving well.

Next afternoon, while I was working at my desk, I heard hooded crows calling faintly. I went out and saw Atalanta floating along below the peaks to the north-east. Chasing her, small as midges against her immense dark form, were two hoodies. Two hundred yards nearer me and high above them, a flock of seventeen young and old crows and four ravens were also flying along, as if accompanying the eagle at a distance but near enough to ruin her hunting. I fought my way up through the high bracken as Atalanta lurched along, with ponderous indrawings of her wings, before she and the flock vanished behind the trees of the woods along the burn. On September 4 I saw her again, this time flying with Melanion over the same peaks, and again beset by ravens and crows. On neither occasion did I see an eaglet with them, and I felt sure they had not bred successfully this year.

Imagine my chagrin two days later, on my first autumn trek to see if the master stags had started rounding up hinds for the rut, when I heard the loud and unmistakable '*k'yew k'yew*' calls of an eaglet! Poised there on the lip of a huge corrie, I could hardly believe my ears. Then I heard the calls again. As I turned I suddenly saw the eaglet flapping eastwards about two hundred yards south of me. I took a photo with the telephoto lens. It was certainly not Diana. This eaglet was smaller, doubtless a male, and its wing patches were quite different in shape from those of either Diana or Apollo. The eaglet carried on, still calling loudly, straight towards Melanion, who was circling above the crests on the far side of the corrie. I then lost sight of them.

I carried on up to the peak overlooking the glen below Guardian mountain, having successfully stalked a group of grazing hinds and a little yearling stag, its 'knobber' antlers still in velvet. Then I saw the eagles again. I raised the binoculars. There were three of them now – Atalanta, so high that she kept disappearing in the clouds, Melanion circling below her, while below him soared the new eaglet.

I now knew for sure that my favourite pair had bred again but, dammit, in an eyrie I did not yet know. It seemed to complete my humiliation.

6 · Far-flung Falcon

On another stag trek a week later I saw the three again. They were circling above the crags containing Eyrie 1. As I watched, the eaglet broke away to travel north-eastwards. Atalanta and Melanion circled round each other twice more before the huge female appeared to make her mind up about something, put her wings back and set off in a 'jet glide' towards the south. At first Melanion hung back, as if watching her departure in surprise. Then he set off in her wake, both eagles travelling at about eighty miles per hour until they vanished over the far ridges across the loch. Once more I had seen them go straight over the territory of another pair of eagles (Pair Six).

On September 17 I took a break from work indoors to walk round my four acres, and was treated to a flight display by the eagles. Atalanta came soaring over the peaks to the north-east and was soon joined by Melanion. For about five minutes they sailed round each other and to and fro across the peaks, with the male often flying close to his mate. Had they got the new male eaglet up there, reluctant or too tired to fly? It seemed not, for they then sailed away to the west. As they went, Melanion made several spectacular 'golden ball' dives. It was the first time I had seen these occur outside spring and the nesting season.

Shortly after that the eaglet came over the ridges and set off in their wake. As I turned for home, I heard a raven croaking and looked back to see this largest of the British crow family mobbing the eaglet as he headed west. Making noisy 'krok krok' calls, the raven pursued relentlessly, and even when the eaglet went into a deep dive to shake it off, it kept up. I had never before seen a raven keep up with an eagle going into a dive. This seemed finally to arouse the eaglet's anger, for he suddenly turned and chased the raven, pursuing it right across the arch of the sky to the east again. Then both birds dived, zoomed and tumbled around each other, as if it were all just a game, the male eaglet almost as manœuvrable in the air as the raven. Finally the raven turned off and flew into the lochside woods to the east, while the eaglet set off once more after his parents.

I went out about an hour later just in time to see Atalanta and Melanion heading back to the east again. Two minutes later the eaglet came flying back from the west, calling loudly as if in despair, still chasing after his parents. I wondered if the two adults were now trying to give their youngster the slip.

For the next few days torrential rains and south-westerly gales assaulted the cottage and began to strip the first leaves from the trees. As I stumped round the woods each morning, Moobli no longer able to accompany me on even this half-mile walk, I felt acutely depressed, as if there was some kind of physical weight on my heart and soul. Just when I thought I had beaten the loneliness which often assaults the isolated wilderness dweller, it had returned in full force. Once, as I climbed the rock escarpments of the west wood, my heart seemed to skip a few beats. I had that feeling of panic again, that I was about to die, and for some moments I could not get my breath. Reason told me it was probably a psychological problem, caused by fifteen years of isolation in the wilds, and that I had ended up in a lonely trap of my own making.

That day I moved back on to my desk the great pile of manuscript and notes I had amassed for A Last Wild Place, on which I had already worked for nine months before shelving it, at the request of my publisher, in order to write the eagle book first. As I sat staring at the daunting mass of the most complicated book I had ever attempted, wondering how on earth I could ever get back into it again, I glanced out of the window.

The pair of black-throated divers were swimming along through the rough waters of the loch just beyond the boat bay. The front bird surged forward, rose out of the water flapping its wings and took off, closely followed by its mate. I dashed out with the binoculars and saw their bodies tilting this way and that as they rose higher and settled into their true steady flight, their slim sharp wings beating smoothly like twanged steel, and then becoming smaller and smaller as they vanished into the horizon. They had failed to breed this year, but were now obeying their ancestral instincts and were away to winter on the sea.

It seemed ironic that a few weeks later I should receive a letter from Roy Dennis of the Royal Society for the Protection of Birds asking for all my breeding records and other data for the divers on this loch, for this was only the third year out of eight that the divers had failed to breed. The letter said that black-throated divers could well be declining. Their breeding success had been extremely low since the R.S.P.B. began collecting information about them in 1971. The Society thought there could now be as few as 150 pairs, and had employed a field worker this year to make a survey; she was to collate data and assess the numbers, distribution and breeding success of the British diver population. Would I be able to help?

As I lugged my hefty yearly diaries down from their shelves I could not help wondering peevishly why no one ever considered me for such jobs. I had missed even applying for the eagle survey post because I hadn't known about it in time. Now here was another job I would have liked to tackle. I dutifully spent a few days sifting through the diaries, and sent Roy all my data – that in eight years the pair had bred seven young, which was a far higher success rate than for most diver pairs. I added the reminder that previously I had supplied the locations of the twenty-seven golden eagle eyries *in confidence*, on the understanding they would not be divulged to anyone else, and would not be worked on without my being informed and my own help secured.

When Roy Dennis wrote back thanking me for the diver records, he told me that the R.S.P.B. was undertaking a full survey of the golden eagle next year. A real attempt was to be made to cover all nests, so that they could arrive at a figure for the total population and also have a clear view of problems like persecution. The survey was to be kept confidential; only those who were already eagle men were being asked to help. It was hoped that I would help, and I would be contacted again for the matter to be fully discussed. The letter assured me that all nest-site data would be kept confidential, which wasn't precisely what I had asked, or been promised. Well, it could all be discussed later. I replied I would be delighted to help, just as I intended to with the Nature Conservancy Council survey, which I now understood was to last for at least three years.

I next saw the eagles again on the day I completed my annual report to the N.C.C. I listed the facts – that out of six eagle pairs only two eaglets had been reared to flying stage, and that the black-throated divers had failed to breed, but that the peregrines had reared three young. I expressed the opinion that while it had been a poor year for the eagles (they had reared five chicks successfully the previous year) the result was not disastrous. As I typed the last words, I heard loud piercing '*keeyoo*' whistles – a buzzard calling from somewhere above the cottage.

I dashed out to see what looked like one large buzzard diving on another, which turned completely upside down and shot its talons upwards. As the larger bird circled, as if for a second assault, I ran back in for the camera. I was out again in seconds, yet they had parted and the buzzard flapped wildly off to the east, calling loudly. The bigger bird came back low over the west wood and I saw it was not a big buzzard at all but Melanion, and it was he who had dived on the large female buzzard in either a symbolic or real attack. I tried to take photos but the camera shutter stuck.

Melanion rose higher and higher on the wind, then I saw Atalanta heading towards him. They re-crossed each other's paths twice before Atalanta headed back towards the west again, while Melanion treated me to a display of no less than eight 'golden ball' dives. He zoomed down with wings closed, opened them, swooped upwards, flapped hard to gain more height, turned over as if on a roller-coaster, with his wings tucked in like a trussed turkey, and zoomed down again. He repeated this fantastic yo-yoing performance to the north, to the east, to the south and to the west, going all over the place and not in a direct line. Again he had made this territorial display in autumn, well after the nesting season, and I was sure he had intended to drive the buzzard away. No wonder she had turned her talons upwards, not in any symbolic food pass but to protect herself from his attack, and had shot away with loud calls. It was the first time I had ever known an eagle go for a buzzard. It was possible Melanion had just been having a brief game, but the buzzard was not to know that.

All through October I climbed and reclimbed the hills to photograph rutting stags, lonesome treks now. Not once did I see the eagles again. Howling rain-filled gales blew my boat off its trolley and into the rising waters of the loch, so that I found it one morning smashed against the rocks, its stern holed at last. My little battery radio broke down so that every time I came off a trek it was like returning to a silent shroud. I suddenly realised how much I had depended on it for company, to hear human voices, enjoy regular programmes. For all I knew, nuclear war could have broken out. Another gale smashed the little windmill generator that powered a 12-volt battery for my desk light, and blew a huge old tree across my fence. There were also production problems with the eagle book, all the photos being put in the wrong places. When it was possible to boat out, I made frantic phone calls to try to put things right.

The only good occurrence at this time was the stag trek at the end of the month – my best ever – in which I photographed over sixteen different stags and their hinds without them ever knowing I was there. As I tramped home, I felt I would make that the Last Trek – I had done enough. I was on the hill, half a mile from home, when a large bird suddenly launched itself from a rock below me. As I saw its dark scythe-like blue-black wings and the way it dived in twisting fast flight towards the loch, I knew it was a peregrine falcon. It levelled out above the loch, flickered towards the opposite hills, then circled and appeared to land in the east wood. I wondered if it was one of the youngsters from the cliff near the sea. At any rate, I hoped it was trying to stake out a territory of its own and that it would stay in the area. There was plenty of bird prey in the loch-side woodlands and many suitable nesting cliffs in the hills around the cottage.

I now had to go south and spend time finding a nurse to look after my aged father in Spain. On the day I left in mid-November, my mail included a letter from the eagle survey field worker, Dr Jeff Watson. He had been in his post for over a month and was busy choosing specific study areas. He wanted to come and discuss eagles with me shortly. I typed a reply in my Land-Rover in the village and posted it there and then. I would be happy to help him all I could and would telephone him in the next few days.

It was at this time that I decided to trade in my battered, petrol-guzzling Land-Rover for a superb Volkswagen camper which contained fridge, sink-unit, wardrobe, ample cupboard space, comfortable beds, and which handled like a bird at ten miles more to the gallon. For twelve years my truck bed had consisted of one inch of foam on a plywood board.

On the telephone Jeff Watson cheerfully admitted he had not worked a great deal with eagles before, just a few in the Galloway area, and he realised it would be different up in the Highlands. I said again that I would be glad to help, but I hoped I could have some kind of sub-contract. In eight years I had financed over two hundred boating, driving and foot-slogging treks round most of my twenty-seven eyries just out of what I earned from writing, and now the cost was becoming prohibitive. Dr Watson said he would talk to the eagle survey's supervisor, N.C.C. scientist Dr Derek Langslow, and get him to contact me. It was agreed that real studies could start around mid-March, when eagles would be displaying in their nesting areas. Dr Langslow told me that he had little personal experience with eagles, but thought I could probably be paid up to £200 per season, just for travel expenses, provided that Dr Watson found my area to be a good one to study. It did not sound to me anything like enough, and I said so, but it was better than nothing. We agreed to discuss the details later. I was sure Dr Watson would find it an excellent study area.

Soon afterwards Roy Dennis sent me documents which detailed all the objectives of the eagle survey and showed that it was being organised *jointly* by the R.S.P.B. and the N.C.C. in the first year, when an attempt would be made to cover every single territory and breeding nest. Dr Langslow of the N.C.C. also wrote to say:

> We would be happy to enlist your help on the Golden Eagle project, and Jeff Watson will contact you in due course over the specific area that we would like you to check. He will also give you details of the information that we require on each eyrie within the relevant part of the study area. We can arrange for travel expenses to be paid for the work.

It all sounded good, and I thought that at last I would get some financial help towards trekking round and monitoring all my usual eyries. Later Jeff Watson wrote to say he wanted to suggest that priority be given to the block of country to the west of my loch.

> Here, as far as I can see, there are few people other than yourself who have any great knowledge of the bird. If there are any other areas, or particular sites, you'd like to keep checking then perhaps you could let me know when we meet so that we can avoid unnecessary duplication.

Again, all sounded well, and eventually a rendezvous was arranged for Jeff Watson and Roy Dennis to meet me by a certain bridge at the end of my home loch on March 25.

Meanwhile, I visited the N.C.C. headquarters in London to renew my usual licences, and to donate two of my wildlife books to their library – and received a slight shock. The licensing staff told me they were issuing no licences for the black-throated diver that year, on the recommendation of Roy Dennis of the R.S.P.B. I said that since all the information Roy Dennis and the R.S.P.B. had about the divers on my loch for the last eight years had come from me, that seemed absurd and grossly unfair. The divers, which often nested on my islet, needed guarding from trippers in boats who could innocently disturb them. It was important that their breeding success should be carefully recorded. They promised to try and make an exception for my application, which finally they did. But it was not to be the last of the unwelcome rebuffs I was to receive in this whole curious affair.

7 · The Killer-trek Eyrie

When I went to keep the rendezvous by the bridge on March 25, two fit-looking young men stepped from a camper like mine and introduced themselves. One was Dr Jeff Watson, tall, bearded and twenty-eight years old, but the other was not Roy Dennis. He was busy with other urgent work that day, I was told. He had sent his assistant, Roger Broad.

We sat round a table in my camper and I produced my map of eagle eyries. The first surprise was to discover that these men knew all the locations. The map of twenty-seven eyries I had given in confidence to the R.S.P.B. two summers earlier had already been incorporated in the list of known sites for the survey – without my being consulted or told about it.

The second shock was that Jeff Watson wanted to include most of my old eagle terrain in his own main study area, one of six that were being set up all over Scotland. They had consulted Greg Hunter and my best friend, a keeper called Allan Peters, who years earlier had first shown me several eyries belonging to two eagle pairs south of my loch, and Dr Watson had already been shown some of the locations. The idea was that Watson would take over monitoring all the eyries south of my loch, and Greg would help with those on his own estate, plus four others which I used to cover to the west. I would be left to deal with five eyries north of the loch, which were only accessible by boat, but at least they included those of my favourite eagles Atalanta and Melanion. Roger Broad then pressed the point that maybe I could search for *new* eyries in the sixty square miles of wilderness behind my cottage.

I was so dumbfounded that I thought only briefly before replying. I had not really been looking forward to slogging round all the eyries again this year anyway, on the vague promise of a few travel expenses. Not even the once-mentioned sum of £200 had been confirmed. I could not really afford to keep doing all that work, and besides my eagle book was due out later in the year, and that meant going away for periods promoting it. I said if that was how they wanted to organise things I would go along with it, fit in as best I could. The two men seemed relieved that I was not angry.

'That's the spirit, Mike,' said Roger Broad, sounding like the corporal I had been in the Coldstream Guards before he was born.

It appeared that some eagle men in salaried jobs had put up a fight to keep monitoring their own eyries, and Jeff Watson had not been finding it easy to set up his study areas. He promised to meet me in three weeks time so that I could take him on Eagle Rock mountain to show him some of the eyries he did not yet know.

As I drove back to my boat, doubts assailing me, I happened to meet my good friend Allan Peters. He told me that Roger Broad had brought Jeff Watson to him when trying to locate the actual eyries shown on the map. Allan, a keeper for the Forestry Commission (another government department like the N.C.C.), had felt obliged to help while I was away.

'The best thing we can do is all co-operate together,' he said. 'And learn from each other.'

'A wise thing to say,' I replied. 'I suppose it's for the eagles' benefit, after all, and that's the main thing.'

Even so, over the next two days I found myself fuming. I felt I had been outflanked, virtually kicked out of my old eagle ground. I even thought of leaving Scotland for good. But for the fact that I had no other quiet place in which to work on my complicated new book, I would probably have made plans to leave there and then.

Far from receiving any financial help for trekking round the eyries I already knew, which had taken years to discover, nearly all the easiest ones were being confiscated, and I was expected to search for new ones in the most difficult mountainous terrain in the region on a vague promise of travel expenses. The only directly attributable travel expenses I could envisage for that work would be boot leather! Surely, the reasonable course would have been to help me with a modest contribution towards my living costs so that I could be free to keep a constant check on the eyries I already knew, while the new young *salaried* men broke the fresh terrain? I had failed to secure that much, but my suggestions to the N.C.C. in Edinburgh that they should work more with the people who actually *lived* in eagle terrain seemed to have prodded them into action, for I discovered that most of my old eagle contacts had been visited. In a way, I should be pleased that the N.C.C. and R.S.P.B. staff were now paying such attention to my area.

I tried to calm down and reason things out. Nothing would be gained by protesting or refusing to co-operate, for I would alienate powerful bodies like the N.C.C. and R.S.P.B. and probably would not receive my eagle licences this year. Certainly I would receive no travel expenses of any kind. Years ago I would have kicked up a fuss, but age had taught me discretion, instead to play the part of the old fox. I decided to hold my tongue, bide my time, and see how things transpired. The truth was that Jeff Watson had chosen the area for his main studies because he had so much information on it, a good deal of it supplied by me.

To hell with worrying, I thought the next day, and I set off to check Eyries 27 and 28. The eagles had used neither eyrie last year, so there was a good chance they would use one of them this season.

I was still over half a mile away when Melanion came over the lower eyrie and carried on to the south-west. He made no territorial or courtship dives this time. I carried on and kept scanning the nest ledge to see if Atalanta was on it, in which case I would have left immediately. In my view, the one unforgivable sin when studying eagles is to put a female off her eggs. In all the years I had been watching eagles I had done it only once, by accident, and had resolved never to do so again. As I came nearer, it was clear she was not there and that the nest had not been newly built up. But the birch roost site was being used, probably by Melanion.

Carefully, I climbed up towards the upper nest in the daunting V-shaped crag. At the last moment I put some grasses over my bush hat and with aching slowness moved my head sideways round a rock. I peered through the binoculars. An unusual sight met my gaze. The winter gales had removed some of the top sticks but among the new twigs added was a long, neat human walking stick, which appeared to have been thrust into the side of the nest. It stuck out incongruously, at right angles over the void below. Surely no human could have put it there. It would have taken a team of at least two professional climbers, with ropes, pitons and other modern gear to have scaled that sheer rugged face. And any humans meaning harm to the eagles would have destroyed the nest. In all other respects the nest looked as if it was being used, or was about to be used. I left quickly, baffled by the stick. I searched for any new eyries over a farther two miles of rockfaces but found none.

I did discover, however, the remains of two old hinds. These, together with two dead hinds and two dead calves I had found earlier within half a mile of the cottage, indicated that the carrion supply was far higher than it had been last year. December and January had been exceptionally cold, so the increased deer carrion would benefit species like eagles. As I tramped home I heard some weird mewing wails, promptly followed by harsh gobbling calls '*powoo, powlyow, powoo, powlyow*', coming from the loch below. I raked the surface with the binoculars and there, floating near a land-spit three miles from my home, were two large dark rounded dots with stout upright grey necks. It was good to know the rare black-throated divers were back from their seafaring winter and had already begun courting. I hoped to find their nest this season, even if they did not use my nearest islet.

At the end of March I called on Greg Hunter to find out why he now wanted to take over four of my former western eyries for the survey. My first surprise was that his door was opened by a woman I had not met before, a gorgeous blonde; the second, after Greg confirmed the N.C.C. had chosen our area because they had more information on it than any other, was that he didn't care if he covered the eyries or not. If I wanted I could continue to do them myself. He already had too much work on his plate. Besides, he was getting married in May – to the lovely young blonde!

'How on earth did you come to meet her?'

Greg grinned. 'She came up here on holiday and heard I was interested in nature. She came knocking on my door, asking about flowers.'

No girl like that ever came knocking on *my* door asking about bloody flowers, I thought bitterly as I drove back to the boat.

A freak cold spell followed, with days of dark drizzly rain and hail showers, and on April 8 I woke to see snow blizzards engulfing the cottage. I used the time to work on my new book and to write several wildlife columns for a Scottish paper – a job I had taken on partly because I liked the paper and also because I needed the money. It was bad weather for breeding eagles, however, for if a bird incubating eggs has to leave the nest, due to its mate not bringing in enough food, or to humans accidentally or deliberately frightening it off, the eggs swiftly become chilled and the embryos die.

April 11 dawned in a clear blue sky and I decided to get down in earnest to the survey. I set off on the trek I dreaded most of all, the real 'killer', which involved 12,000 feet of ups and downs to the northernmost Eyrie 18. I tramped up slowly with my camera pack, taking it easy so as to save my strength, and trying not to tread on the many primroses that festooned the lower slopes. Up in Big Corrie I forded a swollen burn and then kept low in the tussocky bowl for two more miles until I was overlooking the almost sheer near-2,000 foot descent to another river. Bitter, cold winds blew from the north-east. My lips were blue and I was shivering despite my camouflage jacket, sweater, wool shirt and vest, and all the exertions. I had to climb backwards down some rocky faces before wading across the rocky bed of the rushing river. I turned north-west for the final mile-long climb up another 1,000 feet to the side of the eyrie cliff. Not once did I see an eagle.

Below the rowan-tree roost I found five small eagle pellets, mostly filled with sheeps' wool and deer hair from winter carrion, and a few newly preened breast feathers. It looked promising. In case the eyrie was occupied, I climbed steeply a farther 200 feet round to the back of the great buttress, then hiked to a spot where I could look at the eyrie from the hill just north of it. I sidled downhill inch by inch until the nest edge came into view, and slowly raised the binoculars.

My first sight was of piles of thick sticks, some broken in half, scattered over the nest. I thought humans might have tried to stop it being used by piling debris all over it. The top of the nest was a foot higher than before. Suddenly my eyes made out the yellow base of a large hooked beak and the edge of an eagle's face. I raised myself an inch higher, peering through the cliffside grasses, and saw the dark blood-orange eye. It looked like Atalanta! She was clearly sitting on eggs and the nest had a very deep well.

What a good thing I had spotted her and not moved out farther. I dared not even try to take a picture. Slowly I drew back, headed north a further quarter-mile, then struck down to the glen bottom, giving the eyrie face a wide berth of half a mile. I kept looking up but saw no movement. She probably could not see down that far over the edge of the nest.

I forded the river again and began the precipitous climb out, still wondering if it really had been Atalanta. It seemed impossible, for this eyrie was a good three miles, even as the eagle flies, from her other eyries. Twice I had to stop and rest, sure the old heart was going to conk out. By now my left hamstring, which I had pulled during the winter, was playing up again, yet the worst and steepest part lay ahead. I ate an egg sandwich, got to my feet and laboured on. The clouds had rolled away, the winds had dropped completely, and the early spring sun shone down with broiling heat on my back.

I was almost a mile from the eyrie when suddenly I saw the huge shadow of a bird head through mine and go ahead of me. I looked up to see – no doubt about it now – Atalanta zooming over my head, a mere forty feet up. It was impossible to get my camera out of the pack as I needed my hands to cling on to the almost sheer rocks. She went over, head turning from side to side as she looked at me backwards, then performed a lovely airy circle above the ridges and disappeared. Her great wings looked oddly tattered at the tips.

Why on earth had she left the nest? If she was on eggs they would surely get cold. I toiled upwards, zig-zagged over bogs, over slippery green rockfaces, across musical burns with five-foot drops disguised by grasses where they tunnelled under the peat, scrabbled up slopes of gabbro, but now I hardly felt the torture. I was so happy that I had finally not only pinned Atalanta down to this eyrie at last but that she was now actually breeding in it.

As I scrambled over the final crest and began the easier miles of undulating slopes to home, I wondered why she had left her nest and flown so close over my head. Surely she could not recognise me as the man who had worked her twin eaglet eyrie two years earlier, when she had been exceptionally tame, or who had for so many winters hauled dead deer up into the hills from the woods for her and her mate to feed from?

I had just decided to make a detour on the last steeps above the cottage, to check Eyrie 1, when I saw something moving through the grasses on the hill to the left of it. It was a large boar badger romping about in full sunlight – a rare sight. I took several pictures as he sniffed tufts, set his rear-gland scent on others, and worked his way down a burn bank. When I got below the eyrie face and looked up I had yet another surprise.

The whole five-foot ledge had been hugely built up and was covered to a depth of over a foot with woven twigs, some over an inch thick. Draped over the twigs were lengths of dusty grey sheeps' fleece and wefts of deer hair, both taken from carcasses. It looked a very comfortable eyrie now, but if Atalanta was using Eyrie 18 she could not also be using Eyrie 1. Or had I been mistaken? Was there another pair of eagles on this terrain?

I clambered painfully down the steep deer path above the burn ravine, dangerous in places where one slip would mean dropping forty feet on to hard granite, and plodded the last hundred yards to the cottage. All my leg muscles ached, but oddly there was no pain in my 'arthritic' knee caps, just slight twinges in the actual joint of the right knee. Moobli greeted me ecstatically. After feeding him well, I put the eagle pellets into envelopes to give to Jeff Watson for analysis. I was still irritated by the way in which most of my old eagle territory had been taken over. My main concern was that I might actually be prevented from visiting or photographing any of the easier eyries which had taken so long to locate. The prospect of carrying a hide and its materials to Eyrie 18, and of making that killer trek every time I went to and from it, was terrifying.

Nevertheless, it had been a great day, I thought as I finally collapsed into bed. I had been dreading making that trek yet again, had feared I might even drop dead on it, yet I had seldom travelled better over such hard terrain in my life.

Three mornings later I was ambling round the woods, my rested legs feeling even stronger after the big trek, when I saw Atalanta sailing below the peaks to the north-east. As she floated eastwards, her huge black form again looked slightly tattered on the wing tips. Then a female kestrel launched from a cliff and harried her, swooping and diving like a small silver light. Next, two hoodies joined in. Suddenly, Atalanta wheeled and dived on the kestrel, pursuing it for about fifty yards and making it swerve and dodge wildly to get out of her way. She was just seeing it off. Then she circled and went over the crests in the direction of the Eyrie 18 glen. Maybe she had not been on eggs when I had seen her but just sitting on the nest. On the other hand, perhaps Melanion was taking his turn at incubation, so letting her have a break. I would find out later. As I neared the cottage I again heard the mournful mewing wails of the black-throated divers, coming from down the loch, but I could not see them.

On April 16 I decided to go to the nearest big town and stock up with supplies so as to have a really long stint at my book and to make more eagle treks without having to go out again. As I drove along the narrow road south, I was surprised to see Jeff Watson's government camper van parked by the woods below two of the eyries on Eagle Rock mountain, which Allan Peters had shown me and which I had checked for years. Jeff Watson and Allan are probably up there right now, I thought as I drove past. Again I had the odd feeling of being excluded from my old ground. On the way back I called in at Allan's home and found Jeff Watson with him. The exchanged greetings were at least cordial, I noted with relief.

The two men had indeed checked the two eyries but they were not occupied. Jeff was carrying a long polished pole with a mirror on its top which, he explained, enabled him to examine some nests for eggs or young chicks without going too close or trampling over them. Good thinking, I reckoned. I told them the news about Atalanta, and Jeff was pleased. Then he gave me some surprising news.

'Mike, I was walking right round that [Eagle Rock] mountain a few days ago when a female eagle came out of a small cliff above a crevice right in front of me. I looked, and there was a nest with two eggs in it. I left quickly and she soon went back. It's probably one of the nests you have studied.'

'Ah, yes,' I said. 'In a burn gorge? That will be Eyrie 8.'

Jeff frowned. 'I don't think so. I thought you placed Eyrie 8 on the west side of the mountain.'

'That's right.'

'Well, this nest is on the north-west side, in a crevice way down the mountain.'

A map of the eyries I knew there flashed into my mind. It was best to be honest.

'Good heavens,' I said. 'It's probably one I *don't* know.' If so, this would be Eyrie 30.

We agreed to meet in two days' time. Jeff would hoot on the forestry track opposite my home just before 9 a.m., and I would take him up Eagle Rock mountain and show him Eyries 3, 11 and 8. On that hike, I thought, I would find out for sure if he meant to exclude me from visiting eyries over most of my old area.

Next morning, as I was weeding my vegetable garden, I saw a

black-throated diver paddling westwards by the nearest islet. I stalked nearer each time it dived and got three good pictures. It seemed possible the pair would use the islet for nesting this season.

At 8.30 a.m. next day I boated over to keep my appointment with Jeff Watson. I waited for half an hour but he did not show up. Suspicions started forming again. I decided to go and check the eyries myself. I would check *all* my old eyries this year and to hell with the consequences. I boated along in sombre mood until, after a mile, I saw a figure waving frantically from some rocks on the shore. It was Jeff, and he was breathless. He had been unable to open a locked barrier (erected to keep out poachers) at the end of the track and had run and walked a two-mile detour. When I saw his obvious anxiety not to let me down I felt a great deal better. We boated to the foot of the mountain. As we hiked up to Eyrie 11, I noticed he had no trouble in keeping up the pace.

Soon we were below the eyrie, now just a few sticks and wood rush on a triangular ledge forty feet above us; it had been wrecked by human hands four years previously. Jeff wanted to check it, and I told him it was just about possible to go in from the top but that I didn't like doing it, and had only done it once.

'I'll do it,' he replied, and was up there in seconds.

There were no signs of new occupation, he called down. We tramped down a steep gully before the long climb to Eyrie 3 in a large black rockface. I was about to tell him there were two old disused sites on the way when Jeff spotted the first one himself. It was as it had been for five years, just a few decayed sticks on a ledge in a small square crag. I told him there was another on a long cliff up ahead, one I had called the 'roseroot cliff', where the eagles had made a temporary effort to build after Eyrie 11 had been destroyed. Jeff raised his binoculars and located it in a few moments. It had taken me three years of practice to spot such sites as quickly.

Jeff wondered why I had not included these two sites on my map, and I told him it was because they had never showed signs of being used. He said he thought they should be included, and marked them down on his own map. I did so too – Eyries 31 and 32. He wanted to check the second one, and so we headed up to the long cliff. We were still 300 yards away when a ewe, which had appeared to be trapped on a ledge to the left of the eyrie, made a jump for the top, missed its footing and fell.

'God, there it goes,' said Jeff. We watched the ewe fall straight down past the cliff on its back and vanish behind a ridge. We heard a sickening thump.

'She's eagle fodder now,' I said, but when we reached the top of the ridge we saw the ewe jump to its feet and run off, quite unhurt, just momentarily winded. The ewe had survived a fall of at least forty feet, probably because of her thick woollen fleece. Farther on, another ewe had not been so lucky. It had died from starvation in just such a ledge trap.

We reached the side of the cliff. Jeff swarmed up and over the top with the agility of the born climber. He came down shaking his head.

'No. There's nothing new up there either.'

I looked at Jeff Watson again. I could find no fault with him, and it was clear he had unusual talent. There was no bombast, no seeking to prove himself the great 'scientist' over the part-time 'amateur'. He had a broad forehead, sensitive eyes, a quiet manner and, as he had already proved, could climb a great deal better than I could. By now he had located many of my old eyries without help from anyone. Dots on a half-inch map are one thing; finding the actual eyries in the myriad rockfaces and cliffs in this kind of terrain, in just a few weeks, was quite another. He had been working hard and was clearly able to camp out and be alone on the Hill for days on end. I had taken quite a liking to him.

'You *are* the right man for the job,' I said. 'I doubt they could have found anyone better.'

Jeff looked embarrassed, but pleased.

After we had checked Eyrie 3 and found that not one stick remained of the old nest up a steep chimney on the dark rockface, I put some straight questions to him. It seemed that N.C.C. head-quarters in Edinburgh had indicated to Jeff that if he found my area a good one to study he should use it. He thought they wanted to show me the area *was* being looked after.

'I don't think anyone's trying to edge you out, Mike,' he said. 'Anyway, I don't think in those terms. I want to work *with* you, not against you.'

I said I was greatly relieved, for I wanted to check my old eyries so as to complete a ten-year study on the breeding success of the eight pairs.

'Well, I want to check them myself, but I could give the results to you at the end of each season,' he replied. 'Won't that free you, give

above: Atalanta and Melanion
sailed round one another in
courtship flights

below: Wildernesse in autumn.

above: Eaglets are said to leave their parents' territory in December; here Diana was still flying over the area the following May.

below: Moobli on the trek to Atalanta's farthest eyrie.

above: With a woodmouse in its beak, the barn owl flew to its youngsters in the chimney stack of the Yorkshire farmhouse.

below: The lonely whooper swan could not fly or feed itself.

above: A pair of rare black-throated divers, of which there are fewer than 150 pairs in Britain.

below: To prevent pine martens from taking the eggs of divers and gulls, I kept the bird table supplied with their foods.

you more time to concentrate on your photography?'

The more I thought about it, the more the idea appealed. Trekking round many eagle eyries demands physical prowess above all else, and I was not getting any younger. I had sixteen wilderness years behind me, after all. It was really up to me to help the younger generation, especially talented folk like Jeff, who at twenty-eight had most of his life and career before him. Two questions remained. The first was would he show me the location of the eyrie he had found where the eagle had been on eggs?

He immediately pointed downhill to a deep crevasse way below us which, because I had never found a nest in it, I had not checked for three years. The eyrie was just over a small brow on our side of the gorge, he said. I looked. It was certainly an eyrie I did *not* know; it was at a height of some 900 feet and there was only a one-mile climb up to it from where we had beached the boat.

'Can you actually look *down* on the nest?' I asked him.

'Yes. From the opposite hill, about forty yards away.'

It sounded an ideal site, for to find an eyrie on which one can look down, and thus see the eagles' feet, all the nest and all the prey that was brought in, was quite rare. The last question remained.

'Jeff, would you mind very much if I put a hide there when any chicks are well hatched, and did my photography there this year?'

Jeff's face was a study. He actually looked relieved.

'Mike, I'd be delighted. Allan or I, or both of us, could help you. I'd like to know how you build and work from a hide. It's the least I can do for all your help.'

I thanked him, feeling joyful. It was clear that by not protesting at the 'taking over' of most of my eyries, by not making a fuss, I had not only avoided making an enemy, I had made a friend. Also I now knew of a first-class eyrie I would probably not have found myself. I think Jeff liked the fact that I did not pretend I already knew this eyrie, which would have been easy enough. I had the feeling right then that this was going to be a great season. I boated Jeff to my home. We had a good lunch and talk, then I took him back to his camper. Jeff reckoned the eggs at Eyrie 30 had been laid on March 25, so we agreed to meet on May 15, when any chick or chicks hatched would be about ten days old. At that stage, in fine weather, the eagles would leave the nest to go hunting for several hours at a time and, if the situation was as good as it sounded, we could safely build my kind of hide in a very short time.

8 · Blackcocks and Black Throats

April 24 was a fine sunny day with just a few white woolly rounded clouds scudding across the blue vault of the sky, and I was reluctantly at my desk writing a wildlife column. After typing the last words, I went out into the fresh air to scan the peaks above Eyrie 1. There were no eagles in the air, but I did see a fine roebuck standing on a heathery ridge at about 400 feet.

I climbed up the side of the burn ravine, then stalked it cautiously from ridge to ridge. After shuffling along a rocky ledge over a fifteen-foot drop, I came to within forty yards of it, but all I could see and photograph was the buck's velvet-covered antlers, sticking up above the grasses and broken old brown bracken. That was not much good, so I gave a brief sharp whistle.

Instantly the buck shot to its feet. As I took pictures through some heather, I could see it was moulting its dark winter coat. Large patches of hair were falling out so it looked as moth-eaten as a bear just emerged from winter hibernation. It must have got my scent then for it began to make a hellish racket, giving loud fox-like barks, '*boff, bowf, boff, bowf*', as it ran a few steps, paused to look back, then ran a few more. I slid back and down until out of its sight.

I had just turned for home when I saw a large eagle sailing eastwards over Eyrie 1 and vanish over the highest ridge. It did not look dark enough to be Atalanta. As I carried on down a smaller eagle, doubtless a male but too dark to be Melanion, came beating over the west wood, soared over my head and was just approaching the highest ridge when the female returned. As the two flew round each other I was astonished to see another large female come in from the south-east and join them. For several seconds the three eagles circled round each other, none showing the white wing or tail patches of the immature. Then the last female turned, went into a jet glide, sailed across the loch and disappeared into the face of a deep gully two miles away to the south-east.

This was the first time I had actually seen three adult eagles amicably together right in the middle of the nesting season, and I wondered what the explanation could be. Were they poaching on the southern edges of Atalanta's territory, now that she was nesting in her most northerly eyrie? The pair that were left headed west, making occasional shallow dives as they went, and I thought that would be that.

When I reached the cottage, I looked back to see one of the eagles sitting on the peak above Eyrie 1. It had obviously circled back. It flew towards me, just as the female returned. Again they flew round each other. Twice the male dived on the female as my camera clicked and she made an upwards roll. Then they both vanished over the peaks to the north. All this curious behaviour puzzled me. Maybe there *was* another pair on the territory I had believed to be only Atalanta's. I would now have to check all the nearest eyries again.

I began next day first with Eyrie 1, taking a circuitous route along burn gorges so that if there was an eagle on the nest I could spot it before it saw me, and leave again without disturbing it. As I climbed nearer I could make out a small white dot in the centre of the nest. Good heavens! Was it a hatched eaglet? Approaching from the south-west, I reached a pair of rocks in a V shape, a superb hide site, and saw a male eagle heading south over the eastern ridges, a good two miles away. It made two 'golden ball' dives, soared back to the north, gaining height, then was joined by a female. They sailed round each other, far apart, then vanished up into the clouds. They did not reappear.

I was now fairly sure there was a pair of eagles nesting in the great mountains well to the east, but they were beyond the boundary I had set myself. Three hundred square miles was as much as one unpaid part-timer like myself could manage to cover and most of my eagle study terrain laid westward to the sea. But why was that female off her eggs, if she had any? The answer to that question came in my mail a week later, in a letter from Roger Broad of the R.S.P.B. On his part of the survey he had been into those very same mountains with the keeper of that land and they had located an occupied site which was 'already partly hatched'. They were going to check it again in the middle of the chick stage. It was good news. I now knew there were at least nine pairs of eagles in about 320 square miles.

From the V-shaped rocks I scanned Eyrie 1, but found no new signs of occupation. The white dot was just a weft of old sheep fleece. I was about to leave when I noticed something reddish near a small burn below the eyrie. It was an old dying hind, her ears worn and grey, muzzle bare, and her stomach 'blown' from eating too much new grass after weeks of poor grazing. I talked to her soothingly, stroking her head but she was too weak even to stand up. Pathetically, she nuzzled my hand but there was nothing I could do. She would be dead by tomorrow, making eight dead deer so far in the immediate terrain. The eagles had had a good carrion year.

Instead of striking directly over to Eyries 27 and 28, I made a wide swathe to the north-west, checking even unlikely rockfaces for new eyries. I found not a new but an old site. It was on a broad low heathered ledge under a perfect overhang of sheltering rocks, though there was nothing on it now but a few sticks and old wool from sheep carrion. Here was Eyrie 33, and it would have to be checked in future.

It was interesting then to reflect on how eagles come to choose certain eyries for nesting. Eagle literature holds that eaglets cut out of their parents' territory by December, at the latest, but I had already proved that some hang around all winter and even during the start of the following nesting season. Or else they return after months, or even years, away. It stands to reason that the young eagles which take over territories at the breeding age of four or five years old cannot all be strangers. Some must be the very eagles that were raised on those territories. When an old eagle, or pair, dies out these returning youngsters may well not use the sites their parents favoured and those eyries become disused and overgrown. The youngsters fly round the terrain, a memory gene stirs, and they settle on sites that their grand or even great-grandparents favoured.

Eyrie 27 was still unused. Before the steep hike up to Eyrie 28 I went to check the fox den from which Atalanta had taken two cubs to feed her twin eaglets two years earlier. There had certainly been foxes there recently, but without Moobli's nose I could not tell if there were any in the jumbled cairn of boulders now.

I puffed up, in and out of wraiths of mist, to Eyrie 28. It was still in the same built-up state, the walking stick still projecting from the front of the nest. There were no new signs of occupation, however, nor any little white splashes to indicate a hatched eaglet. I headed back along the top of the cliffs above the lower eyrie, wondering if I would find Apollo's body, or a few feathers, even now. Then I saw something white to my left, and received one of the most startling shocks I have ever had on an eagle trek.

There, on a flat mossy rock, lay a complete eagle's egg! It had a small, shallow half-inch dent in the white rusty-marked shell, and there was a crack along one side. The contents were still there, but the inner skin had been punctured, and fluid seeped out when it was touched. There was no smell. It looked just like an egg in which someone could have stirred a little strychnine and left it out for a fox. Surely such an idea was preposterous: there was no evidence in recent years that the farmers or keepers on this land would do such a thing. It was clearly an egg that Atalanta had laid earlier in the season, and it had been kept fresh by the unusually cold weather. Well, I would send it away for analysis, for there was no chance of the eagle taking it back to the eyrie. Eagles do not seem able to return young chicks to the nest once they have fallen out.

I wrapped the egg carefully in my hat and a handkerchief. On the way home I found two more dead hinds, each only partly scavenged. Once indoors, I found that the eagle's egg measured 7·4 cm and weighed just over a quarter of a pound. Next day I wrapped it up carefully and sent it to the wildlife analysis unit at Eastcraigs, Edinburgh. I also telephoned the news to Roy Dennis and Dick Balharry, with whom I had always liaised on eagle work.

I was fairly sure about what had happened. Atalanta had been about to lay the egg in the nest in late March or early April when perhaps the farmer and one of the keepers had appeared on their usual and legal clearing out of fox dens before the lambing season got under way. They had accidentally startled her from the nest, and she had dropped out of its far side. Unable to hold on to the egg, she must have swooped down and laid it on the mossy rock. After that scare, she had gone to her farthest eyrie (no. 18) and had laid another egg, or even two. This would explain why, after building up Eyrie

28, I had found her on the farthest nest on April 11. Well, I would find out whether she had been successful after all when I checked Eyrie 18 again in mid-May.

It was some time before I received confirmation that this was indeed the likely explanation. I met a young friend who had once helped me work eagles from a hide and who had become under-keeper on the estate earlier in the year. He told me that he and other fox hunters had gone to the big cairn den below the eyrie with guns and terriers a few days before I had, but the eyrie had looked deserted. They had certainly seen no eagle leave it, or any eagles at all. They had shot a vixen which had bolted from the den, and the terriers had killed some cubs. They had only been there about half an hour. He also solved for me the mystery of how the walking stick had come to be lodged in the nest. During the winter hind-culling season, an assistant stalker had left his stick stuck in the ground while they had eaten lunch and then forgotten it. When the stalker had returned to the area two days later to look for his favourite stick, it had gone. Clearly one of the eagles had found it, decided it was ideal nesting material, and had woven it into the nest structure.

On the day I posted off the eagle egg, my eagle, diver and pere-grine licences arrived.

In early May, during a break in days of cold rainy weather, I built a new eagle hide for what I hoped would be a lying-down situation up at Eyrie 30, the one Jeff Watson had found. I made it 8½ feet long so that I could lie well back in it and avoid the long telephoto lens sticking out of the front, where its artificial appearance could scare the eagles. I tied on mail-bag canvas, painted it to resemble lichened rocks, then covered it with plastic mesh into which vegetation could be woven to match the surrounding terrain. While working, I twice saw a black-throated diver submarining along near the islet on which the colony of common gulls were now breeding. I did not go over to the islet; if the divers were nesting there, they would be laying eggs before long.

As I finished the hide I saw the buff-white rump patch of a small red deer showing conspicuously on a ridge above the cottage. I climbed up, stalking carefully. It was a yearling stag, probably late-born, for there were as yet no antler knobs. It was lying down on a ledge. As I came close it got to its feet and just stood there, shiver-ing, not looking at all well. I took a few photos, then decided to get it down to the cottage to see if it would take a feed of Nutrilamb milk from a feeder bottle. It charged me weakly but I caught it and with one arm gently round its neck, the other supporting its rump, I tried to walk it down the slope. After thirty yards it fell to the ground, too weak to walk any farther. Experience told me I was too late; it would not survive.

In late afternoon I went up to look at it again, but it had gone. Knowing that such weak deer always move downwards, I made a brief search and found it lying under my fence, even closer to the cottage. It was dead. I dragged it up to a shelf at 300 feet as food for the eagles. Two more hind carcasses lay in dells immediately below small rockfaces. It had been the worst (or best from the predators' view) deer carrion season for six years.

May 6 was a fine sunny day for a change and so I set off on a six-mile zig-zag trek through the lochside woods in search of buzzard nests, badger setts and fox or pine marten dens. For some weeks I had been attracting a pine marten with titbits of bread and raspberry jam on my bird table after one of these rare animals had moved into our small woods. Sometimes, however, it spent periods in the long woods to the west, where it used a deserted otter holt. I wondered if it was back there now, as I had not seen it for a week or more.

As I set off through the trees, the air rang with sound; the cheerful songs of chaffinches, the staccato salvos of wrens, the sweet plaintive descending scales of willow warblers, the belling of great tits and the squabbly notes of spotted flycatchers. I had never seen so many tree pipits. They seemed to be everywhere, exalting in the spring sunshine, flying up high from the trees, tilting their tails right up, then parachuting down on widespread quivering wings, feet extended like little twigs, singing '*see you, see you, whiz whiz, whiz*'. It was as if the trees had sprung yo-yos. Then they landed and made little '*tch tch tch*' notes, as if saying it had not been a very good courtship performance really, and they would do better next time.

I was in the open, a quarter of a mile past the little west wood, when I saw an eagle heading east towards me, flying just below the lochside ridges. It was far too light in colour to be Atalanta, the tawny buff and brown parts of her plumage were more vivid, yet she was about the same size. Then a male came behind but well below her. They both circled over my home, doubtless seeing the deer carcasses. Then the male went into a jet glide to the east and vanished over the distant ridges. The female circled round again, rose higher and higher in the westerly breeze until she was about a mile up, then headed back towards the south-west. Suddenly another male eagle came along below her line of flight, quite near to her, but she appeared to take no notice. He too glided to the east and disappeared. The female made one more circle before going into a jet glide towards Eagle Rock mountain.

I was sure she would go down into the new eyrie Jeff had found, so I kept the binoculars on her. But she did not. She went on and on (oh, my aching arms!) and disappeared over the last ridge of that mountain. Right above the eyrie another smaller eagle was soaring, probably the male from that nest, yet he appeared to take no notice of the female, even though she had passed quite close below him. Once again I had seen four eagles near each other right in the middle of the nesting season, yet none had shown any animosity, or even apparent interest in any of the others.

On the trek I located my eleventh occupied badger sett, three more dead deer and one dead sheep, but none of the buzzards' nests were occupied and the marten was not now using the old otter holt. On my return I found one of the marten's new sweet-scented twisted scats on a rock near my boats. That night the marten came to the bird table, took two titbits, then dashed off as if it was not really hungry.

Next day I saw a black-throated diver near the islet in the setting sun. It kept turning on to its right side, showing its creamy pink underbelly. This was courtship behaviour. Then it preened its wing feathers, reaching back with its snake-like neck to tug them through its dagger bill. Another diver was sitting on the water only twenty yards away. I sneaked back to the cottage for my camera. When I got outside again I was just in time to see both birds flying to a bay a mile to the west, where they cavorted about in the water again. I was working on my book the following morning when I heard weird, strident metallic calls, 'keh kerlyee' repeated three times. I looked out to see one of the divers steaming along to the west. These were not the normal mewing wails, like those of a large lost cat, nor the gobbling calls of pre-courtship. I wondered why the diver had made them.

On May 11 I went out for supplies then called on Allan Peters, to find out if he had seen anything of Jeff Watson, because I was now anxious to get the hide up on the eagle eyrie. Allan told me that Jeff had been very busy, not only locating the last of my old eyries to the west but some of Greg Hunter's too. Greg was getting married in three days' time, and eagles had not exactly been his first priority recently. Jeff had told him he would contact me in a few days as he wanted to help me with the hide.

As he often did, Allan now capped that lot of good news with some more.

'Have you ever seen a blackcock lek?'

I said I had not. For years black grouse had been rare in our part of the west Highlands, and were mostly concentrated on the eastern moors. In fact, I had only seen one blackcock (the male black grouse) in all my years here, when it had scurried across a road above the west end of the loch in front of my Land-Rover.

'Well,' said Allan, 'I've got some lecking in my cow-field right now!'

Soon we were on our way. As we drove up a narrow road through Forestry Commission plantations I felt a mounting surge of excitement. The courtship rituals of the black grouse are among the most spectacular of all British birds. The 'lek' is actually a sort of displaying or trysting ground, often traditional, where the glossy, black-plumaged twenty-one-inch males assemble for the rites. Each cock occupies a tiny 'court', or territory, about three yards or so in diameter, which it defends against other cocks. The displays are mostly ritual, but occasionally fights occur. The more central courts on the lek are apparently the most desirable, and are occupied by the dominant, more vigorous cocks. Once the initial intensity of the first displays dies down, the fourteen-inch females, dowdier with barred buff plumage and forked tails, wander in among the courts. Each cock tries to court a female as she passes through his court, but the females, known as greyhens, generally make for the central courts. In this way most of the matings are made by the dominant cocks, thus the finest birds in the main are the ones to pass on their genes. The whole lek acts as a magnet, attracting females from all over the area, so giving each cock a better chance to mate.

As we came to the lek area we saw two blackcocks perched on the tops of young spruce trees at the edge of the plantation. One flew down to the display area, then the other. We parked, sneaked along a gully, and sat below some trees near a tiny holiday cottage.

The first two cocks were already on their courts, standing at the edges of their respective boundaries, facing each other and looking

73

fierce. Then two more cocks, followed by another three, flew in and the lek proper began.

The cocks strutted in their courts, and spread out their long, dark, outer tail feathers downwards into lyre shapes, so they looked like pairs of burly arms, like boxers clenching fists and measuring up to opponents. Wings were lowered and also held out to the side to increase the posture of aggressiveness, and the dazzling white under-tail feathers were held bolt upright in the shape of fans. It was ostentatious, magnificent, primordial and beautiful. The only trouble was that our vision was obscured here and there by small clumps of rushes covering the ground.

Then we heard soft bubbling '*roo-coo, roo-coo*' sounds, rather like those made by wood pigeons, but louder and deeper voiced. Two cocks came out more into the open, facing each other on the edges of their courts. Their throats were puffed out, their short, sharp and strong beaks opening and closing as they inhaled air to make the bubbling sounds. When they got closer they puffed their plumage out even farther, looking even more belligerent, and we heard odd hissing noises, '*tash-kee*' and '*tash-kay*', the latter syllables ending in flat '*ayee*' sounds, just like the air brakes of a lorry giving out. As they made these noises their beaks jerked upwards and their wings flicked as if to warn the other not to come any closer. The scarlet wattle combs above their eyes seemed even more inflamed. I tried to take photos, then swore as my film ran out. Without my glasses I had mistaken thirty-three on the dial for twenty-three.

From what we could see, the outer cocks were trying to work their way into the centre courts but were repulsed by the threat displays and the loud hisses of the dominant birds. At first it seemed that all this was taking place without a single greyhen present. Then we saw two on the edge of the courting ground. One greyhen began walking towards the centre and in turn each cock tried to court her, circling round and making short chases, at which she would lower her tail and swerve away. When she neared the centre, a dominant cock walked alongside, comically tilting his whole body and tail towards her almost coyly, as if saying 'How about me, eh?' We did not see any mating, but that could have been because of the rushes. After half an hour the hissings ceased. We heard a few more bubbling calls, then as the sun began to set one cock flew back to the spruce plantation, followed by another, and we could hear the whirring of their wings. Soon all had gone, and silence fell upon the lek.

I thanked Allan for the impromptu show and we promised ourselves to come again with a hide, which we would enter before dawn. We went over to the courting ground and found many droppings, some filled with larch and spruce needles but mostly with young pine shoots. In large numbers birds like black grouse can cause havoc in young plantations, but in small groups like these they are an asset — for their interest, their beauty and, from the pure conservationist view, for their culling effect on large monocultures of close-stacked conifers.

Forestry agencies, especially the Forestry Commission, are often criticised by conservationists for planting large areas with blanket conifer forest where little light seeps down to the woodland floor, wildlife finds no foothold, and the hunting areas of species like eagles are reduced. Allan had often told me he thought many of the forests did more good for wildlife than harm. So far as our area of the west Highlands was concerned, he was certainly right.

In this harsh, steep, hilly terrain there were many small areas where young trees cannot be planted at all, or would simply not 'take' and grow. In these clearings, natural indigenous trees like ash, oak, alder, willow and rowan had sprouted and had been good for mice and voles. This in turn had helped species like buzzards, hen harriers, wildcats and pine martens to flourish. Indeed, the once-rare pine marten was becoming quite common in the region. But for these plantations, with their frequent clearings, the blackcock would not have spread back to the area. Our local Commission has done much to provide picnic sites and nature walks, and now there were more wildlife species to be seen than if the land had been left completely alone. The Forestry Commission was also the first large body to ban snaring in its forests and to declare its lands otter havens.

Two days later I was walking round my east wood when I saw three large birds sitting on the water in the lagoon by the nearest islet. They were too big for red-breasted mergansers — but three? I rushed back for my camera, sneaked through the wood and stationed myself behind a large larch trunk, peering through the telephoto lens. They were three black-throated divers. They were dipping their heads in and out of the lagoon, ignoring a colourful male merganser that was sleeping on a rock, its head behind its wing. I was now treated to a rare part of the divers' courtship ritual, one I had never seen before.

They seemed to be extremely peaceful, every so often two of the divers pointing their stout bills at each other, a mere inch or two apart, and staring intently into each other's eyes. Then they would waltz round in a half-circle, before looking away and dipping their heads in and out of the water again. Sometimes one paddled over to the third and repeated the process, and at other times all three pointed their bills together, completely horizontally, and swam round, their short tails making the points of an equilateral triangle as if they were conversing in some silent language. Then all dived under the water, not throwing themselves up first like cormorants but with a gentle slide, head and chest first.

They came up a hundred yards away and made a waltzing triangle again. Two of them broke away and circled each other, while the third looked on from the sidelines with a gloomy air. Then one dived, followed by the second, and finally the more distant third. They all came up together, and the farthest diver rolled on to its side, tucked up a wing and exposed the soft creamy pink of its underbelly, which flashed across the loch in the sun. They drifted east of the islet and I lost sight of them as they entered the nesting bay. This behaviour could not be part of true courtship, for surely any female among them would have laid her eggs by now. Perhaps the real pair were asserting their bond, informing a newcomer that they were already matched.

My eye was distracted then by something in the sky. I looked up to see three mergansers flying eastwards at tremendous speed. The one in front was making loud squawly duck-like calls. They wheeled upwards, then down, then veered sideways. Through the binoculars it was clear a hen was in the lead with two cocks after her. One cock stayed close to her tail, as if trying to take a beakful of feathers out of it. She was swerving all over the sky, wings beating rapidly, up and down, dodging, covering a great distance. She switched north, wheeled to the west, swerved to the south, went higher, dived down again, and always the first cock stayed close to her tail while the second seemed to get left behind on the rapid turns. Maybe this was one way a male wins a female, by being the one to keep close to her. Finally the trailing cock seemed to decide he could not keep up, gave up the chase and drifted away. I had never seen mergansers behave like this before.

Two hours later I returned to see if I could spot the divers again and was just in time to watch the pair stand up in the water, run hard across the surface, flapping rapidly and taking a long time to rise into the air on the southerly wind before wheeling away to the west. With their 9 lb bodies and short pointed wings, which are so ideal for underwater diving, these birds need long 'runways' to get airborne. But why did this pair keep flying to the west?

I woke late on May 15 and saw the headlights of Jeff's camper van flashing above the shore on the opposite side of the loch. Cripes! It was 8.30 a.m. I dashed out, boated over and brought him back for breakfast. As we ate Jeff gave me the eagle news so far.

Five pairs in my old area had chicks, one pair was still incubating late eggs in a larch-tree nest, and there was one pair he still had to locate and check. It was likely Atalanta had a chick or two in Eyrie 18, which I still had to check again. Then there were two chicks in the nest Roger Broad had located, which was not in my old or Jeff's new study areas. It looked as if it would be a good year for the local eagles.

It was a fine calm hazy day and Jeff said he would gladly help me build my hide overlooking Eyrie 30. We crossed over to Eagle Rock mountain, left the boat in a hidden rocky niche and began the mile-long climb up the northern side of the crevice. Hell, it was hard going after the first quarter of a mile, with the camera pack, tripod, lenses, food, pint of milk, sleeping bag, plastic foam to lie on, and the hide with all its hazel-pole bracers. The ground rose steeply with deep drainage ditches topped with ankle-wrenching tussocks every two or three yards. I could not keep up the pace Jeff was setting. He grabbed the hide from me, which made things easier. As we climbed the last forestry fence, the mother eagle launched herself from a dead oak snag where she had been perched opposite the eyrie, flew over our heads and disappeared. Against the hazy sky she looked as dark and massive as Atalanta. Could I have been mistaken earlier? This nest was nearer to Eyries 27 and 28 than was Eyrie 18, I realised with slight shock.

We checked below the oak snag and Jeff took three regurgitated pellets, mostly filled with wool from sheep carrion, to analyse. Finally we were overlooking the nest, on a ledge screened by small rowan trees on the far side of the crevasse but only forty yards away. There was one eaglet in the nest, all clad in white down but quite big, about two weeks old. It was crouching down due to the sounds we were making. The situation was perfect, the best I had ever known, for I could see right down into the nest. There was a large boulder to the left of a slightly sloping ledge before the ground rose steeply again. All we had to do was bridge that gap with the hide. I could then lie in the gap between the boulder and the hill.

We soon had the hide poles in place, anchored invisibly by cords and small stakes at each end. As we hurried to gather moss and armsful of heather and weave them into the hide's meshes, I saw one of the eagles' kill-rocks below us, some blue-grey feathers scattered round it. Jeff went down and returned with the skull of a heron. It was the first time I had known eagles to take heron as prey.

In less than an hour the hide was complete and it was indistinguishable from the surrounding terrain. I told Jeff I had evolved this type of hide to be virtually impossible for either eagles or humans to detect. The monstrously artificial square canvas hides that some bird watchers use not only scare the eagles but alert any passing human to the fact that there is a nest there. The other great virtue of this site was that the rear flap of the hide faced on to a steep hill, so that I would be able to enter or leave totally obscured from the eyrie. Indeed, such was the shape of this hill that it would also screen my final approach from the rest of the mountain as well. Any eagle sitting on one of its peaks would not be able to see me either. Only an eagle flying behind me would know I was there, and I could easily guard against that happening.

Invisible though the hide was to human eyes, I now had to make sure the eagles accepted it, or did not notice it. If neither of the pair came in, or did and showed signs of stress, I would strike the hide and abandon the project. Naturally, I hoped this would not happen, not only for the sake of my own observations and photos but because Jeff wanted a full list of prey brought in to help the survey. If an eagle was watching from somewhere behind us as Jeff was now leaving, his departure would help it believe the coast was clear.

I slid into the hide, set the camera on the tripod and, while Jeff fixed disguising heather on to the front of the lens, climbed into my sleeping bag. Then, wishing me luck, Jeff left. I heard his boots clumping down the hill and settled down to wait.

9 · Tragedy of the Divers

Soon the eaglet rose from its prone lying position and made a great effort to stand up on the trippy twigs of the nest, just managing it with much waving of its little white embryo wings. At this featherless stage it looked comically like a penguin, and I took some pictures. Twenty minutes later, I was about to lay my head down to ease my aching neck muscles when there was a rush of air above the hide and my lens was filled with a mass of great feathers. The mother eagle was floating into the eyrie.

She landed lightly on the nest, folded her long pinions above her tail and, lifting her great booted yellow feet with exaggerated care, tramped over to some prey which lay behind a large sprig of heather. I was astonished. She had come in even before Jeff could have reached the boat! She craned her head down, gripped the prey with her huge blue-black beak and as she lifted it with ease and hauled it nearer to the chick, I saw that it was a greyhen. Not only had the oft-maligned forestry plantations attracted black grouse back to the area, they had also provided a new source of food for the eagles. This was most interesting.

The eagle clamped her long black talons on the greyhen, easily ripped off slivers and tendered them delicately to the chick, which was making weak 'kyew' cheeps all the time, with the tip of her beak. She turned her head to the left, to the right, and sometimes held it straight on, helping the chick to get each scrap just right. Not once did she appear to notice the hide or look towards me (except in natural looking about) as I clicked away. The hide was clearly the minor masterpiece we had felt it to be. With each morsel she watched to make sure the eaglet was getting it down all right before she pecked off another. When it appeared to have trouble in swallowing, she watched with maternal concern, and once took a feathery piece right out of its beak as it seemed about to choke. If she cut off bits that were obviously too large she just swallowed them herself. She fed the youngster fifty-one slivers, until its white crop bulged in two portions like a halved tennis ball.

As the eaglet laid its head over the nest twigs and went to sleep, the mother did not sit beside it but sort of crouched down like a great winged cat, overlooking it with arched neck and a most tender caring look. She was a big heavy bird, though certainly not Atalanta, for she was much younger and had an even wider face. This was the most beautiful eagle I had ever photographed; the fawns, golds, russets and browns of her thick plumage were all superb and rich and rather light in colour. She must be the big female I had seen flying along the lochside near my home on May 6 when two males had also headed along, one above and one below the line of her flight. I had the feeling she could be one of Atalanta's daughters, which might explain why she had then been on the veteran eagle's territory.

After an hour of just looking about she tramped over to the left of the nest, showing her huge yellow feet, to the remains of a ptarmigan. As she got up I saw a white scrap under the nest twigs where her tail had been – the corpse of a small eaglet that must have perished in the competition for food. Hearing its mother move, the chick woke up, tried to walk towards her, tripped and completed the brief journey by shuffling along on its hocks.

The eagle pulled a long yellow-pink sliver from the ptarmigan, presented it to the chick, then fed it twenty-one more slivers where it lay irritatingly obscured by a sprig of heather. When it was full up once more, the mother took a nap standing up, dozing in long snatches, her bluey-white eyelids, unlike a human's, closing upwards from beneath. Only then did I relax enough to realise I had just had my best first afternoon watching an eagle's nest. What a sterling fellow Jeff Watson had turned out to be. Not only had he found this nest, he had carried my hide up most of the way, had worked very hard to help me build it in record time, and in doing so had made himself an hour late for an appointment. He also faced a far longer walk out, as he was leaving the boat for my use. Any 'debt' he or the N.C.C. owed me for the map of eyries had already been repaid in full!

As the light faded the eagle woke up, looked twice towards the edge of the nest, then jumped upwards and flapped away in the windless air. I took two photos, surprised that even at forty yards I was too close to get all her outstretched wings in the frame. In half an hour she swept in again with a great leafy spray of birch in her beak. She dropped this at the back of the nest, then re-arranged a few twigs, picking them up in her beak and dropping them near the chick, as if trying to build up a slight screen. She now spent a lot of time just looking down at the eaglet, all her movements slow and intent, as if drinking in the sight of it, her baby! Then in the soft light of dusk, facing away from me, she went to sleep standing bolt upright, her head tucked right back below the upper shoulder of her left wing.

After 10 p.m. she woke up in the near dark and preened her tail feathers, reaching right back and stroking each one out to its full length with her hooked bill, zipping up the barbules and making sure each feather was where it should be. Satisfied with this, she looked around for something else that needed doing, then started weaving some loose sticks into the nest structure. She really did *weave* too, holding each stick in her beak, forcing one end between other twigs and twisting sideways, then doing the same with the other end. This evidently was hard work, for she had to stand with her powerful legs wide apart and her whole body and tail waggled to and fro with the effort.

By this time the male eagle had landed in the oak-tree snag below and to the left of the hide, for I could hear him making 'k'yow' calls, rather like those of an eaglet but louder and deeper in tone. The mother eagle took no notice whatever. She took another brief nap and then began to preen the chick, quibbling her great beak delicately all over and through its short white down. As I clearly saw again all its short chunky round body I was sure it was a male. What a splendid little chap he was, full of beans, avid for his grub and able to stuff away three times as much as his enormous mother. He stood up like a child in a bath, staggering about under his mother's massaging bill, as if saying, 'Hey, it tickles there!', and flapping his little white wing stubs with ecstasy and glee. Sometimes, just like a human kid, he tried to dodge away.

Once this toilet was completed, the mother brooded the youngster all night, sometimes by sheltering him under her left wing, at others by half crouching over him, heedless of the strain this position must have been on her legs. Before I lay down to try to get some sleep myself, I saw that all her head feathers were frowsted up, giving her the look of a harpy eagle.

My own night was uncomfortable. What had seemed a gentle slope when I had lain on it for a few seconds before building the hide, now appeared much steeper. My sleeping bag kept slipping backwards over its plastic sheet. Bit by bit, careful not to make any rustling sounds, I removed the plastic. Then the grass became polished. I had to keep hauling myself up into position again with the sore tips of my fingers and toes. The cold seemed Arctic, wind blasting through the hide's meshes. Minor projections hurt my ribs and hips and when I lay on my stomach a swell in the slope tried to dislodge my kneecaps. I had no sleep at all.

Around 5 a.m. the eagle tramped to the greyhen and pulled off more slivers, often presenting them with her head upside down, so the chick could take the meat snippets from the inside of her hook more easily. After the feeding, she preened her pinions with her bill, setting a few feathers neatly above the ones in front where they had overlapped wrongly, then moved back to massage the down on the eaglet's head. She seemed quite unable to leave him alone. When she was not feeding, preening or tucking him in with twigs, she just kept fondly gazing at him. Once, as she stood with arched neck, the eaglet stretched upwards then turned his head to one side so his eye gazed into hers. The rapport between them was overwhelming.

I once wrote that there is no love or compassion in the animal world, only maternal, and occasionally paternal, care – and even that is short lived. I was wrong. That eagle loved that chick as surely and strongly as any human mother could love her baby. Three hours later, as I threaded the third film into the camera, I heard the chick giving its weak 'k'yew' calls. Then the cheeps not only rose in volume and frequency but were joined by much louder, deeper 'keeyow' calls.

What a rising crescendo of wild sound now rang from the great granite cliff above the nest, 'k'yew, keeyow, k'yew, keeyow,' and I lifted one eye back up to the camera viewer. The mother eagle was crouched on the edge of the eyrie stickpile, her wings hunched and half open, her piercing orange eyes glaring into the sky, the red of her throat showing as she made the louder calls, which seemed both supplicant and demanding at the same time.

Suddenly there was a loud swish of air above the hide, then the lens was filled with a pair of mighty mottled brown wings, a wide spread tail, and the male eagle landed with a hooded crow in his talons. He dropped the crow, stood briefly at the right of the nest looking at the remains of prey, the eaglet's half-full crop, then flew off again. I took pictures of all this, but the light was poor in what was now a blustery cloudy day and I felt the shutter speed would prove too slow.

After a few minutes the mother eagle began plucking the crow. Holding it down with one set of talons she twist-tweaked wing and breast feathers off with remarkable speed and tossed them into the air. Then she fed sixty-two slivers to the eaglet, giving him a few small feathers and bones as well, as if knowing his digestive system could now not only cope with but needed them.

By 11 a.m. the wind was blowing the camera off focus, the first drops of rain were smearing the lens, and it was so cold my fingers had turned white. The mother eagle showed no inclination to leave the nest. In my twenty-one-hour stay in the hide she had been away for a mere half-hour, the longest I had ever known an eagle stay beside its youngster. I decided to leave. Ignoring leg cramps caused by the cold and the tight conditions inside the hide, I got my boots on, stuffed the sleeping bag and camera gear in my pack, then with infinite care so as not to make any sound, I slid out of the back of the hide. Out of sight of the eyrie, I crept backwards down the steep hill for forty yards before turning to descend the tussocks down to the boat. As I reached the bottom of the long ridge that shielded me from view I looked back at the eyrie a quarter of a mile away. The mother eagle was still there and again feeding the chick. In all that time she had been completely unaware of the hide or my presence. It was, thanks to Jeff Watson, the best observation place I had ever enjoyed.

Back home after a bouncing boat ride, Moobli greeted me with loyal whining fuss, but he had eaten all the food I had left in the woodshed for him. I bathed myself down, noting the blue bruises on ribs and hips, and kept falling asleep as I typed up my notes. It was as much as I could do to force myself to make a proper meal before collapsing into bed.

Three mornings later I went out early to buy some new films and supplies in the nearest town and found I could not launch the boat. A pair of black-throated divers were floating offshore, only forty yards out, and although they saw me they refused to budge. For such rare and shy birds this was extraordinary behaviour. There was something oddly depressed about their demeanour and they kept dipping their long dagger beaks in and out of the bright surface. Ludicrous though it might sound, it was as if they were appealing in a silent animal way for some kind of help.

I felt sure, as I had seen them near it often before, that the divers would now be nesting on the nearest islet. Because I had wanted to make sure they were well ensconced there, I had not yet gone over to check. As I now had a unique licence to watch and photograph the divers at their nest this year, I certainly did not want them to fail. Perhaps they were just two males, while a female was somewhere incubating eggs. I moved down to the boat, but still they stayed. I waited twenty minutes, even took a few pictures, then decided as they drifted slightly to the west that I could not stand there all day. As the engine burst into life and headed over to my van, they barely bothered to move out of the way. Now I *had* to check the islet.

On my return I boated to its northern edge, hidden from all the nest sites of the common gull colony by a rising rocky mound on which grew long heather and a small collection of stunted Scots pines. I wriggled up through the heather on my belly and peered through the topmost sprays. There were over a score of gulls on the islet's far side, making their usual ringing clamour, but not one appeared to be sitting on a nest. There was no sign of any incubating diver either. The gulls knew me of old for I had monitored their breeding success, along with the divers, over the last eight years. Often they came winging across to snatch scraps from my bird table, or to catch food I threw into the air. I showed myself and climbed down to check. The gulls had made their usual nests amid natural cups among the tussocks but not one contained any eggs. Puzzled, I climbed back up to the heathery mound below the pines and started searching round.

I found one gull eggshell, then another, then three more broken ones by a burrow that was almost as large as a rabbit's. Five yards farther on, round a bluff to the west, I found another burrow and outside it the remains of seven more gulls' eggs. I peered into the dark burrow and felt a surge of disappointment. Lying on the earth was the unmistakable olive-brown, black-speckled thin end of a black-throated diver's egg. Hell! A yard away, on top of a small mossy rock, was a dark twisted tapering scat. I knew the look of this type of animal dropping well, and when I picked it up and sniffed its almost scentless sweetish smell, my initial recognition was confirmed. It was the scat of a pine marten.

I had little doubt it came from the marten which had moved into our woods two years earlier and which, in early spring, I had managed to attract to the bird table at night by setting out titbits of bread and raspberry jam. For three weeks the marten had not appeared on the table, nor had it left scats in the woods; and now I knew the reason why. Obviously, it had been attracted by the raucous calls of the nesting gulls, had swum over to the islet and was now feasting sumptuously on their eggs. I then found a dead gull with deep neck wounds lying between some outlying rocks. Perhaps it had died trying to defend its nest. Predating on common gulls' nests was one thing, but wrecking the breeding of rare birds which numbered only 150 pairs in all Britain seemed quite another. Now I understood why the divers staying close to me this morning might have been making a mute appeal for help.

I boated home, prepared a stack of jammy titbits, went back to the islet and left a trail down to the shore, then up from the mainland shore to the bird table. This ploy to lure the marten back off the islet proved futile. Before I got back to the cottage I saw the gulls were swooping down to snap up the titbits themselves. I then put up a makeshift hide in the long heather overlooking the burrows, but though I waited in it for a few hours before and after dark, no marten appeared. I left the hide there in the hope that it and my scent around it would scare the marten back to the mainland, where I could try and keep it satisfied with food. This ruse also failed, for the marten did not return to the bird table again until the autumn.

In the early morning of May 20, as I was packing the eagle gear and a sandwich, the skies darkened and a rain storm swept over from Eagle Rock mountain and drenched the cottage area. As I looked out, thinking twice about going, I saw three black-throated divers paddling westwards beyond the boat bay. What were *three* doing together in what should be the nesting season? Suddenly the front two reared up, began beating their wings hard and pattering their feet over the surface. Because of the head wind they rose into the air quicker than usual, and I watched the round dots of their bodies get smaller and smaller as they disappeared round a land spit three miles away. Were they looking for a new nest site in which maybe to lay another egg?

The skies brightened and I decided to go after all. I boated over, trekked up in a wide arc and, from behind a tree near the bottom of the long screening ridge, scanned the eyrie with binoculars. It looked empty. I felt momentarily sick. If anything had happened to the chick I would never work eagles again, I resolved. In fact I would leave the Highland wilderness life altogether. From the dell below the hide I scanned the few peaks and all the sky I could see. No eagles were to be seen anywhere. I ran up the last yards and got into the hide as quietly as I could. To my great relief the eaglet was fine. It had just been lying low.

I was still setting up the camera when there was a great rush of woofing wings above the hide and the mother eagle landed on the nest. Two minutes later and she would have seen me getting in, and that would have been that, for many hours at least. I had to wait for the moment when she was looking away before poking the lens through the front meshes.

She fed the chick from a fresh hooded crow, ate some bits herself, yawned twice with her huge beak wide open, then did some preening. After an hour I heard the shrill bleatings of a small lamb coming from the top of the cliff right above the eyrie. The mother eagle looked down into the crevasse, up into the void above the hide, jumped upwards and flapped away. My god, I thought, I hope she is not going after that lamb! Just then I heard the deeper bleats of a ewe, apparently calling the lamb back to her side.

Eagles are blamed, often erroneously, by farmers and shepherds for killing lambs. Research by the Animal Breeding Research Organisation in Edinburgh has proved that 17 per cent of all lambs born on Scottish hills are either dead at birth or die within twenty-four hours, due mainly to poor ewe nutrition in winter. And this figure can rise to as high as 40 per cent in the harsher sheep runs of the north and west Highlands. Most of the lambs taken by eagles, great carrion feeders, are already dead. By now I had put in 541 hours in eagle hides and all this time, plus all the visits to other eyries, had resulted in my finding five lambs on nests, only two of which, judging from the typical wounds, had been actually killed by the eagles. There had been a third lamb from which eagles had been feeding near Eyrie 27 two years before but, judging from the throat wounds, it could have been killed first by foxes which had a den below the eyrie. I did not want the mother eagle to kill the lamb I now heard bleating, nor did I want her to spoil the statistics.

Half an hour later I heard an air noise near the hide and in swept the mother eagle again, not with the lamb but with a large spray of rowan leaves in her beak. She put it all round the chick, picking it up and dropping it again, finally leaving it to the rear. Then she dropped a heather twig in front of the chick, slightly obscuring my view of him. Just before 3 p.m. she began feeding the chick from the body of a ptarmigan. She kept this up for twenty-four minutes, all the time with her rear end and tail towards me. Trying to make her change position so I could photograph the actual beak-to-beak transfers of food, I gave a few breathy blasts on a deer bleater, a device made to lure foxes to waiting guns at night. It did not work with the eagle, however; she merely looked up at the first bleat then ignored the others. It was a natural enough sound in the hills and there was plenty of food in the nest anyway. Once the chick had received enough, she flew away again.

Almost an hour later the male arrived with a dry heather twig in his beak. As he stood with it, alert and still, I saw he was considerably smaller than his mate, had darker plumage and his eyes looked black in the lens. His legs seemed more slender and longer in proportion, so his body seemed higher off the nest. Although males do help incubate the eggs, he did not seem to have grown the thick warm incubating and brooding under-plumage of the female. He dropped the twig, looked carefully at the chick's crop, then at the prey remains with careful scrutiny, tramping from one carcass to another like some avian Ministry of Food inspector. He appeared to be assessing whether any more food was needed. He made no attempt to feed the chick which, in turn, made no solicitation cheeps as he did when his mother was on the nest.

Shortly after the male left the chick shuffled over to the remains of the crow, made two or three weak symbolic sort of pecks, then twisted a bit off and jerked it back. At three weeks old it was beginning to feed itself. It could now also walk a few steps, but it still had to flap its wing stubs, on which the first dark feathers were sprouting. Ten minutes later the mother came in with a small rowan spray which she dropped right on top of the chick! The chick shuffled it off and squeaked, but instead of feeding him she started to doze.

Seeing her resting like that made me feel drowsy too. I yawned, and to ease my aching neck muscles I laid my head on one arm. I must have dropped off, for at 7 p.m. I was startled awake by a loud woofing of wings, '*whush whush whush*', above the hide. I shot up to the viewer, just in time to see the male coming in with a small birch twig.

For the first time in all my years of eagle watching, I now had both the male and the female on the nest with their eaglet – and found I was nearing the end of a film! I dared not risk moving the camera by putting in a new one for fear of scaring one of them away, so I chose my photos carefully.

Now the male appeared impatient. He walked round the nest on the six-foot-long ledge, again looked at the prey items in the full 'larder' then back to his mate. He knew the chick had been amply fed and it seemed as if he thought the female should take a break and come away with him for a long float together. He kept looking at her, then crouched down with half-open wings, as if about to take off, so conveying his wishes to her.

She was not going, however. A cold north-west wind was blowing on to the eyrie and there was something that had to be done first. She glared meaningfully at him with her bright sagacious eyes. Something was communicated. He crouched, jumped and beat away, to return in a few minutes with a bare stick in his beak. She took it from him, dropped it as if in disgust, then gave him another meaningful look. Off he went again, this time returning with a long thick spray of heather which he dropped at her feet. She picked it up like a banner bearer, stepped across the nest with exaggerated care, lifting her feather-booted talons high, then with a ponderous wiggling movement of her whole body, wove it into the nest, deliberately screening the eaglet from the wind.

Twice more the male flew off and returned with heavy sprays. Then he flew straight towards me and landed on the rock beside the hide. I could hear his great talons scratching to gain purchase on the rock a mere two feet from my head! My heart thudding with excitement, I heard a brief brushing noise and then saw the top of the hide's roof lifting up slightly. There was a loud '*tunk*' sound as if something had been tugged free, and a loud woofing of wings, rapidly receding. I got to the viewer just in time to see him landing back on the nest – with a big heather spray he had tugged from the hide. Now I knew for sure they did not know I was there, or even that it *was* a hide. What moments. What blissful self-satisfaction.

What was just as astonishing and in a way more exciting, was to witness the extraordinary yet apparently silent communication between the two great birds. The male watched his mate weave one spray into the nest beside the eaglet before picking up a dry twig and holding it near. She looked at the twig and then at him, as if he needed his head examining, then tramped over the nest to pick up another leafy rowan spray. The male dropped the dry twig, stood there for a second or two with his beak open, as if in disappointment, then picked up a leafy birch spray from near his feet and held it out to her. This she took from his beak – just as my film ended. Somehow I put in a new one in record time without moving the lens.

The mother placed this spray right in front of the eaglet and he, watching all this, reached out with his beak from his lying position, picked up two small twigs and also dropped them near himself. He was copying his mother's actions, for sure. The mother now picked up two more pieces of heather from the back of the nest and dropped them right on the eaglet, until he was almost completely hidden from my view. Only then did she finally obey her mate's wishes and fly away with him.

The dying sun was now gleaming on the eyrie, giving the youngster a final warm up before the cold night ahead. The parents would not be back for a while. After the nine most rewarding hours I had ever spent in an eagle hide, I left. When I was a mile away, and nearing the bay where my boat was beached, I saw the two eagles, soaring along together above the eastern peaks of the mountain.

Next morning, on my usual early walk round the woods, I saw another dead gull lying on the islet rocks. As I watched, a black-throated diver paddled eastwards, and again took off into the wind and flew down past the long land spit three miles away. Was the female now on a new nest somewhere there? I would make a search soon. I boated to the islet. Only one gull was on a nest containing a single egg. Three others stood about disconsolately, giving hopeless 'kee' calls. Of the rest of the eighteen gulls that had returned this season there was no sign. The dead gull again had neck wounds.

Hoping to attract the marten off the islet, now the egg supply was all but finished, I placed the gull on the mainland rocks opposite the islet. If the marten became hungry enough to want the gull it would just have to swim over for it.

During the next few days, I spread titbits of food in the east wood to try and help satisfy the marten's appetite. This final ruse worked, for the titbits kept disappearing and the gulls must have laid a few more eggs, though they only raised two late young to flying stage that season.

Blustery, showery weather followed and I did not return to the eagle hide until May 30. This time I took with me a short length of one-inch plastic foam, just enough to protect ribs and hips from the rough ground. As I freshened the hide with new long heather sprigs, having made sure the eagles were not about, I saw that some of the biggest sprigs were missing from the front. There were two eagle breast feathers on top of the hide and two more actually inside it. Certainly the eagles had found it easier to take loose sprigs from the hide for their nest than to pluck growing ones. Had one of them sheltered *in* the hide from the recent rainstorms? If so, and it came back and found its new shelter occupied by a human, that would really blow the gaff, as they say. The more likely explanation was that the two feathers had been blown in by the wind.

The eaglet seemed fine, slept for the first hour and a half, then set a few twigs round himself with his beak. When he climbed to his feet I saw that pinions had started to grow; dark-brown feathers were sprouting along the scapulas and a few half-inch-long ones were sticking out of his white pin-cushion of a tail. He preened these for a while, pulling off little tatters of white down with his beak and watching some of them float away on the slight breeze. He then flopped down for another long snooze. After two hours he clambered on to his feet again and preened the down of his neck and ruffled through the new scapula feathers before flapping his stubby white wings, dislodging more down.

After looking round the eyrie he moved towards some light-coloured prey lying at the back of the nest which, from my obscured point of view, looked like a lamb. I hoped it was not. At just over a month old the eaglet still could not walk over the rough twigs without stumbling, and once he put a wing down on the nest to stop himself from falling over, like a man would put out an arm when negotiating the side of a steep hill. He tried to pull off some morsels of meat with his beak but with little success, as if there was not enough meat left.

By this time the sun had moved on to the eyrie and the eaglet was hot. He sat down on his hocks with his beak wide open, panting in the heat, and with his huge talons sticking straight up into the air. An eagle's powerful yellow feet and long black talons are its killing tools, and during the early stages of its life they grow proportionately faster than any other part, so at first the eaglet finds it hard to cope with and walk on them.

At about 5 p.m., after a fruitless seven-hour wait, the eaglet began to squeak and glare up into the sky. Then in swept the male eagle with what looked like a snake in its beak. It was of an odd dark-coppery colour and its tail appeared to be moving slightly as if it was still alive. As I took pictures, the male dropped the 'snake', looked at the eaglet, then back to the 'snake' again. He moved forward and put his hooked bill close to the chick's with a solicitous inquiring gesture, looked down at the new prey again, then back to the chick, which was still squeaking, anxious to be fed. The male, however, seemed unable to feed the chick and soon left, diving away down the gorge.

Presently the eaglet walked over to the new prey, seemed to decide he could not feed from it himself and sat down beside it. He had now waited all day to be fed, without luck, and the twin pouches of his crop hung down like an old man's jowls. He then moved over to the remnants of what I had taken to be lamb, lay beside it and picked a few bits off. He did not try to hold it down but luckily it seemed a hefty chunk and gravity helped him tug off a few tiny scraps. Finally he stood up, clamped one foot on the 'lamb', probably the first time he had done this, and began to tug. Still he got very little of what seemed just a pile of bones and lightish wool.

At 7.15 p.m. the mother eagle came in at last. As she looked around the eyrie and I saw again her magnificence, I named her Juno, after the Greek goddess of the sky. She tramped over to the 'lamb' and at first appeared to ignore the cheeping eaglet, for she swallowed the first four morsels herself! She then fed him with great deliberation and tenderness, pausing often to make sure one scrap was going down before proffering another. In all she fed him 173 slivers. As she pulled the prey up between her talons I saw with relief it was not a lamb at all but a rabbit. From a distance the whitish belly fur had looked like the wool of a lamb. Once she paused over a four-inch thigh bone, held it near the eaglet, decided it was too big and gulped it down herself. Now and again the eaglet copied his mother, and also grabbed at the rabbit with his beak as she held it in her talons and pulled a few bits off for himself.

It took Juno a full twenty minutes to feed the eaglet until his crop seemed fit to bust. Then she walked about, lifting her great booted feet high, until she found what the male had brought in. She picked it up by the neck in her beak and I saw then that it was not a snake but a full-grown *stoat*. I got one fine photo of her standing with it, poor thin killer in the beak of a mightier predator. Since stoats average 1 ft 4 ins in length and are efficient carnivores in their own right, capable of killing rats and rabbits three times their own weight, I could only guess at how and why the male eagle tackled and killed this one.

Among the old eagle legends is a story from the mid-1800s of an unnamed stalker who saw an eagle rise high into the air and then fall back to the earth. When he got near, he saw a stoat run away from the dying eagle. It was believed the eagle had seized the stoat as prey but the stoat sunk its teeth into the eagle's neck, held on tenaciously and so brought the eagle down. I can't help feeling, if true, the 'stoat' must have been a pine marten.

Be that as it may, as Juno held this stoat high in her beak the eaglet looked at it with evident distaste, his facial expression seeming to say, 'I am not eating that!'

I took two photos of Juno leaving the nest in the dying sunlight, withdrew the camera and packed up all my gear. Just before leaving, I peered out and saw that Juno was back on the nest. Good. Once again I was able to slide out of the back of the hide, creep down the hill, then trek down to the boat without being seen from the nest.

I launched the boat into still water, lit golden by the setting sun, and went to check the wooded islet beyond the land spit, towards which I had three times seen the black-throated divers flying after losing their first egg to the pine marten. There was just a chance they might now be nesting on it.

As I boated over quietly I saw a black-throated diver ahead of me in the water. I swerved to make a wide circle round it. It did not even dive. Keeping well out from its shore, I cruised slowly right round the islet, paying particular attention to any flat little grassy area above shore level, as I knew divers do not like to walk far from water to their nests.

Two small grass platforms on the islet's west edge contained nothing but a female red-breasted merganser, which stopped preening its breast and watched the boat with a very sharp and beady red eye. I turned the north corner to head east and had gone only a few yards when I saw the female diver sitting on what was clearly a nest a mere two yards from the water line. She must have laid again.

What wonderful luck! Knowing birds like divers can assess whether they have been seen or not, and are more alarmed when your eyes are actually on them, I looked away and puttered almost silently past. She did not even leave the nest.

As I continued homewards, my happiness was tinged with more than a little fear, for if it was a fine day tomorrow I would need all my wilderness skills. The diver is not only three times as rare as the golden eagle but is just as wary, and somehow I had to erect a hide overlooking the nest and watch and photograph these unique and superb water birds without disturbing them.

10 · Discovery at New Island

I woke to a calm day of sunny haze and prepared a rough screen type of hide. Already I felt my nerves tingling with excitement. I had no clear idea what the hide situation would be, but I knew the divers' islet was covered with thick undergrowth. I was certainly not going to set up one of those artificial square canvas hides to overlook the nest, in the hope the divers would accept it, or even move such a hide nearer in gradual stages (the usually recommended method) when each visit to do so would frighten the birds.

Instead, I made a three-foot square of hazel wands and tied green close-mesh netting across it to screen me from frontal view. To this I lashed a seven-foot hazel pole and tied more of the netting along its entire length. That should screen me from a side view of any diver out on the loch waters. Then, with lunch sandwiches in the camera pack, I boated to the north-east corner of the islet and paddled quietly into a small bay, out of sight of the nest, which was over two hundred yards away round a bend. I slid the boat silently to rest over a submerged tree.

As I climbed out with the pack and hide materials there was a sudden whoosh, and on whistling wings a female mallard shot out of some upended tree roots and winged over the water. She had been on a nest containing nine pale-khaki eggs, all warmly swaddled in as much dark-brown down as an eider duck would use. I was too keen to get to grips with the black-throated divers to pause and extract the camera from the pack and take photos of the mallard's nest. As I crept about, working my way towards the divers' site, it was almost impossible to keep quiet because broken brown dead bracken stalks lay everywhere, together with dead birch twigs and heather sticks, all crackling underfoot.

On hands and knees I moved round the south side of the islet and then cut back, forced to cross or go under great white snags and stumps of ancient fallen pine trees which were obscured by long heather, bracken and grasses. Over a bluff filled with crow berry, I came to a standing pine and cautiously peered round it. The diver was on her nest, but it was no place for the screen hide as there was too much foliage in the way. Quickly I wove some heather into the hide netting.

I withdrew about thirty yards to the south-west and then cut back to the north again. Suddenly the frame of the hide dragged over two tall bracken stalks. Whether she saw or heard me, or just the bracken moving, I did not know, but the diver slid over the rocks into the water and paddled out to join her mate fifty yards offshore. Damn. Both birds held their dove-grey heads and dark dagger bills up in the air, alert and full of suspicion. They clearly knew there was *something* odd on the islet and neither would return to the nest until their fears were allayed.

There was only one thing to do – show myself, act naturally and innocently, check that there *was* a nest with eggs, walk back along the shore in full view of the divers, get into the boat and take off.

On the short way down to the shore I found the perfect hide site, a big flat mossy rock at the end of a natural tunnel in the long heather, right next to a thick birch trunk. I stuck the side wands of the hide's front on either side of the rock, which was itself two feet high, then draped the pole of the waterside screen backwards, resting its end amid the branches of a small pine which was conveniently growing in just the right spot. This took mere seconds. I then ambled along the shore with my hands in my pockets and saw there were two olive-brown darkly-speckled eggs keeping nicely warm in the hazy sunlight in a small grassy depression. I did not go right up to the nest, or give any indication I had actually seen it, and did not attempt to photograph it. I turned, looked up at the sky as if assessing the weather, walked back to the boat and, still in full view of the divers, puttered away to the east. I kept the engine just loud enough for the birds to hear it receding and boated round to a spit of land below a pine wood over half a mile away.

I spent nearly two hours in the woods to give the divers time to settle down, and even photographed a wild tawny owl regarding me with sleepy sloe-black eyes from a high branch in one of the trees, then rowed quietly back to a bay in the south shore of the islet. On hands and knees I crawled through the tangle of fallen snags until I was by a tree above the hide. Down the last hundred yards I had to slide on my belly through the heather like a snake. There was one rise in the ground where I had to push the camera pack ahead of me. The diver might have seen it moving on the skyline if I had kept it on my back. I had to flatten my toes outwards so she would not see my heels moving – assuming she *was* back on the nest. The last slope down to the heathery tunnel behind the flat mossy rock was steep. As I slid down it my belt somehow came undone, so that my trousers ended up round my ankles. I dared not pause to hitch them up, so I completed the journey with them like that, only hitching them back up once I was at the rock. Slowly, I raised my bush-hatted head above the long heather.

The diver was back on the nest and was actually dozing, the eyelids coming up from beneath, the whole eye folding inwards like a rubber submarine closing down its port-holes. The sky was now clouding over, the air had gone still as if there would be thunder later. The loch was the colour of khaki-green slate, reflecting the varying greens of the hills, trees and woods.

Now came the tricky part. For the first time in my life I had to complete a hide in full view of a rare and wary sitting bird. Moving my hands like a sloth, inch by slow inch, I adjusted the height and position of the front wands so that the camera on its tripod commanded the only possible clear view of the diver between some tree branches ahead and braced them with cord to the roots of heather. I wove heather, bracken and bilberry fronds into the green netting screen, and tied the side pole to the little pine. Then I could concentrate on pictures.

The diver was a beautiful sight. She sat there motionless, patiently incubating her eggs, amid a perfect setting of white lichened granite rocks, small trees, flowers, grasses and gently lapping waters. The colours of her summer plumage were so startling they seemed unreal, as if they had been painted on by a great artist. The white zebra-stripes flanking her neat purple-black throat patch merged delicately with the curving ones that framed the white chest and creamy-pink belly feathers. Her dusky blue-black wings

opposite: a black-throated diver on her nest amid marsh marigold 'kingcups'.

above: The diver sat motionless, patiently incubating her eggs.
below: A black-throated diver on a nest amid marsh marigolds.

above: The rapport between Juno and her chick was overwhelming.

below: The male flew in with a long, thick spray of heather as Juno covered up the chick.

above: Juno picked the heather spray up like a banner bearer, then stepped across the nest with exaggerated care.

below: The male returned with a bare stick which Juno took from him.

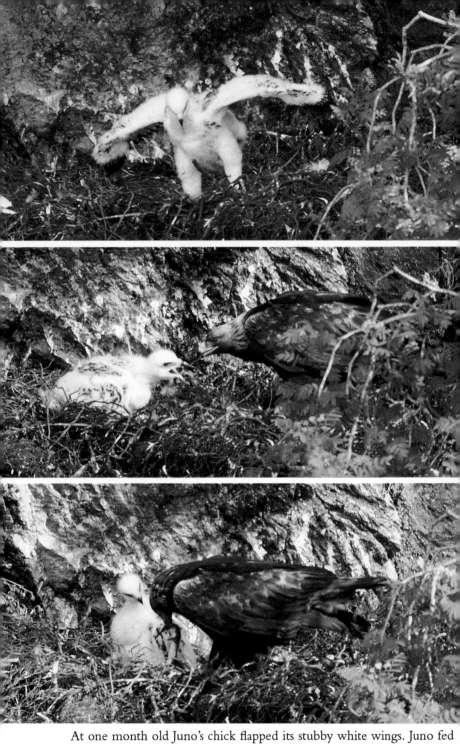

At one month old Juno's chick flapped its stubby white wings. Juno fed 173 slivers from a rabbit before she picked up an unusual item of prey brought in by the male – a stoat. The eaglet seemed to regard it with dis

shone with greenish highlights, and were divided by symmetrical white griddles, below which was a profusion of white squares, rectangles and oblongs that shone as if lit from within. When a hooded crow called harshly from the mainland shore, she woke up and looked towards me, her graceful head more like that of a snake than a bird. I would never have forgiven myself if my attempts to photograph and record the behaviour of these rare creatures had resulted in desertion of the eggs. I would certainly never try it again.

Suddenly I heard the whine of a powerful boat engine coming nearer and nearer. The boat slowed down with a roar, and the year's first fisherman began trolling his lure along the far side of the lagoon. The diver heard it before I did and slid quickly into the water, as if not wanting to be seen on her nest. Then the fisherman came back, trolling up my side of the islet. It was not any of the fishermen I knew and I hoped he was not going to keep trolling up and down this particular lagoon. Luckily he did not. He went right round the islet, trolled along the far side once more, then shot off to fish the far side of the loch with more roaring of the engine. In the silent watery world of the diver the alien noise seemed an abomination, yet I could not really complain about just one fisherman. It was Whit Monday, after all.

After twenty minutes, the eggs still warm in the hazy sunlight, the diver returned. I looked up just in time to see her standing by the nest and turning one egg over with snake-like movements of her neck and beak. When sitting back on the eggs she held her full body weight off them by lowering the 'shoulders' of her wings to the ground. She shuffled from side to side with both feet, swaying slightly as if waltzing, to get her incubating plumage all over and round the two eggs.

Half an hour passed. Suddenly her head bent low in alarm after I too heard a stick crack in the mainland woods opposite. She jerked herself forward and down the slight slope with two powerful kicks of her legs and swam out a few yards into the loch. From the hide I could see nothing that could have caused a stick to crack. Possibly it had been a falling branch. A few minutes later I heard something striking the ground, and there was the diver trying to walk out of the water back to the eggs, making little struggling jumps which enabled her to get one leg off the ground at a time. I took pictures, and she soon settled back on her eggs.

Time ticked by – four hours in fact – before the skies clouded over again. Once the diver turned one bright orange eye upwards. Was she assessing the weather, or had she seen Juno or the male eagle flying overhead? I could not see because of the thick tree foliage above me. The light was going; time to pack up. As she dozed, I carefully extracted the camera and made the long belly-crawl out. It is hard work going uphill when your only 'engines' are your elbows and the very tips of your toes.

While boating home I was greeted in close flight by a common gull I had come to call Cedwig. He was the tamest of the gulls from the colony on the nearest islet and often perched on my chimney, waiting to snatch titbits from my bird table and take them down to his mate paddling in the loch below and making squeaky supplicant '*klee*' calls with upward jerks of her beak. He was the only one of the gulls who would swoop down from the sky to catch scraps I threw into the air.

Cedwig kept landing on the surface right in the path of my boat, only flying up a split second before he would have been run down. Clearly, he wanted food. I tossed out some crusts left from my lunch sandwiches. He dived closer and closer for them, even snatching one from the roof of the half-cabin two feet in front of my head. As I neared my bay he veered off and flew back to the denuded colony.

I hauled the boat out on to its trolley and heard a muffled thumping behind me. Moobli had hauled himself down from the woodshed to greet me home, whining more than usual after my long absence. His rear legs were bad now but I made a great fuss of him for an hour and fed him well. Poor Moobli!

Next day, hot and steamy, I rowed the last half-mile to the divers' islet and put in another five hours, face and hands smeared with insect repellant to keep off the hordes of midges and the first of the biting deer flies known as 'clegs'. I took some photos of the diver on her nest, and an hour later I heard two soft yet oddly harsh '*gull*' or '*gowl*' notes. The other black-throat was swimming offshore. Evidently this was a call to his mate, for she slid off the nest and paddled over to him.

I decided not to risk moving the camera in case they saw the movement, but then I wished I had, for as the female drew near to the male he raised his long bill from the water with a small silvery fish in it and presented it to her. She swallowed it with two backward jerks of her neck. To my surprise both divers started swimming together out of the lagoon to the west and into the main loch, until I could no longer see them. How long would she leave the eggs in even this weak sunshine and warm air?

Half an hour went by and I became concerned. Then I saw the two divers paddling back and, to my astonishment, they had another pair of black-throated divers with them! Evidently these birds are not strictly territorial, even in the nesting season. Perhaps the other two were their own youngsters from a previous year. All four swam peacefully along together, making soft muted '*gowol*' sounds, before one left the party and swam close to my position as I crouched low behind the loch-side screen.

A few minutes later I heard the familiar thumping sound and looked through the view-finder, just in time to see the diver squat on the eggs. Again she turned one over with her bill, drooped her wing shoulders to the ground and gently lowered herself down. By then the other three divers had left the lagoon. I wondered if the second pair were nesting farther west. Why had the four got together for what seemed a brief social occasion?

Before leaving on June 2 to buy more films and supplies, I realised I had heard nothing about Atalanta's egg from the Wildlife Analysis Unit in Edinburgh. It had been sent off on April 26, after I found it on the mossy rock near Eyrie 28. I wrote a quick note, posted it when shopping, then hurried back to join Allan Peters, who helped me build a fine hide overlooking a buzzard's nest with two chicks that he had found in an oak wood. A week later the Unit's Dr Douglas Ruthven replied to my reminder, confirming that the eagle egg had arrived safely.

Since this has been a particularly busy spell, much of it deliberate poisoning cases unfortunately, the analyses are not yet complete. It is most uneconomic to do this type of sample on a one-off basis and I have waited until more egg samples accumulated. I expect 2 more eagle eggs this week from N.C.C. Aberdeen and I hope to complete all the analyses by the 18th of June. I will send you a report as soon as possible.

While I felt disappointed at the delay, it did not matter much really. As Roy Dennis of the R.S.P.B. had once told me, unless you can prove THAT person put THAT poison into THAT egg and killed THAT protected creature, there is little chance of bringing the culprit to book. I hoped for the best, for I was fairly sure no livestock owner in my immediate area would stoop to taking an eagle's egg and add insult to injury by putting illegal poisons in it. What the letter did tell me was that, despite the energetic campaign in recent years to bring home to public, farmers and keepers alike the fact that illegal poisoning was one of the biggest problems facing the golden eagle today, the practice was still occurring, mostly in the grouse moors of the east. In my book, *Golden Eagle Years*, I published the fact that between 1973 and the spring of 1981 there had been sixteen *proved* cases of golden eagles being poisoned in Scotland. Since then, and up to the time of writing, fourteen more eagles have been found poisoned, eleven by alpha-chloralose and three by Mevinphos.

Early on June 4, a hot, sultry and humid day, I laboured back up to the eagle hide with perspiration stinging in my eyes. Half-way there I stopped and lay down, trying to melt into the background, as I saw Juno hanging like a huge cross-shaped kite in the sky above the eyrie. She circled twice then glided on to the nest, doubtless to give the chick a feed. She did not stay long but came out, circled, then landed in a birch tree farther up the crevice. She showed no sign of leaving. I struck north, down towards the loch, as if visiting the eyrie area was the last thing in my mind. I skirted a few more bluffs, then caught a glimpse of her flying again before she vanished beyond the high peaks to the west. It was safe now to enter the hide.

At first I thought the eaglet had gone. Then, through the lens, I spied him sitting behind a curtain of rowan leaves and white flower sprays that decorated the right of the nest ledge. He was now in the 'chocolate and cream' stage, with blackish-brown feathers well sprouted on his primaries and secondaries, dotting his back and chest, while the tail feathers were about two inches long and tipped with a fringe of white. It was surprising how all the whites of his down mingled with the white flowers and the lichens on the rocks and the patches and dots of dark feathers merged perfectly with the dark grey of the granite behind the nest. Without a strong lens one could pass by on my side of the gorge, a mere forty yards away, and never know he was there.

Twelve more hours I waited, but neither parent came in. There was no real need, I realised with chagrin. At five weeks old, the eaglet could feed himself well, his crop was more than half full and

there seemed plenty of prey on the nest. However, he now enter-
tained me as only an eaglet can, and also obliged me by picking up
the prey items in turn so that I could identify them precisely for Jeff
Watson's N.C.C. survey.

After forty minutes he got up, walked into the centre of the nest
and looked round for food. Seeing something, he made a clumsy
sideways jump and fell over, only righting himself by violent wing
flaps. He picked ants off his legs with his beak, yawned a lot, sat
down with his beak open while panting with the heat, flirted his tail
feathers up in a fan and reached back to preen them. He performed a
few 'Hottentot' stretches, arching his wings right up above his head
with his beak almost on the nest twigs, then squatted on his hocks,
his wings opened and lowered to the nest floor, while preening his
belly feathers.

Bored with that, he had another snooze, then tramped awkwardly over to a dead greyhen (kindly provided by the Forestry
Commission plantations), tried to tweak its foot off but failed. A
little more preening, then he stamped over to a gingerish wing and
lifted it, revealing that it belonged to a red grouse. He made an
abortive attempt to pull off one of the grouse's furred feet, delved
into its chest cavity and came up with a redly fleshed bone from
which he tugged morsels of meat before swallowing the bone itself.

He had another long sleep, during which he lay half on his side,
his head stretched over the nest twigs and his great crayon-yellow
feet sticking out to the side like a dog. Then he roused himself,
tramped round the nest, lifted a wood pigeon which one of his
parents had partly plucked, but lost interest in it as if it was not
normal prey. After that he fed himself some more from the grouse.
With all the prey they had brought in, no doubt the adults felt they
had earned the right to a long float together. I was disappointed but
not surprised; from this stage onwards an eaglet is left alone for long
periods once food has been provided. During his next preening
session, the light fading, I left. I saw no eagles in the sky on the walk
out. The air was still burning hot. I arrived home at 9.30 p.m., to
bathe myself down and prepare meals for Moobli and myself.

I had never known such a long hot spring and early summer in the
Highlands. I decided to take no desk breaks and to keep on with the
outdoor work. Next day I put in a five-hour stint in the divers' hide.
As I rowed to the south bay on the islet I saw a bright yellow fishing
boat, with an elderly couple in it, at the east end of the lagoon. I was

half-way through the undergrowth when I heard their engine start up and the boat travelling to the west. Knowing it would put the diver off her nest, I took advantage of the noise and disturbance to get down to the hide quickly without the birds detecting my movements.

I had to wait only ten minutes before I heard a soft '*gowl, gowl*', and there was the diver stumbling, with a few belly flops, up to the nest. The light was excellent now. As she sat there, I watched her breathe in six times and then hold her breath for seventy-six seconds before breathing seven times more. This is clearly a breathing adaptation that has evolved in a diving bird which cannot breathe for quite long periods while chasing fish underwater.

The sun shone on the rocks near her but the nest itself was in shade. She had chosen a spot under two Scots pines where the early morning sun got to her, while at the end of the day, the sinking sun would shine on the nest too. Just when most needed, there was a morning warm-up after the cold night, and an evening warm-up before the next. It was an ideal spot for the big eggs that a diver lays.

At about 2.30 p.m. she went off the nest as I was having a brief rest from the uncomfortable propped-arm position I had to maintain to look through the view-finder, and sailed out into the lagoon. There was no alarm; she just wanted a break from sitting on the eggs. She preened her wings, dipped her head and threw water on to her wings and back, wriggling it upside down as if to clean the feathers against each other. Then she reared up in the water and flapped her slim, pointed but powerful wings. This time I did extract the camera and tripod from the rock, crouch low behind the heathery screen, and take a few pictures.

Suddenly the diver reared again, beat her wings harder and, with a far shorter run than usual, took off into the west wind. I was afraid I had made a mistake and that she was gone for good, but twenty minutes later I heard a loud metallic '*gleek*' call, one I had never heard before, and felt sure she was coming back. I was lying low, boots covered with heather and camouflage jacket hiding my body and head in case she flew low overhead. Then I heard the soft '*gowl*' note and saw her paddling in towards the nest. I took a sequence of her flop-walking over the flat rocks and grasses, then of her arching her neck in a superb bow to twirl and turn both eggs before settling down on them again.

After five hours I slid out and crept as quietly as I could over the dry stalks and gnarled white skeletons of the fallen pines to the mallard's nest site. To my surprise, all the eggs had hatched and the family were just leaving. The mother duck was waddling very slowly to the water's edge with two tiny ducklings following her. Then another ran down the mossy stump, staggered after them and also entered the water. The duck swam out slowly, the first duckling racing through the water to try and catch up and be close to her, while the other two straggled. After taking photos I saw a fourth duckling, brown with greeny-yellow stripes like the others, still on the nest. This one feigned death, lying completely still on its side, one bright dark eye wide open and regarding me with terror. As I turned quietly to leave I wondered what had happened to the other five eggs. At least whatever predator had taken them had left four, an easier number of young for the mother to look after in the wild conditions of the loch.

As the boat burbled homewards, Cedwig came flying up for lunch crusts. I watched him wheel and dive for them, then thought no more about him. Nearing home two miles farther on I felt myself being watched. I turned slowly – Cedwig had landed on the flat top of the engine! He was standing there quite calmly on his knock-kneed yellow-green legs, as if waiting for another scrap. Only when I reached the boat bay did he fly off and beat his way back to the islet colony.

On nearly every trip up and down the loch after that Cedwig 'hitched a ride' in this manner. Apart from saving himself a bit of wing flapping, I am sure he liked to feel the vibrations of the engine through his flat webbed feet. Even when I tossed him food, once he had had enough he would still hitch rides for the rest of the journey. I found such tameness endearing. If only the eagles and divers behaved like that!

Next day an eagle almost did.

I was up early, as I had arranged to meet Allan Peters, who, after all my descriptions of eagles at the nest, was now anxious to watch them from the hide himself. As a keeper who also owned his own sheep, Allan had all the necessary wilderness skills and cared about eagles as much as I did, and this pair was also on his terrain. No photographer himself, he would only watch through a telescope from well back in the hide and could record all new prey which we needed for the survey. After putting him into the hide I could spend five more hours with the divers (surely their eggs would be hatching any day now) before going to fetch him out again.

We toiled up the hill, and this time I felt better than he did; for once, I was carrying only binoculars.

'Here we are,' I said.

'Here? Where? Where's the hide?'

'Right there.' I indicated the humped combination of granite boulder and hide a mere four yards away.

The look of astonishment on Allan's face was wonderful to behold.

'I don't believe it,' he said. 'I thought that was just one big rock. I can't make out the hide even from here. It's a masterpiece.'

We improved the hide with a few fresh heather sprigs, then quickly checked the eagles' nearby kill rock. There was now a raven's ravaged skeleton on it and, to our dismay, four legs of a lamb. There was not enough evidence to show that eagles had actually killed the lamb. There was equally no evidence to show they had not. I would have to register this one as doubtful. The heron's skull I forgot to photograph earlier had now disappeared. After seeing Allan into the hide, I descended the hill and rowed over to the islet.

The diver was *still* on her nest, motionless but for an occasional turn of her graceful head. After an hour and a half she made some soft gulping noises. Were the eggs now hatching beneath her? She reached her dark blue-grey beak forward, plucked several grasses and swept them round to her rear, as if to screen the eggs. A few minutes later she slowly humped herself down, pausing to look round twice for danger, slid into the water and dived when only two yards offshore. I peered out to see her come up beside the male, who had again brought her a fish, which she took from his bill and swallowed. I noticed that the male seemed slightly bigger. I lay my head down to ease my aching neck muscles for a couple of minutes, and was surprised when I looked up again to see her back on the nest.

At 3.35 p.m. I heard a double '*gowowl*' note, quite loud, and saw the male swimming past close in. Then he dived and vanished. Soon he reappeared opposite me and the female again left the nest to join him, the sun now shining on the eggs. This time they stayed together for nearly twenty minutes, she sleeping with her head tucked into the cleft between her wings on her broad back. He seemed to be keeping guard. After her cat-nap, the male had a sleep too in the same way, while she remained by his side. As they bobbed like little grey gunboats out there in the blue water, I felt privileged to be sharing their secret silent world, to witness the trust which would last the lifetimes of two of our rarest birds.

Once the female arched her wings high over her head for a long stretch, then her mate lifted his left wing, rolled over on to his right side, showing his huge creamy belly, and shuffled round in comical circles by paddling with the other foot. They both drifted to the west before diving in unison. Moments later one of them was shuffling back up to the nest. I felt sure it was the male, for it looked larger. He had a little more trouble making the shuffle-walk, frequently dunking his breast on the ground, and when he stood up to probe the eggs gently, as if to ascertain whether they were hatching or not, I saw there were reddish water grasses stuck to his chest. I took a few more photos, then left to fetch Allan out of the eagle hide.

I had just beached the boat when I saw the huge form of Juno floating down from the eyrie and about to head northwards across the loch. I gave her a cheery wave and made two imitation eaglet calls. To my astonishment she abruptly changed her flight and came low, right over my head. I could see the terrible talons bunched up beneath her broad tail, and I imagined the paralysing terror any prey animal would feel at so close a sight of nature's dark angel of death. Then she circled and flapped away on her original path, three beats and a glide, three beats and a glide, three beats and a glide, into a slight easterly breeze, until she vanished right over Atalanta's Eyries 27 and 28. Yet again the theory of strict territoriality during the eagle nesting season had taken a knock, and again I had the feeling she was one of Atalanta's daughters, had perhaps been reared in one of those two eyries. Or perhaps she knew Atalanta herself was breeding in one of her two farthermost nests. I would have to make the 'killer trek' soon to find that out for myself.

Allan came out of the hide, his face ecstatic, saying the time had just flown by and he could have stayed until dark. He could hardly believe all the antics of the eaglet, which had fed himself well from what looked a rabbit at the back of the nest. Once he had started to call loudly and to glare into the sky. Not realising the full significance of this, Allan had almost missed seeing the male eagle sweep in, dump a grouse and leave almost immediately. I boated him back to his van and, as I carried on home, Cedwig arrived from nowhere to hitch a ride on the engine, a fitting end to another tiring but rewarding day.

After a day devoted to Moobli and writing business letters, and two days spent painting my roof, I sallied out on June 11 to check the peregrine falcons' nest – if I could find it – and to photograph the adults. But here, it seemed, my run of incredible good luck was to come to an end.

11 · *The Peregrine Cliff*

As I drove the miles of mostly single-track roads to the peregrine cliff on a dull but rainless morning, I naturally hoped the falcons would be at least as successful as last year, when three young were reared. I doubted all three were still alive, for up to 70 per cent of large raptorial birds die before reaching breeding age, often in their first winter before they have fully mastered their hunting techniques.

There were several reasons why I had not visited the birds until now. I had been preoccupied with all the studies of eagles and divers; besides, the cliff was many miles away, and I had not wanted to cause any disturbance during the egg-laying and incubation period. I also knew that the new keeper and under-keeper, a young man who had helped with my eagle work, were as keen as the estate owner to ensure that they bred successfully. Their nesting cliff rose precipitously above a small public road and their return two years earlier (for the first time since 1947) was a sort of conservation status symbol for the area among those who knew about them. In a way they were symbolic of the peregrines' fight to survive and re-colonise many of their old haunts after years of adverse circumstances, throughout Great Britain.

Between 1930 and 1939 it was estimated there were 650 pairs nesting on coastal and inland cliffs in Britain, despite harassment by some keepers and egg collectors. During the Second World War they were heavily shot and persecuted, for they were a threat to the carrier pigeons which were used to carry messages when radio silence was essential, such as when planes were trying to spot and locate enemy submarines. After the war their numbers began to recover, but in the late 1950s and early 1960s they were decimated by the use of organochlorine pesticides in agriculture. These persistent poisons built up in the bodies of their prey, usually flying birds, causing sterility and addled or thin-shelled eggs which broke in the nest, and even fatally poisoning some adults. By 1963 the number of occupied territories was estimated at sixty-two, rising to sixty-six in 1964. In many of its former areas the falcon was facing extinction.

Alarmed by the decline, scientists and conservation bodies conducted tests and surveys (notably by Dr Derek Ratcliffe of the N.C.C.), and the most lethal pesticides were voluntarily withdrawn in the late 1960s before the legal ban of 1974. Numbers began to rise again but, despite being given special protection (like eagles, they are Schedule 1 birds) they have come under increasing threat in recent years from egg collectors and those who steal fledgelings, known as eyasses, for illegal falconry. Publicity in press articles, radio programmes and TV films concerning the vast sums that can be paid on the black market for both has not helped. There are a dozen chick- and egg-stealing gangs working in the Highlands alone. At least 275 peregrine eyries are known to have been robbed between 1976 and 1982; a further seventy were robbed in the 1983 breeding season, forty-nine in 1984 and forty more in 1985. Thieves struck at many more sites than these but the cases were not proved. Despite this, there are estimated to be some 1,600 individual wild peregrines in the United Kingdom today.

It is well known that the peregrine is one of our most spectacular birds of prey. The nineteen-inch falcon is four inches longer than the male, or tiercel, and stories abound in natural history books of its breathtaking downwards 'stoop'. Moving at speeds of up to 180 miles an hour, it is said to be able to snap off a pigeon's head with its talons in full flight. Actually I doubt if it can attain a speed greater than ninety miles an hour, even in a stoop. I have seen a peregrine flying rapidly along the face of a cliff easily overtaken by an eagle gliding on a strong wind; the eagle's speed is deceptive to the human eye due to its large size. Greg Hunter once saw an eagle chase a peregrine, catch up to it with ease, forcing the falcon to swerve all over the sky to get away before the eagle lost interest.

As I drove towards the nesting cliff on this day, however, I realised my experience of the peregrine was far from extensive. I had seen my first pair in the bare hills a mile above my home eight years earlier, in May. The falcon had been flying in a weird way I have not seen described, beating her sharp scythe-like wings with strong spasmodic jerks, yet covering large areas of sky at great speed, while the attending tiercel beat his wings at three times the speed as he flew all round her. Then both had gone into a power dive and had vanished over a ridge. That October I had seen a peregrine easily overtake a soaring buzzard near some sheer cliffs east of my home, but only ravens used the cliffs for nesting. Seven years ago to this very day I had been in the garden when a falcon had arced across the sky like a meteor in violent winds and had snatched a fledged gull chick from the islet colony. The long-term decline of the peregrine in the Highlands and Islands up to the mid-1960s was believed also to be the result of a gradual decrease in the overall food supply. That I found no nesting falcons in the region of my home I put down to the scarcity of suitable prey. And that, apart from last year's observations, was my sum total of peregrine experience.

As I pulled in to my usual parking spot by a white gate half a mile from the nesting cliffs, I saw an older van like mine already there. It contained four tough-looking young men dressed in camouflage hues of greens and browns. Were they an egg- or chick-napping gang? As they obligingly moved to make room for me I asked inno-cently if they were the R.S.P.B. party I was meant to be meeting. They exchanged glances and said they were not, but had been for a walk along the river to see if they could see any otters. I wished them luck and went on my way, hoping that if they were such a gang my casual remark would dissuade them from their intended operation. As I struck off to the left and began climbing the steep long-heathered hill to overlook the nesting cliff, the men got into their van and drove away.

It was at this point my luck ran out.

I emerged from the oak wood at the foot of the hill, climbed the last shallow cliff and started to wade through the heather, which was three feet high in places, just as a thin drizzle began to fall. This was unusual in the easterly breeze and it would also blow droplets into the camera despite the long lens hood. I settled my camouflaged form amid the heather on a small bluff, located the twin ravens' nests through the binoculars and started to search for the falcon's eyrie from there. In some places ravens and peregrines will continue to nest on the same length of cliffs, if they are big enough. Indeed, the two birds will fly round each other in territorial displays and mock-mob each other as if in some kind of game. As far as I know, the raven is never taken as a prey species. It is not listed among the 117 species recorded by Derek Ratcliffe in his 1963 paper,* yet all the other British crow species are; as are, very rarely, birds as large as barnacle goose, heron and both short- and long-eared owls. Whether this implies some kind of symbiotic relationship between the cliff-nesting falcons and ravens I do not know, but certainly since this pair of falcons had arrived the ravens had cleared off. Both nests I now saw were unused; they had not even been appropriated by the falcons, as sometimes happens. Last year's granite perch in the rocky overhang to the left of the nests was being well used, however. The bottom wall of rock was garishly splashed with white falcon faeces.

Suddenly what again looked like a large kestrel (except that its underside was silvery) came soaring over the peaks above the ravens' nests, but with the rain getting worse I did not try to take a photo. Then I heard young chicks calling '*kree kree kree*', again like young kestrels but louder. Sure the falcon would fly into the nest ledge, I extracted the camera from its wet pack as the peregrine flew over the peaks again and did not return. The chicks were still calling but try as I would I could not locate them. From the noise it seemed they were on one of the small ledges to the right of the roost but fringing heather hid them from my view. Two more hours I waited, scanning the innumerable crevices and ledges amid the dwarf trees of the sheer cliff where it was impossible to erect a hide. Then the rain came on hard and I was forced to give up. I climbed down, trousers soaked to the waist, but it was good to know the falcons did have young.

After a day at my desk, I set off on June 13 for the 'killer trek', to see if Atalanta had managed to re-lay and raise a chick or two in her farthest eyries. It was the last time I would make that trek, I resolved, especially if she had not. I would never have another season as good as this, and to keep slogging the same hard hills at my age, repeating all I had done for twelve years, never mind the Canadian treks, would probably lead to mental atrophy and early death.

* *The Status of the Peregrine in Great Britain* (B.T.O.)

It was a sunny day with occasional high fluffy clouds and I took it easy at first, up over the tussocky crests to 1,500 feet, down 1,000, up another 1,500, down to near sea level, and there I paused to slake my thirst at the river before climbing the final 1,000 feet up to Eyrie 18. No whisky ever tasted as good as that fresh burn water. To my surprise, I found I was feeling no stress, no knee pains, despite the almost sheer inclines.

As I climbed to the eyrie buttress, I found the nineteenth deer carcass of the year, a large stag calf, three hundred yards south-east of the eyrie. There was little meat left on it. That would have helped the eagles – if they *were* using the eyrie – and foxes too, judging by the big hair-filled scats nearby. Up at the rowan-snag roost site were many downy incubating feathers, doubtless from Atalanta, who would probably be spending nights there instead of on the nest. It did not look promising, but beside an old pellet filled with deer hair was a small fresh greenish-black one.

I stumped upwards below the eyrie crag itself. The nest was as hugely built up as before. On the rock below it were a few white splashes that seemed too small to have come from an eaglet in mid-June. Then I saw a blackish lump on the nest, as if some intrepid eagle-hater had somehow got up there and put a rock on it. My heart sank. I climbed up farther, well away from the eyrie, to get enough height before training the binoculars down on it.

The 'rock' had a big head with a dark-brown eye and a huge blue-black hooded beak. It was an eaglet! It seemed to be in fine shape, with hardly any white showing on its head. It was certainly older than Juno's youngster in Eyrie 30. After losing an egg below Eyrie 28 early in the season, Atalanta had clearly laid another and raised a chick. The old lady had done it again!

Over at the kill rock I found two lamb legs but close inspection revealed the hooves to be unformed, with white on the pads. The lamb had probably been still-born; certainly it had never walked. The eagles had found it dead. I pocketed the few pellets for the N.C.C. survey, as I had the others. Two yards away were many tatters of grey-brown fox-cub fur – the fourth fox cub I had known taken by eagles. One of the birds had partially plucked it there before carrying it up to the nest.

For half an hour I lay hidden in the grasses over a small ridge, hoping the eaglet would shift to give me better photos, but it just lay as flat as a pancake, refusing to move at all. For eight weeks old it was highly intelligent, but being Atalanta's I supposed it would be. Even now, I saw no trace of the adults. Doubtless one of them was perched below the skyline a mile or two away, watching my every move.

I left, taking a more gently sloping route to the east. Just before the river I came across a huge flat slab of granite from which wafted the strong ammoniac scent of fox. Keeping to leeward, I circled round it. It was a den in full use all right. There were small cub scats everywhere, a few bits of lamb skin and a large play area of flattened grasses. I waited behind a rock fifty yards downwind for an hour but nothing came out. Then I set off to cover the part of this trek I most dreaded, the great 2,000 foot almost sheer mountain wall that sealed the yawning glen off from the south. I had to stop twice to rest. Then I went straight up, no zig-zagging this time, clambered over the final crest and tramped home, weary but happy that Atalanta had not failed this year after all. This was good news too for both the surveys of the N.C.C. and the R.S.P.B., but it meant I would have to tackle the 'killer' one more time – to check the eaglet was flying safely.

I spent three days re-organising the rocks of the boat bay, varnishing my oars, photographing insects and writing letters, and was feeling fit and strong again when another hot day dawned on June 17. I resolved to pay a long overnight visit to the hide overlooking Juno's nest. The first part of this trek was covered in deep forestry drainage trenches and the herbage of the tussocks that grew along their tops was now fully grown, obscuring where the trenches were. I was carrying a heavier load than before – sleeping bag, length of foam and food and drink to last the night, as well as all the camera gear. I had to watch where I was putting my feet. One false step would result not only in a wet foot but a sprained ankle or broken leg. I climbed up the steep sides of the burn that ran through the bottom of the gorge, more hidden now by the summer foliage of the trees. I paused before the last steep open stretch, saw no eagles in the sky, and was sure my entry into the hide had gone undetected.

The eaglet was now well beyond the chocolate and cream stage, with brown flecks sprouting on his white head and down his chest; the browny-black feathers of his wings and back were now well grown. He stood there looking bored, beak open in the heat, yawning a lot. Beside him lay some large flat browny animal. After two hours a cold east wind began blowing through the hide and the eaglet began to squeak loudly. His head was going from west to east, down, up again, then east to west. I thought he was watching one of his parents circling, checking the eyrie from the air but finally he called louder and Juno soared in. She looked sleeker, had lost much of her incubating plumage but the young yellow-orange eyes and wide face were unmistakable.

With her beak she momentarily picked up a large reddish-brown creature at the right of the nest and I was sure I glimpsed the brush of a fox! She fed the eaglet 111 slivers from it but kept her back to me so that, annoyingly, I had to snatch what few shots I could when the chick and her head and beak could be seen. When he had swallowed almost enough the eaglet walked to the left, Juno to the right, then both of them reached right across the nest with their beaks for the last transfers of food. I had never taken better feeding photos but it was amazing how the eagles' colours blended with those of the cliff face behind them. Even from forty yards both would have been hard to see with the naked eye. After twenty-five minutes on the nest, Juno stepped off airily into space and I got two more pictures of her flying away.

As dusk fell I ate some sandwiches before trying to sleep in the bag on the plastic foam. Juno returned in the near dark and fed the chick once more. It was too big to brood now and she just spent the night beside it, at first dozing with her head and neck feathers frowsted up so that she looked like a huge owl, then slept with her head back behind one wing. She got more sleep than I did for the bitter wind kept my feet and hands freezing cold even inside the bag.

At first light Juno tramped to the back of the nest, lifted up the head of a red grouse, dropped it again and then went over to the big brown prey on the left of the nest. To my surprise she reached down with her beak and with a great heave lifted the entire creature, but for its head, twelve inches off the floor of the nest. As I took a picture, I could see the four bloody stumps of its legs and a long ridged backbone before she dropped it again. After that she looked at the eaglet, apparently decided it was not yet hungry, and stepped off the nest. She would be away hunting for a good hour or two now.

The early sun gleaming like a low diamond in a yellow sky, I slipped out of the hide at 5 a.m., anchored its rear flap in case the wind blew up again later, and tottered on cold legs down to the kill rock. On it now lay the skull and beak of a red-breasted merganser. The serrated edges of the sawbill which the merganser has evolved for holding on to its slippery fish prey, were unmistakable. How had the eagles caught this? I was sure it was the work of the sleek manœuvrable male. Perhaps he had even snatched it from the very surface of the water.

I picked up three pellets from below the male's oak-tree roost perch to give to Jeff Watson, then put on some speed to warm up my legs as I climbed down towards the tiny speck of my boat. I had only gone two hundred yards when Juno came sailing by, quite near and unperturbed, then turned and rocketed into the eyrie.

I boated out into an increasing wind, intending to take a wide arc round the islet to see if the diver was still on her nest. I never reached it. There across the shimmering loch, in the lagoon between the islet and the mainland shore, I saw her swimming along. And keeping close to her, looking like tiny burnt brown corks bobbing along next to her great battleship of a body, were two little chicks. They could not have been more than a day or two old and were so small that even the little wavelets sometimes obscured them from view. Bringing up the rear, proudly swimming along in echelon, was the male. By moving to the new islet after losing their first egg to the marten, these shy but intelligent birds had transformed failure into what was, so far, complete success.

Despite the sleepless night, I boated home feeling at one with the universe, each crashing wave just part of a greater exhilaration, and received an enthusiastic reception from Moobli. I intended to push my luck on this golden day so I set my alarm clock for just one hour ahead, enjoyed a brief but deep sleep, gulped down some breakfast, and then set off to have another look for the peregrines' nest. This time I took Moobli, helping him into boat and van.

I climbed up the steep gully in the oak woods, scrambled over the top and was soon esconced amid deep heather below a small screening birch tree. The wind had increased to near gale force and the tree began to bend. Here I was, thirty miles from home and up another mountain. An odd life some would say. The gale was so strong I could not hold the long-lensed camera or even the binoculars steady. When I put my ear flat to the birch trunk I could hear the tree sighing with the strain, and also a metallic clinking noise as the twigs and small branches brushed against each other.

I scanned the great face ahead, with its hundreds of crevices and tiny ledges to which dwarf trees, mainly birch, clung precariously. Then I was sure I had located the nest site, with two white downy chicks in it, moving slightly in the wind. I took a photo. Then, as the sun slowly crept round and shone into the ledge, I realised it was not chicks I had seen but two similarly shaped patches of lichen; the movement had been the shadows of the leaves of a small birch playing on the lichen. Damn.

After an hour I was about to give up when two small dots appeared over the ridges to my left, a good third of a mile away, moving fast. It was the peregrine pair, I was sure. They were flickering along like arrows of flame, and now they turned towards me.

The larger of the two, the falcon, came nearer and circled overhead as I took photos. She gleamed grey and silver in the sun, like a bullet with wings, then flew across the cliff where I lost sight of her in the frosted glass of the viewer. I dropped the camera, reached for the binoculars and got on to her again as she landed with a flurry of wings in the gale on a rock much higher up. I dropped the binoculars and grabbed the camera but as I lifted it my sleeve caught on the film-spool winder and the back of the camera opened. I had lost some of the photos I had just taken! I swore I would never buy that flimsy make of camera again. By the time I had set all to rights, she had left the rock.

Twenty minutes later I was about to pack up when she came soaring over the peaks to the left and again began to fly along the side of the cliff. Again I got on to her with the binoculars, hoping above all that she would land on the nest and thus actually *show* it to me.

Suddenly she began to flap faster, to fly at great speed into the teeth of the gale, when to my surprise I saw a buzzard sailing over the higher cliffs away to the right. The falcon mounted higher into the air then like lightning turned and stooped downwards on to the buzzard's back – zap! Feathers flew, the buzzard made a clumsy somersault, tried to slash at the falcon with its talons, but missed. Then it flapped awkwardly, as if stunned, and vanished again behind a small ridge. Somehow I found the camera in my hands and that I had taken a photo but I was sure I had mistimed it. The falcon's attack had happened so fast. By now she too had disappeared behind the ridge, but higher up.

It was obvious she did have a nest on that cliff. I had not just imagined the calling of chicks on my last visit, for she would not have acted in such a protective territorial fashion if there were no chicks. She was certainly not going to have that big buzzard anywhere near the nest.

A few minutes later a peregrine came over the ridges to the left and circled twice for a couple of photos before I saw it was the smaller tiercel. Even over the wind I was sure I could hear chicks calling, but he did not fly into the nest either. Instead he looped upwards and landed on a rocky spur beside a sheltered recess. Judging by the white splashes below it this was one of his favourite perching places. I saw him get settled, then lift one bright yellow foot, tuck it into his barred breast feathers and go to sleep. Lazy beggar, I thought. Why didn't he fly in and feed the chicks? I left, resolving yet again to return on a windless day.

As we drove back along a winding sea loch, I pulled up behind some trees as I could see four common seals out in the water. I sneaked down to the shore, took my closest-ever picture of a pair of sandpipers on a rock, and looked over the brimming waters. The seals were paired up and were clearly mating. They swam close to each other, huffing and snorting with pleasure, even entwining their leathery front and rear flippers together, seemingly oblivious of the camera clicks. Now a heron flew past and I got a close picture of it, too.

As I drove on to visit the buzzard hide, I saw Jeff Watson's camper van parked outside Allan Peters's home. I delivered my note about Atalanta's breeding success for Jeff to pick up, and Allan's wife told me he had just rung to say they would be late back. They had some work to do in a boat. I had a good idea what they would be up to: Jeff was probably going to ring the eaglet in Eyrie 30.

Up at the buzzards' hide my luck still held. In one hour I saw both adults on the nest with their remaining chick and watched one comical moment when the female shoved the male off the nest, as if telling him to go and get more food. Later, on the way home in the van, I took two photos of a roebuck barking in the woods.

As I stopped to unlock the poacher barrier on the last section of the forestry road, Allan and Jeff drew up. They had indeed ringed the eaglet successfully.

'You'll never guess what we found on the nest today,' said Jeff.

116

'I was in the hide yesterday and this morning,' I replied. 'And I'm pretty sure there was a fox there. I saw its brush.'

'That's right,' they said together, surprised that I knew.

'And there was a grouse,' I continued, 'and some biggish brown animal I could not quite identify. I took a photo of the eagle lifting it up.'

'There was a grouse,' said Allan. 'And the other thing was a big roe-deer fawn. It must have weighed eleven or twelve pounds when it was caught.'

Later my photo revealed this was indeed the prey Juno had lifted in her beak. There had also been a young raven in the nest, which must have been caught after I left.

I told them the good news about Atalanta's chick. Jeff said he would like to make the hard trek with me in two days' time and try to ring the chick. I told him he would need to be a very good climber to get up to Eyrie 18, and anyway the eaglet would be well fledged by now, as it was older than Juno's, and so it might not be possible to ring it. I suggested he should have a spell in the eagle hide himself, for apart from collecting all the circumstantial and statistical evidence surrounding their lives, it must be a good idea for a scientist to watch the actual *behaviour* of eagles at close quarters.

It was only when I was cooking supper later, relaxing with a few drams, that I realised what a fantastic day I had just spent. In the space of twenty-four hours I had watched and photographed a golden eagle with its chick, black-throated divers with twin youngsters, peregrines flying and one defending its nest against a buzzard, mating seals, sandpipers, buzzards at the nest, and a barking roebuck. It might even have been some kind of record. Could I have had such experiences with rare wildlife anywhere else in the world than in these wild and beautiful Highlands?

12 · The Invasion

The following day I dawdled about in the hot sun, doing nothing constructive except cleaning the cottage, washing my trekking gear and hanging it out to dry, and giving Moobli a happy day. I was not looking forward to trying to keep up with a fit twenty-eight year old like Jeff Watson on the 'killer trek' tomorrow, for after all his mountain rangings since the start of the season he must be one of the fittest hill men in Scotland. Unconsciously, I suppose I was saving my energies.

After hooting on the loch shore opposite early next morning, I was not too dismayed when Jeff said he did not want to do the trek after all. He reckoned Atalanta's eaglet was now just too old, and would fly if he tried to ring it. We both agreed it was wrong to cause a well-fledged eaglet to leave the eyrie prematurely. Instead, he would like to go into the Juno hide and watch the eagles at the nest he had been the first to find. I was delighted at this, but first boated him home for lunch. I gave him the full list of prey brought in so far, the pellets I had collected and the fox-cub fur from Atalanta's kill rock.

The situation in my old area, most of which was now in Jeff's main west Highland study area, was as follows: Pairs 1, 2, 5 and 8 all had one healthy chick each, while Pair 3 had two chicks. Pairs 4, 6 and 7 had laid eggs which had failed due to, respectively, the disappearance of two eggs from Pair 4, the disappearance of a healthy chick from Pair 6 in mid-June, and one unhatched egg for Pair 7.

118

Even so, six healthy chicks in my old area was the best record I had known. In addition, in the rest of Jeff's study area (covering 600 square miles and in which he had located thirteen more pairs) there were four more healthy, well-fledged chicks. He reckoned at least three clutches had been taken by egg collectors. There was also the healthy eaglet in the eyrie east of my old area which Roger Broad of the R.S.P.B. had located with the help of a local keeper.

I recalled the first year trying to locate eagle eyries and regarded Jeff with increased admiration. I told him he had done a tremendous job, whether he had had my map or not, and far better than I could have done it. He seemed pleased at that. I then asked him the question that nagged at the back of my mind – had he found a single *new* pair on my old area? He said he had not.

'Not bad for a part-timer?' I said, giving way to a moment of pride.

'Very good indeed,' he replied, which from laconic Jeff was a compliment indeed.

To my surprise, as we stormed up to the eagle hide, Jeff flagged a bit and suggested I should take the lead. We quickly improved the hide with a few fresh sprigs and Jeff slid inside with his binoculars, eager to watch eagle behaviour and to note the new prey brought in. I hoped they would 'perform' for him and so help with the insights one cannot get from merely collecting material and data. I boated home and, to pass the next hours before fetching Jeff again, went to the divers' islet to fetch that hide away.

As I stalked carefully through the undergrowth I heard a slight '*gleek*' sound. The diver pair were floating out in the lagoon. Now they had only *one* chick with them, bobbing through the wavelets between its parents. I kept watch, taking photos through the heather. It seemed the second youngster had perished.

When I next met keeper Allan, he told me he had been walking along the lower western slopes of Eagle Rock mountain that same afternoon and had seen the second diver pair, also with one chick. They were near a small wooded islet, two miles west of mine, where he felt sure they had nested. At least the two pairs had enjoyed a 50 per cent breeding success, far better than on most Scottish lochs.

When I went to fetch Jeff his face was almost as ecstatic as Allan's had been on his first time in an eagle hide. He had watched all the eaglet's antics and seen the male eagle come in with a grouse. On the nest, too, were a young raven and a new roe-deer fawn, well grown. He felt he had been highly privileged to see all he had.

Jeff now had to dash north, to liaise with Stuart Rae on the northernmost of the N.C.C. survey's six main eagle study areas. As I boated him back to his van he told me he had looked up the 'killer trek' on his map and seen that it was indeed a terror. He would be back in July, he said, and would be grateful in the meantime if I could check that Atalanta's eaglet had flown safely. I said I would, gave him some jars of my bottled fruit to swell his camper provisions, and we said goodbye.

I spent a few days on business letters and garden chores, then on June 25 went to check the eaglet was all right. As I beached the boat Juno again sailed over from the west, came low, hovered motionless on the wind, circled once and again flew straight over the loch and Atalanta's two nearest eyries, again disproving the rigid territorial theories. The first rain for nearly a month began to fall as I hiked up. A roe doe startled me by leaping from the long grasses and ran into some alders, barking her head off. I looked round for her fawns but found none. Perhaps it was her two that the eagles had taken. The eaglet was fine and had a new young rabbit in the nest.

Next day was fine again and I decided to pay another visit to the peregrines. I had an old friend from London staying with me, and as he also had a peregrine licence, I took him along, hoping he would get some photos of the flying birds. As he had his car with him, I took advantage of the situation to drop my van in at the village garage for a service, and we went in his vehicle to the parking spot. My pal was older than I, basically a city man, and he was slow on the hill, so I was well ahead when I emerged on the top and waded through the deep heather.

Suddenly I heard loud shrill rasping cries, '*raik raik raik*', and saw one of the falcons swerving wildly about the sky, sometimes diving down towards the single-track road three hundred yards below, then swinging madly up again. What on earth was going on? I headed farther on and then heard human shouts mingling with the falcon's cries. I looked down.

To my horror I saw below a big light-blue minibus with two men and half a dozen youths beside it looking up at the peregrine cliff. They were shouting instructions to a climber who, judging by *his* voice (I could not actually see him amid all the dwarf trees) was not more than thirty yards from where I estimated the nest ledge to be.

My friend caught up, we waited a little longer as the men below still occasionally shouted, the climber replied, and the falcon kept up its wild flying and shrieking clamour.

I took a picture of the van and men and said, 'We'd better go down and stop them.'

'I'm not going down there,' said my friend. 'They look a rough lot. Besides, it's not our business.'

'It *is* our business,' I replied. 'I've got the licence on this nest. That climber may be after stealing a chick or two. You can stay here but I'm going to stop them if I can.'

As I hurried down the steep hill, it occurred to me that while the side of the minibus had the name of a town youth club on it, this could just be a front for a professional in their midst. It would take a very good climber indeed to get up that cliff. If they were just on a country jaunt, why had they chosen the falcons' cliff when there were so many others nearby? The climber could easily come down with a chick in a bag inside his jacket and none of the others would be any the wiser – for a while anyway. I came out over a marshy area and bid them good afternoon.

They bid me the same in return, then one of the men asked, 'What is that bird up there? A buzzard?'

The other man said, 'I thought it might be a hen harrier.'

As politely as I could I told them it was a peregrine falcon, a specially protected Schedule 1 bird, and they were illegally disturbing it at its nest, an offence for which there were hefty fines.

The first man said they had just been driving along the road after visiting the beach at its end, had seen this big cliff and one of their number had gone 'for a wee climb'.

'But you can see the falcon up there screaming, and you must know you're disturbing it. Your man is climbing towards its nest.'

They claimed they had no idea there was a nest on the cliff.

I told them it would be a very good idea if they got their climber down fast, that I was watching the nest for both the N.C.C. and the R.S.P.B., the estate owner was fishing up ahead, and we were now about to meet a policeman who was coming to inquire about some poaching in the area the previous night. Surely they didn't want to get into serious trouble?

I bid them good day and walked fast to where the owner and the new keeper Duncan were fishing over half a mile away. They both agreed we should get the police to check the innocence or otherwise of the disturbers. Duncan drove me back to the garage, where I phoned the police station twenty miles away. A constable assured me he was on his way. I then rang Roy Dennis, who was not at home, but his wife thought I was doing the right thing; the police could at least tell them off, and Roy would probably get someone to visit the club and give a talk on our rare birds. By the time the constable arrived the minibus was gone. We caught up with it outside a local community hall, where the climber turned out to be a lad of sixteen who, the others said, could 'get up anything'. Innocence was soon established and I said I was sorry to have brought in the police, but faced with such a situation there was little else I could do. They *might* have been after the chicks. After all, they had been exchanging shouts right under the falcons' nest for a full thirty minutes, despite seeing the flying bird's distress, and such disturbance could easily discourage the peregrines from nesting on that cliff another year. I explained the problems these rare birds had endured over the years, they were a valuable part of OUR heritage, and the affair ended amicably.

I rejoined my friend for tea at a local café before he drove on to the north and I set out for home. As my boat neared its bay I was sure I saw a peregrine flickering along the shoreline and vanish into the east wood. I stole through the trees, hoping for a second look, but saw nothing. I must be getting peregrines on the brain, I thought.

June 27 was dull but warm. I hiked up to the eagle hide without seeing either of the adults. The 8½-week-old eaglet was now covered in dark-brown plumage, with white flecks still on the back of his head, front neck, chest and legs, but the golden mantle was growing well. There was a roe-deer leg on the nest, which looked big enough to have come from an adult deer. There was little meat left and, after a few tugs at it, the eaglet gallumphed over the nest to a large item of furry prey. As he half-opened his wings, I saw they were almost fully grown. If anyone went too close to the nest, he could fly away now. Unless approached by an ill-intentioned human with a gun, he was safe. Before pecking at the new prey he lifted it briefly with one set of talons. At first I thought I saw a wide pine marten's head but it was too large. Then I made out the auburn fur and the conical black-tipped ears. It was another almost fullgrown fox!

I was amazed, for in seven previous seasons of watching nesting eagles from hides, I had not known such a pair as this. Not only had the female been an exceptionally devoted mother during the chick's early stages, but apart from their normal prey they had brought in two well-grown fox cubs, two large roe-deer fawns, an adult roe's leg, an old heron, a merganser, a fully grown stoat, two ravens and two hooded crows. While it is wrong for us to question too closely what 'good' or 'harm' such rare and magnificent species do to man's interests (they were on this land before we were), all these creatures could be classed as 'vermin', depending on whether you were a shepherd, farmer, forester, fisherman or poultry-keeping crofter. This pair had definitely proved that eagles can do a great deal of 'good' from the human point of view.

After feeding from the fox, the eaglet went behind the screen of rowan leaves to the right of the nest ledge, preened his front neck feathers, flopped down on his belly after raising his tail high first, then went to sleep with his head tucked back behind his left wing. In the late afternoon Allan Peters arrived for his second and last visit to the hide, determined to wait until an adult came in. (He was rewarded, for he again saw the male eagle dump an unplucked red grouse.) When I pointed out the adult roe-deer leg on the nest, Allan said he had shot a roebuck a few days earlier in a forestry plantation lower down the north side of the mountain but had been unable to find it. Evidently the eagles had done so, and had been able to cut off one of its rear legs, and carry it back up to the nest.

I was picking cherries with a long, forked hazel pole from a tree in my garden the following afternoon, when I heard crows calling. I looked up through the dull showery air and there, against the dark backdrop of the hills near Eyrie 1, was a hoodie in fast swerving flight. From high above it and descending in echelon at great speed, with wings up and talons extended, were what looked like two large kestrels. I had never seen kestrels attack or mob a crow in this way before, and there was no time to get my binoculars for positive identification, for in seconds all three birds vanished behind a hump-backed hill and did not reappear.

I wondered if the kestrels had appropriated the nicely built-up ledge of Eyrie 1 as a nest site and climbed up the deep wooded gorge of the burn with its tumbling waterfalls to take a look. Before the top of the ravine I struck off at a tangent to check the eyrie, but the nest looked as deserted as before with a few sticks, blown off by winds, lying below it. As I cut back to the top of the burn gorge I heard thin high-pitched squeaking noises coming, it seemed, from below the last high birch trees. Was I about to find the pine martens' den at last?

As I neared the trees I saw what looked like a newish hooded crow's nest in a fork of the second highest birch. It had the appearance of being used, but surely any young crows would be flown by now? I climbed up a knoll which reared over the edge of the ravine, and from its top my head came almost level with the nest. I saw something white moving in the well of the nest – the head of a young chick, but this was no young crow. It was undoubtedly the head of a young bird of prey for I could see a small dark hooked beak. The head vanished and then came up with another one beside it.

Just then I saw two fast-moving dots heading towards me over a cliff on the far side of the gorge. The one in front was coppery coloured, a kestrel. The bird behind it, higher in the air, dived down on the kestrel at great speed and, as the first bird swerved away to my right, I saw the slatey-blue back, the barred chest feathers of a peregrine falcon! It was clearly chasing the kestrel away. The two birds vanished behind the trees. I took two photos of the nest and the top of one chick's head before climbing back down the knoll, meaning to cross the ravine and go home down the easier far side.

I had only gone a few yards when again I saw a fast-moving dot hurtling towards me. It was the peregrine again, flying with a few rapid flicks of its wings, gliding while holding them back and rolling slightly from side to side, then a few more rapid beats and another rolling glide. It was homing straight into the nest, and I cursed at having put the camera back in my pack. It came so close I could see the dark eyes, yellow cere of its beak and the dark moustaches on each side of its head. I stood frozen in my tracks, but the falcon must have seen me for, when only yards from the nest, it swerved away and disappeared behind the knoll.

I hurried away downwards, making myself as conspicuous as I could, my heart beating with excitement. In a few days, when the chicks were bigger, I would put a hide up on that bracken-covered knoll, a perfect position. Imagine, peregrines nesting right behind my cottage! Would there be any end to this wonderful season? Obviously, I *had* seen a peregrine flying into my east wood after my last visit to the falcons on the cliff near the sea.

Yet two things puzzled me. While my books said that peregrines would annex old or deserted nests of ravens or other birds, these were of species that nested on ledges of sea or inland cliffs. There was no mention of them using a crows' nest up a tree, and they had certainly left the eagles' ledge severely alone. The other oddity was the lateness of these falcons' nesting, for the chicks could not have been more than two weeks old. Perhaps the first one to arrive had not found a mate until relatively late in the season.

Next morning, battling with long-overdue desk work, I looked out of the window and received another delightful surprise. Floating in the calm blue water, just a few yards from my boat bay, was the black-throated diver, and right beside her was her remaining youngster. It was still in the downy brown stage, had not grown its full plumage and certainly could not fly yet. There seemed to be an oddly expectant air about them.

I put my camera and long lens together and wandered casually down to the shore without trying to hide or to stalk them. Still they stayed, paddling gently round each other, as I took pictures. Soon the male joined them, popping up from below the surface like a giant blue-grey cork. Anthropomorphic though it may sound, it was as if they had not only brought the chick back to their originally intended breeding area, but had brought it close for my inspection, as if to assure me they had succeeded after all.

After a few days of gales and rain, causing the burns to seethe down the mountains like white snakes, I returned to Juno's eyrie, sure that the eaglet would now be gone and that I could take the hide away. In case it had not flown, however, I kept out of sight and slid gently into the damp and gloomy cold hide. I did not want to scare it away prematurely. Slowly I poked the lens through. The eaglet was still there. He was now fully grown, with all his plumage but for a whitish band down the back of his neck, and the normal white patches in wings and tail of the immature.

At this stage the parents leave the eaglet alone for hours, even days at a time, just dumping prey, knowing it can feed itself, and immediately flying away again. The male does most of the providing, as if the female has told him she has done her bit and it is now up to him to take over the main duties. Towards the end they try a little judicious starvation, bringing in less prey than normal and flying past the eyrie, often with food in their talons, to induce the eaglet to take its first flight.

This eaglet was now as bored as hell and his behaviour was comical to watch. He sat on his hocks and nibbled his huge yellow toes with his beak, pulled heather sprigs about and arranged them round himself or just over the nest. He lay on his right side dozing for over an hour, his legs stretched across the nest towards the cliff face, and kept stretching his left wing right over them. Then he rolled over on to his belly and rested his head, beak vertically down on the twigs, opening his eyes and blinking, as if having serious thoughts.

After his rest he got up, scratched his eye with amazing accuracy with just the centre talon of his right foot while keeping the protective nictitating membrane, or 'third eyelid', tightly shut. Then he walked backwards to the edge of the nest, tilted his tail up and squirted white faeces well clear. He tramped round the nest then made a lightning strike with one set of talons at some prey. As he started to drag it about I saw it was the remains of the leg of a large lamb. It seemed too big for the eagles to have killed its owner but there was no real evidence one way or another. This was the second 'doubtful' case. There was little meat left on the leg. After a few pecks the eaglet dropped it, tramped to something else, made another fast stab and lifted the remains of a raven, doubtless a youngster. He pulled at the bloody carcass, swallowed a wing blade bone, then brought it up again.

Twice during my eight hour stay he glared into the sky, making '*kyew*' calls with a reproachful air, as if trying to call one of his flying parents into the eyrie, but they were clearly trying to tempt him out. When this ploy failed, he stabbed the raven remains several times with his right foot, then stared out into the distance as if dying to get *out there* and do it for real. For a while he trampolined right round the eyrie, flapping his huge wings to strengthen their muscles, looking out into the void, yet clinging desperately to the nest twigs when he felt in danger of going over the edge. Then he preened the undersides of his wings, holding each out to the front or to the side, as a matador holds a muleta. When he next lay down for a sleep I left the hide.

Three days later I returned to collect the hide but he was still there, looking really dejected. My fears that the adults might have left him to his own devices were assuaged when I saw the remains of a big rabbit in the nest. Oh well, I would have to trek back yet again later.

I decided on the spur of the moment to get the killer trek over for the very last time and check Atalanta's eaglet had flown safely. With luck, I might even see it flying. On July 10 I set off in fine but cloudy weather with a heavier burden than usual, for I was carrying a new hide to set up over the peregrine nest. When I came abreast of it, however, it looked deserted, and a thick twig seemed to have been rammed into the centre of the nest. It was a good way off, so my hopes were not completely dashed. If I had enough steam left on my return, I would climb up the knoll on the other side of the ravine for a final check. I dumped the hide between two large rocks and carried on.

Two hours later I puffed up to the rowan roost, thankful to find many new white splashes and small feathers below it, as well as two very small pellets containing deer hair which I collected for the survey. As the roost was being used, I hoped it meant nothing drastic had happened at the nest. I hiked on up below the nest crag and looked through the binoculars. The desiccated foreleg of a red-deer calf projected from the front of the nest, grotesque against the sky. I climbed higher to the north and looked again. The nest seemed to be empty, with no sign of the wings, head or yellow beak cere of an eaglet to be seen. There was no damage to the area round the nest; all the little ferns, grasses and mosses seemed unbroken and undisturbed. There was no sign of shot on the cliff wall or of feathers, apart from those dislodged by normal downy preening. I hoped the eaglet had got away safely.

Twenty minutes later, as I sat eating an egg and bacon sandwich and looking about, I saw two little specks appear over the high crests to the north and put the glasses on them. The first one was Atalanta, I was sure, travelling in a fast even glide to the south, followed by another eagle which was a lot wobblier and uncertain in the air. It was not quite so big as Atalanta but was a good deal bigger than Melanion. Its awkwardness was quite apparent, for it kept shifting and adjusting its wings, whereas Atalanta's flight was sure and steady. Although they were really too far away I took some pictures. At their nearest point they were below the bright sun and my naked eyes could not pick out any white immature patches on the rear bird. They had probably intended coming to the eyrie area but had easily spotted me sitting there from two miles away, so had turned slightly to the south-west, sailing right over the great glen and finally vanishing in the direction of Eyries 27 and 28. If only Melanion would now come over I would *know*.

I took the shortest route up the great 2,000 foot wall out of the glen and twice found myself in precarious situations, having no choice but to climb almost sheer wet faces or go right back down again and come up another way. Half-way up the last pitch I remembered I was supposed to be afraid of heights, managed not to panic, refused to look down, concentrated on the rock, and finally scrambled over the top. As I slumped there on hands and knees, puffing like an old bear, I saw an eagle land awkwardly on a rock above to my right.

I thought it must be the eaglet but it took off, sailed over the glen, then dived behind the eyrie buttress with its wings closed. I could see no white patches at all. It was smaller than Atalanta, looked too dark for Melanion, but with the sun now obscured behind clouds I decided it must have been him.

As I slogged back over the undulating hills, I was accosted by eight golden plovers, all calling mournfully and flitting on to various rocks round me. I had never seen so many together on these hills. Some uttered the normal liquid '*tluee*' calls, others sounded the louder '*cleeyou*' alarm notes, and when they flew fast in pairs they made bubbling musical trills '*berlioz, berlioz, berlioz*'. No bird sounds are more evocative of the high, solitary wastes and moors. As they flew, I saw the rich black velvety bars across their chests, the flashings of yellow-gold in their speckled wings. One of them followed me for a good half-mile, landing on rocks and calling as I took pictures.

Tired out, I had to force myself to climb the burn ravine and the high knoll overlooking the nest which had contained the peregrine chicks. It was silent, empty, deserted. I climbed down to the foot of the birch which overhung the deep gorge. There I found two distinctive pine-marten scats, and there were small scuff marks on the white bark of the slim trunk. The thick twig which seemed to have been rammed into the centre of the nest was just a nest stick which had been hauled upwards, perhaps by the claws of a marten. There seemed little doubt that the martens had been up the tree and taken the chicks, probably at night. Little beggars! My heart sank. The first pair of peregrines to try and nest near my home and they had failed. I saw no falcon in the sky. Wearily, I collected the hide and descended the knee-cracking route to the cottage. I realised too that I was not totally *sure* I had seen Atalanta's eaglet. Maybe I would have to make that trek yet again.

13 · Soaring High

Amid a host of gaudy orange fritillary butterflies dancing among the summer flowers in hazy sunlight, I hiked back up to Juno's eyrie two days later. This time I took a chunk of butcher's meat in my pack in case the eaglet had been left and was hungry. Again I saw no adults in the air. Nearing the hide, I moved with extreme caution, knowing that at this stage the eaglet could well have flown yet have returned to the eyrie cliff and now be perched on a rock, hump or tree near it – in which event I would drop the meat where he could see it and return home.

I scanned the area through binoculars, saw no eaglet anywhere and slid into the hide. He was still on the nest, standing bolt upright, a fully grown young eagle now, his crop full to almost bursting point, and ready to fly. Pieces of rabbit lay around his feet, as well as a young ptarmigan. He had certainly not been deserted.

For four hours I photographed him trampolining about, standing on one foot and flirting the other, one wing and his tail out to the side, and smoothing his secondary wing feathers through his huge hooked bill. Once he went to the front of the nest, crouched down and half-opened his wings as if about to fly, but then thought better of it. When I left the hide I knew I would probably not see him again. He would be away any day now.

On a supply trip next day I received at last the report on Atalanta's egg from the Department of Agriculture and Fisheries for Scotland analysis unit in Edinburgh. Dr Ruthven had written:

129

There was no evidence of development of an embryo in this egg and the contents were very fluid. Analysis of the contents showed the presence of – 0·16 ppm of DDE, 0·2 ppm of dieldrin, 0·5 ppm of PCB and 0·01 ppm of mercury. These residues are very low and should not have been a threat to the development of this egg.

I sent off a letter with a few more queries, and Dr Ruthven replied:

There is no doubt that the egg was laid this season and I would suspect that it was not more than a few weeks old. The contents were very fresh looking, both in colour and consistency. It was certainly much fresher than some other raptor eggs I have received this year.

The analyses failed to reveal the presence of any agricultural pesticide which might have been responsible for non-fertility of the egg and, as the report shows, it was a relatively unpolluted egg. There was also no evidence of any attempt to bait the egg with poison or 'doctor' it in any other way.

During the past 10 years we have analysed tissue samples from about 200 raptors of various species (which died from a range of natural and unnatural causes) and also many eggs from these species. Although these results have not been published and are not an organised survey but rather an opportunist collection of samples, it is apparent that golden eagles are among the least polluted species and very few show any significant residues of organochlorine pesticides or other persistent compounds. In general the bird-eating species, sparrowhawk and peregrine etc, show much greater evidence of contamination by these compounds.

This was good news about eagles at least. A nice letter also came from Roger Broad of the R.S.P.B. saying that he had again visited the eaglet in the mountain eyrie well east of my home, and it was ready to fly.

It was good to know, if I was right about Atalanta's youngster, that the three pairs of eagles nearest to me had all successfully raised eaglets this year.

I now also heard from Roy Dennis in response to the full report I had sent him on the human disturbance at the peregrines' nest near the sea, which he described as 'quite awful'. He added:

I get the impression actually that they didn't know what they were looking at, but they were clearly trying to find the nest. They sound to me to be complete novices who were just out having a good bash up of the countryside. It is very good you happened along otherwise they could have easily exploded the brood which is not a good thing at all.

On July 16, a dullish day with sunny intervals, I drove down to the parking spot near the cliff, determined to stay until I *did* either locate the peregrine nest or see any chicks. After climbing up and wading through the thick heather, clouds obscured the sun and threw the whole cliff into shadow. The fully grown vegetation and foliage on all the little trees made locating the nest an even more difficult task. Hidden in the heather, I waited over an hour but not a single falcon did I see.

Suddenly the clouds parted overhead briefly, a shaft of sunlight beamed on to the cliff and I saw a fluttering movement among the dwarf birches. I raised the binoculars and there, shuffling awkwardly on a tiny pinnacle of rock, well above the two raven nests, was a lovely young peregrine. All its feathers were fluffed out so it looked like a soft football, the bright light giving its chest feathers a creamy pink hue. There was a fair breeze blowing on to the cliff, enough to buffet the youngster, and it had to make constant adjustments of its wings to retain its footing. Just then I saw another movement above it to the right and through the glasses spotted a second fledgeling, perched in a birch tree. This one was rocking to and fro, clinging hard to a thick twig, the wind rustling its feathers and occasionally its tail up over its back. I kept scanning the cliff but could not locate a third. Just as I got the camera ready and was about to take a photo, clouds blotted out the sun again and this time it did not reappear. I took pictures anyway, but at that distance in that light they would not be much good. Well, the peregrines had raised at least two young, and that was good to know.

The mail I collected at the post office on the way home included a telegram from my publishers. It said that Brian Jackman, the award-winning travel and wildlife writer for the *Sunday Times*, wanted to come up to Wildernesse in a week's time and write an article about my life and work in the wilds. I knew something of his excellent work and felt highly flattered. My publisher added, when I phoned, that Jackman had asked to spend at least two days with me as I went about my work; above all, he wanted to go on a hard wild trek. That gave me an idea. I still wanted to doublecheck that Atalanta's eaglet was indeed flying safely, so I would take him on the killer trek.

'Well,' I said, 'I think that can be arranged.'

I would meet him at Inverness airport early on the morning of July 23. I hoped the weather would be good when he was with me.

Two days later I hiked up to the Juno hide, sure the eaglet would be gone, and it was. I climbed down the almost sheer gully and over the rock slide at the end of the gorge to see if I could get near the nest and record the final prey. When I was half-way across, a boulder slipped beneath my feet and went down a few inches. There was an ominous rumble; the huge rocks above were loose and threatened to come down on me. I had not been so nimble and fleet-footed since I was a kid, and I shot back across the rocks with the speed and lightness, but not the grace, of a ballet dancer. Knowing eaglets sometimes fly back into the eyrie after their first flight, I decided to leave the hide where it was for a few days longer rather than even slightly alter the look of the area by its sudden removal.

After a hard climb the other way I came to within three yards of the nest. There was no new prey on it, just bones and wisps of white down clinging to twiglets. I was now on a broad grassy ledge fringed with small birches. It would have been a good place for a one-day hide from which to take dramatic pictures of the eagles flying in, though it was really too close. One may get a few superb photos by such methods, but not without causing the birds stress, and I am always careful to avoid that. Besides, it was too late now. I removed a large pellet from below the male's oak-tree roost for the survey and went home.

Someone once asked me if I had any great ambition left regarding eagles. I said there was. One winter I would like to excavate a big room in the rock right beside an eyrie that overlooked a superb view. There would be a thick camouflaged screen through which I could take close-ups of the birds incubating eggs, brooding and feeding chicks, and flying in with prey. In this room there would be a comfortable bed, central heating, electric light, a phone, a colour TV set with earphones to cut out the sound, a microwave cooker and a hot-water shower unit! However, since I had not enjoyed any of these amenities in my remote homes for the last sixteen years,

I reckoned I could probably get along without them at an eyrie.

On July 22 I camped out near Inverness and next morning met Brian Jackman at the airport. He turned out to be a tall ranging character with a quiet and pleasant manner. He was sunburnt, having just returned from Africa, where he had been researching for what was to become his fine and most evocative book, *The Marsh Lions*. I drove him back and at once took him to see the peregrines at the sea cliff. We climbed up and had only been waiting half an hour when a peregrine came over the cliff to the north, belly and under-wings gleaming silver in the sunlight. It treated us to a few circlings, then went back behind the cliff. Shortly afterwards we saw two buzzards wheeling round each other in the sky near a crest to the south. As we watched what looked like a bigger buzzard headed towards them. They showed no alarm. As the new bird turned I saw it was a male eagle, which then performed a perfect 'golden ball' dive, hurtling down behind another ridge, and vanished. Not a bad show for Brian's first hour!

As we drove beside the winding sea loch towards the buzzards' nest in the oak wood, I pointed out the seals lying on the rocks in their mating lagoon. A redstart flitted along beside us on the climb up, which pleased Brian. Near the hide we heard piercing, ringing '*kee-oo*' calls and looked up to see the female buzzard soaring over-head. Soon she was joined by the male, also calling loudly, and he gave us a territorial display of several closed-wing dives like a small eagle before drifting away. Then the female performed an even more spectacular dive, of which I managed to take a good photo.

I was sure the birds' agitation indicated that their chick was still in the nest, though it would now surely be ready to fly. Carefully we slid into the large hide. The nest was empty. It was probably in the nest tree somewhere, I told Brian. He got out first, poked his head round and, sure enough, saw it – flop-flying from branch to branch, a dark dot in the shade of the wood.

The following day I took him on the quest for Atalanta and to try and see her eaglet flying. With the vast terrain that eagles cover it was a hundred to one chance, but I had a ruse up my sleeve – the one seemingly infallible wilderness law: if you want to see a rare bird like an eagle, leave your camera at home. You are almost bound to see one then. So I left mine behind, and we carried only lunch packs and binoculars.

The day was hot, muggy and overcast, and as we slogged our

way up the first 1,500 feet through the tussocks and golden carpet of bog asphodel flowers, Scotch argus butterflies hopped through the air on orange-spotted chocolate wings. Then came the two miles of undulating hills over the big corrie, where we did, as Brian was to write later, 'gasp our way from crest to endless crest'. Red-deer hinds with their cream-spotted calves paused from eating to watch us, huge ears twitching like radar scanners. One barked '*hough!*' — and away they streamed, moving over the harsh terrain like dancers. On the tops the air was colder, cooling the sweat on our faces. A flotilla of golden plovers flew round us, strutting on rocks and giving their melancholy calls. We floundered through peat hags, squelched over marshes and through bobbing cotton grass until the hills plunged 2,000 almost sheer feet down into the last desolate glen.

'Where *is* the eyrie?' panted Brian as he came up to me.

'Over there, in the next mountain range,' I said, pointing to the river far below and up the last 1,000 foot climb to the buttress that contained the nest.

'Shit!' I heard him mutter.

It was the only time I heard him come anywhere near to a swear word. His spirits were lifted though by the sight of two stags, their antlers in velvet, heading over the ridges to our left. We caught back our breath, zig-zagged down the steeps, slaked our thirst in the river, then made the final climb up past the massive eyrie crag. The nest was as before, the dried leg of the deer calf still sticking out from its front.

We sat down. It was only twenty minutes before Atalanta came sweeping over from the north and airily circled the glen in front of us, a bird galleon on seven-foot wings. The tips of her primaries were bent upwards, the now-bright light shone her head and mantle into grey-gold fire, and I heard Brian gasp with awe. She circled once more, then soared along the rockfaces to the south like a dark avenging shadow.

Just then we heard the shrill '*keeyew*' calls of an eaglet and there it was, gliding along in its mother's flight path but still more unsteady than she had been. It turned towards the eyrie as if coming in, but must have seen us for it carried on over the top, the white wing patches and tail band showing clearly. After a minute the eaglet came out on the far side and headed off towards its mother, still calling. The hundred to one chance had paid off, and Atalanta's eaglet *was* flying safely. Now, at 4.30 p.m., we could eat our lunch.

On the killer climb out, up what Brian called a *diretissima*, I was proud of him. While he was seven years younger than I was, he was still not a young man, unused to these harsh hills, and he kept up pretty well. Back home, as we sank a few needed drams and I cooked supper, he said it was probably the hardest trek he had ever undertaken. Certainly it ranked with one he had made in Norway with Klaus Helbjerg, the real-life hero of Telemark and the wartime raid on the heavy-water plant at Peenemunde. In postwar years, Helbjerg (whose role in the film *Heroes of Telemark* was played by Kirk Douglas) was put in charge of long-distance footpaths and hiking in the Norwegian government and he had taken Brian on a horrendous trek in the Rondane mountains, covering miles of scree and tumbled boulders in an area known as 'Odin's graveyard'. Brian said he felt as done in now as he had then. I felt good about that too, but resolved that was indeed the last time I would make the killer trek.

Brian finished interviewing me next morning. Before I drove him back to Inverness airport, I took him over to the big mountain to try and see Juno and perhaps her flying eaglet too. Again, to *ensure* success, I left the camera gear at home. As we boated out I worked the engine from the rear while Brian sat at the front so that his body and the roof of the cabin partly obscured my view of the water ahead. After a mile I told him to keep his eyes peeled, for he might be lucky enough to see the birds that were so much rarer than even golden eagles – the black-throated divers.

'There is a black dot ahead,' he said a few minutes later.

I slowed down and looked. There, a quarter of a mile in front of us, was the diver paddling along with her chick. They had appeared right on cue. When they dived I speeded up so that we would be quite close when they re-appeared – ideal for unusual photos! The chick was greyish-brown now, having grown most of its feathers, and was almost as big as its mother. We cut away from them and landed the boat on the shore of Juno's mountain.

As we hiked up the burn gorge to take the hide down, the alders, willows, ashes, oaks and birches seemed filled with the young birds of the year and their parents. We saw roe does, coal tits, great tits, chaffinches, grey wagtails, siskins and even a wood warbler. We were about to start the final steep climb to the hide when Juno came sailing over our heads from the west. I said the eaglet could be with her; then Brian said he could hear it calling, just as I heard it too.

We could not see the chick but we now saw that Juno had something in her talons, the browny-grey speckled form of a headless ptarmigan. She circled and soared, swept past some cliff faces and then landed with casual sweepings of her huge wings on a broad flat rock at about 2,000 feet, near the skyline. Brian located a dark hump on an adjacent rock which he thought was the eaglet. I glassed it too; the colours were right but it did not move. It was hard to see, as the birds were over half a mile away. Juno appeared to tear at the ptarmigan for a short while, as if opening it up, then launched into the air again and disappeared beyond the ridges to the south-west. When we looked back the eaglet had disappeared, apparently having walked into a cleft. Was there something wrong with him?

We reached the hide and began to take it down. Juno again came over us, high up, then headed away to the east. I said that she might have gone to fetch the male. A few minutes later we saw her heading back, followed by a smaller eagle. She had indeed gone to get him. Juno hovered briefly over the ptarmigan as if showing it to her mate, who landed beside it. Then she angled her wings back, went into a jet glide, began to move like a meteor across the arch of the sky and finally vanished over the highest peak of a mountain range seven miles to the north. Again she had gone right over Atalanta's territory and that of another pair of eagles as well.

When we looked back we saw another eagle soaring slowly over the skyline almost directly above the ptarmigan. I prayed it would have white wing patches, and soon saw that it had. It was undoubtedly the eaglet. Then we were treated to one of the finest sights I have ever witnessed in wild mountain nature. The male rose effortlessly into the air until he was beside the eaglet, then both hung in the air like a pair of giant black bats. The male seemed to be trying to teach the youngster a certain manœuvre. After bending his wings back he spread out the front alula feathers, which are designed to smooth the air-flow over the wings to prevent the bird stalling at slow speeds, spread his twelve tail feathers out like a fan and, with his talons extended, descended very slowly to land on the ptarmigan. As he performed all this, the eaglet copied his every movement, then landed beside him. It was superb to watch.

Then both birds launched themselves into the void, rose into the air, hung there again like great dark kites and repeated exactly the same manœuvre, parachuting down with talons stretched out below them. This time the male landed beside the ptarmigan while the eaglet landed on the other side. It appeared this was not what the male had intended, for he was clearly teaching the eaglet how to hunt, how to kill. Once more he rose into the air, watched by the eaglet on the ground, and again descended slowly, hitting into the ptarmigan with great force. Then he hopped gawkily to the side. The eaglet now appeared to understand what was required. Again it rose into the air, hung momentarily, came down faster, landed on the ptarmigan and began to feed. The male watched for a few moments more, then sprang from the rock, went into a jet glide and followed in Juno's wake.

We lowered our aching arms with the binoculars and Brian looked at me.

'What a fantastic sight! *What a life you lead.*'

'Yes,' I replied with an ironical laugh. 'And I left the bloody camera at home! Imagine *filming* that.'

'You ought to get a movie camera.'

'I should have had a movie camera from the very first day I went into the wilds, but I could never afford the kind of gear one would really need.'

That was the climax really, the incredible end to the most marvellous rare bird season I had ever known.

I had not long to wait before the inevitable and deadly blow struck.

PART TWO

14 · *Troubled Times*

It was in early autumn that I lost my beloved Moobli. Although I had known that it was inevitable, I was not prepared for the grief and the pain and the misery that followed upon the death of my only companion for the last eight and a half years. For more than eighteen months I had watched his slow decline. A year at most the vet had given him, when I had taken him south in March the previous year for treatment for what I then supposed was an arthritic growth. Slowly, but not painfully, the giant Alsatian's hind-leg muscles had wasted away. The injections had kept him going a long time, and even when I could not take him on the long treks he remained active and contented in the woods nearer home. When the paralysis in his rear legs became complete in the early summer, he had gamely continued to haul himself around on front legs and bottom. He could manage surprisingly well down gentle grassy slopes, and up them if I supported his rear end with a towel. So long as he was happy I had tried to make his last months as enjoyable as possible. Although I knew it would come, I never seriously anticipated the depression that followed his death.

I buried Moobli on the hill above the cottage. Somehow I got through the journey south alone for the interviews arranged by my publishers. Even there everything was changed. My personal editor was still there, but a new boss was installed. They said they still wanted *A Last Wild Place* when it was finished, the complicated book on which I had worked for over three years without pay, but the advance they could offer was now far less than I had been led to expect when asked to set it aside to write *Golden Eagle Years*. I had been less than happy with the arrangement and printing of the pictures in that book, and I could have no guarantee, it appeared, that any at all would be included in the new one. (A wildlife book without pictures to illustrate its truth, drama and beauty is a cheat to the reader.) Since I had spent nine years taking photos specially for *A Last Wild Place*, the book about the whole cycle of nature in the Highlands I had always planned, it was now clear I faced the long and weary business of finding another publisher.

I returned home and mooched about on stag treks in the hills, but my heart was no longer in them. I had done more than enough already. I broke down frequently beside Moobli's grave, my days a void, filled with an aching loneliness I had not experienced since the early years in the wilds. Rarely had life appeared so bleak, and matched by such appalling weather. In the wettest October for thirty years, my boat was torn from its trolley in a storm, its roof smashed in and the engine ripped off and battered. It took a whole day battling with the elements to recover and restore them to use. On a supply trip, the worst storm I had ever experienced almost ended my life too. I confess that it crossed my mind to wish it had.

In late November I gave up the unequal struggle, certain that my life in the Scottish Highlands was at an end. I stood in whirling snow by Moobli's grave and vowed one day to write a book that honoured his gentle nature and extraordinary life. I packed up and boated away, unsure that I would ever return except to retrieve a few possessions. Long before the year was out I was in Spain. There, so recently it seemed, my father had also died. The weeks of unravelling his affairs and settling his estate buffered the pain slightly, but I could not face a lonely winter at Wildernesse below Moobli's grave in my present frame of mind. I made instead for the vast and infinitely wilder Spanish mountains, tracking after rare lynx, wolf and brown bear. A new challenge, far away, was my one hope of survival.

I drove back to Scotland amid rain-filled gales in early April. For the first time, I was not looking forward to going home. If, indeed, I could still bring myself to call it home. The book on which I had lavished over three years of devotion, with which I had hoped I would win a little recognition for what I had discovered in Britain's last great wilderness, had now been rejected by two more publishers since taking it away from the first. I left the typescript at the offices of the literary publisher, Jonathan Cape, on my way through London. I was certain they too would turn it down. If I could not get work like that published, was there any point at all in carrying on? So sure was I that my life in the Scottish wilds was over that I advertised the remainder of my lease for sale. There had been many inquiries, but most people cried off on learning that there was only access by boat, even though they only wanted Wildernesse as a holiday place. Two families, however, were still interested, and I arranged to meet them and show them round together on April 16.

I boated home with a sackful of mail under a leaden sky. After carrying up the first of eleven loads from the loch shore, I climbed the hill to Moobli's grave. Any illusion that I had recovered from the grief after his death dissolved in childlike tears as I lay on the damp earth in the rain. How much I had loved him, and how much I missed him. A strange keening sound issued from my throat. I had never felt more alone.

Somehow, I forced myself back down to carry up the rest of my gear and supplies, for there was much work to be done. The winter storms had raised the loch level to record heights and my wooden boat runway had been washed away, presumably smashed up, for I never found it. I now had to make a new one. Two of the corrugated iron sheets from the porch roof had been torn from their foundations by the gales and were lying in the woods a hundred yards away. A chunk of guttering had also been ripped off and broken. The water pipe from the burn had been dislodged by the winter torrents and was hanging over the gorge, writhing up and down like a snake in the waterfall. Despite the chimney being covered, rain had seeped in and half-filled the wood-burning stove I had made from an oil barrel.

I busied myself with chores and repairs for the next two days before boating out to meet the two families who were interested in buying my lease. I still do not understand what happened to the weather that day. It had been dull but calm all morning, yet as soon as I got the two men and one of the wives down to the boat, huge black clouds appeared over the loch from the north-west. Rain pelted down, the surface was whipped up to a green froth and we had to wait it out for twenty minutes. No sooner had I got them across, their faces paling slightly in the whirling, bucking boat, than the gales subsided again.

For about an hour I showed them round the land, the boundaries and inside the cottage in perfectly calm weather. Over tea, both parties said they were extremely interested and would write to me with their final offers. As we walked back down to the boat, another freak squall frenzied the loch into foam and we had a bouncy, spray-filled trip back to their cars. I had the weirdest guilty feeling that the whole place was telling me not to go, and my lone trip home was accomplished in beaming sunlight. I heard no further word from either family.

If the winter storms and late snows had inflicted minor damage on the cottage, they had wreaked havoc among the red-deer herds in the area. On the usual morning walks round the woods, I found one dead hind, almost all skeleton after being eaten by foxes, lying below the rock escarpment in the west wood. Near her, newly dead, lay a calf, probably hers. Another calf had fallen recently by a tangle of fallen tree roots in the east edge of the wood. I hauled this one up to 300 feet in case Atalanta came by on a hunting flight. One huge old hind lay curled up like a dog, as if just asleep, beside my vegetable garden. I hauled her down to rot on the shore. Two more hinds were caught up among torrent-scoured tree roots along the banks of the burn. If these deaths were a reflection of the mortality out on the open Hill, it had been an even worse year for the deer than last – or better for all carrion-eating species, including eagles.

Finding these bodies did little to alleviate the depression caused by the yawning gap Moobli's death had brought into my life. But I found a new source of slight consolation – my mail. In the full sacks were scores of letters from readers of my eagle book, saying how much they had liked it and begging me not to give up the wilderness life but to keep writing such books. These warmed my heart, as did many fine reviews which had piled up during my absence.

After writing my full eagle, diver and peregrine reports for the government, the R.S.P.B., and the remaining prey list the previous year, I had exchanged several letters with Jeff Watson. In one, he told me the fascinating news that Pair 3, whose eyrie was near the sea, had taken a peregrine, a kestrel, a merlin and four herring gulls among their prey.

He also informed me that out of the twenty-one pairs in his main west Highland study area (which included much of my old area) eight eaglets had flown successfully, and this included Juno's. As Atalanta and Roger Broad's pair east of my old boundary had also raised one eaglet each, this meant ten eaglets fledged from 23 pairs in the region. The results in my old area were: Pair 1 (Atalanta) raised one eaglet; Pair 2 (Juno) raised one eaglet; Pair 3 raised two eaglets; Pair 4 laid eggs which failed to hatch; Pair 5 raised one eaglet; Pair 6 hatched a chick but it vanished from the nest in mid-June; Pair 7 laid one egg which failed to hatch; Pair 8 raised one eaglet; and Pair 9 (east of my old boundary) also raised one eaglet. This added up to the best eagle season I had known in my immediate area. The remaining eleven pairs in Jeff's larger study area raised three eaglets between them.

I suggested to Jeff that he had no doubt by now concluded there were more eagles in Scotland than was generally admitted, but that I had deliberately not updated numbers in my book as the few die-hard enemies they had left might feel less guilty about persecuting them. He must have persuaded the N.C.C. I was worth supporting, for they sent me £100 towards my petrol costs and other expenses. It was not a large sum, but since I had only gone about the work I would have done anyway, I was pleased to receive it. Recently, Jeff Watson had written: 'If you'd like to continue with the same arrangements as last year re eagles I'd be very happy. Again we can make a contribution towards your petrol costs.' He added that he had been unable to find Juno's nest on Eagle Rock mountain this year but she might be in the deep burn gorge to the west. He would be back in the area at the end of April and hoped to meet me then.

I smiled sadly as I filed away his letter. Right then I did not feel I had another eagle season in me. My wilderness life seemed truly over. With Moobli's death, an era had ended. Part of me now wanted nothing more than to be with him again. I went into the kitchen and brought a bottle of whisky back into the study.

Next morning I woke late to a day of short bright periods which were frequently blotted out by black snow showers. I sat at my desk with aching head, annoyed with myself for drinking so much the night before. I had no real writing to do, apart from a weekly wildlife column for a Scottish paper which took a mere half-day a week, but now provided my only income. I had not the vaguest notion of what my next book would be about, or indeed whether I was still capable of another. Certainly in my grieving state I could not contemplate the book I had promised Moobli at his graveside. If I could not now get my best book published there seemed little point in writing any more at all. Half-heartedly I started answering my mail. At 3 p.m. the sky brightened and pale shafts of sunlight began to beam through the cloud cover. Without thinking, I pushed back my chair and heard a voice say:

'To hell with it! I'm going to check Atalanta's best eyries.'

It did not sound like my own voice.

Twenty minutes later, as I began the two-mile climb up through the tussocks, I told myself to take it easy, expecting to be quickly weary after my long lay-off and a mis-spent night. A few primroses made little suns on the ground but as yet no bracken heads or tussock grasses had started to sprout. I was acutely conscious of the silence behind me, knowing I would never hear again on any trek the scuffing steps of the once powerful, gentle Moobli. I reached the first 500-foot ridge after the steepest part of the climb with my heart hardly pounding at all, and found a dead hind north of the long wood's burn. The heart, lungs and part of the gut had been eaten from a neat hole behind the ribs, and tufts of plucked-out hairs lay round the carcass – eagles' work. I cut away north to check Eyrie 33. Apart from a few new sticks that had been brought in, it was empty. I was sure Eyries 27 and 28 would be empty too.

I tramped upwards mechanically, keeping well north of the eagles' glen. I decided to head round the back of the mountain at 1,700 feet and come at the highest eyrie from the north-west before heading down to check no. 27, where Atalanta had raised twin chicks three years earlier. The first shower of sleety snow hit me on the summit, blown by a squally gale and stinging my face like tiny icicles. It was so cold I had to put on gloves. I stumbled on through the gloom, hardly able to see more than a few yards ahead, sure that my depression must have caused my judgment to fail in allowing me to tackle these hills and dripping granite faces in such chancy weather. I was now on extremely steep ground. Between the black crags were sheer drops to my left. After another fifty yards I was on a steep runner of tawny grasses above a precipitous drop and realised I must be right above Eyrie 28. Another gust of wind made me stagger. I shrank back against a wet granite face for meagre shelter.

When the snow passed and the gale had lessened temporarily to a stiff breeze, I took a few steps forward to see if I could look into the nest. I could see nothing because the cliff face bulged out below me. Far below stretched the whole terrifying expanse of the eagles' glen. I stood there as if rooted to the spot, thinking of the desolate lone-liness that had invaded my life, the failure of my book, Moobli in his cold grave. Suddenly I was seized by a fit of giddiness, panic. My head whirled. That was replaced by a fierce desire to let myself go, actually to throw myself off. A quiet voice was insisting go on, go on, Moobli's waiting. Let the eagles have you.

Some preservation instinct took over. I threw myself backwards, crashed into the granite face, dropped to my hands and knees, scrabbled up the runner and, cursing myself for a fool, climbed rapidly away from the awful cliff to the north-west until my breath came in gasps. As I tramped over the almost level ground on the far side of the summit I gradually calmed down. I told myself I had come out to do one job — check the eyries. I would do just that, thoroughly, then get home and start making plans to leave Scotland and return to Spain. I hiked on, examined all the rockfaces at the head of the glen in case the eagles had established a new eyrie, then set off back to reach a point from where I could overlook Eyrie 28.

Clambering over ridges, round rockfaces, up and down slanting shelves of orange turf overlaid with dead white grasses, I was drenched by two more snow showers before I reached the last little cliff. As I approached cautiously from behind it I saw another shower coming up behind me, as yet a quarter of a mile away. Slowly I peered round and saw the nest, slightly above my level and nearly two hundred yards ahead, rearing out into the sky upon its lone crag, still buttressed in front by the small rowan tree. It looked much tidier than ever before, with straight edges along the top, over which were draped long tussock grasses. Carefully, I raised the bin-oculars.

Suddenly my eyes made out the whole head, eye and blue-black beak of an eagle. Atalanta was sitting deep in the nest, looking side-ways towards me! Clearly she was on eggs, or maybe a newly-hatched chick or two. I thought she must have seen me but she turned her head away and casually preened her neck feathers for a few seconds. I took two cautious photos, then shrank slowly back behind the cliff, my heart thudding involuntarily from excitement.

Last year she had somehow been put off this nest when about to lay and had been forced to leave an egg on a mossy rock well to the south-east of the eyrie. Then she had laid another in her farthest nest, three miles over the high hills, and had successfully raised the eaglet. Now she was trying in this nest again. All thought of leaving Scotland fled from my mind. I knew I had to watch this nest as often as I could, try to make sure she succeeded. I now *had* to do one more eagle season, no question of it. I smiled grimly as I recalled the odd title on Brian Jackman's evocative *Sunday Times* article – 'Prisoner of the Eagles'. It had puzzled me at first, though I had been deeply grateful for his sensitive appreciation of what I was trying to do in the wilds. He paid me the compliment of taking my work seriously; now I saw how perceptive his headline had been, for it was undeniably true.

I heard a slight rattling sound, felt small ice particles hit my neck. The sleet and snow shower was upon me. I saw its grey wall advancing ahead as I peered from behind a tuft on the cliff, and saw Atalanta and the eyrie swallowed up by it. The sleet and flakes settled upon her plumage so that she was visibly whitening before my eyes, but she just sat tight, taking it as if it was normal enough.

I slid behind the cliff. Keeping out of sight of the eyrie, I climbed back and then down again, looking for a hide site. Incredibly, I found the ideal place. It was a broad flat grassy ledge beneath a sheltering overhang, where I could erect a low lie-down hide only forty yards from the eyrie. What was more, if I built it far enough back on the ledge I could easily get into its rear flap without being seen from the eyrie. To do this, however, I would have to climb the full 1,700 feet of this mountain on every visit, in order to come down to the hide from above. It would be the highest eyrie I had yet worked. While I could not see all the nest, as half of it was behind the wall of a crevice, it seemed the ideal situation for superb flight photos of the great birds coming into and leaving it. All the background around this nest and crag was open sky.

I walked away. Then in full sight of the nest, yet four hundred yards away from it, I tramped quietly downhill and passed below the crag. Eagles are intelligent and *discreet* birds and seem to divine if you intend to approach too close or wish to cause trouble. I walked as if I had not seen her and, sure enough, she sat tight. I was also reasonably sure she 'knew' me as an individual, for in the ten years I had followed and watched her, hauled deer carcasses into the winter hills for her and worked her from the nest, I had always worn the same kinds of trekking clothes.

I checked Eyrie 27, which, naturally, was empty. Below it was a dead hind and a calf from which the eagles had also fed. Half a mile nearer home I found another dead hind. It had been a good carrion year for the eagles, and I had not needed to haul that last calf up into the hills at all. That year the tally of dead deer came to eleven hinds and twelve calves, within a half-mile semi-circle of the cottage, as well as four hinds and seven calves found on normal treks within three miles – the second highest mortality I had known in ten years at Wildernesse.

I arrived home, not one whit tired, and went up to Moobli's grave, as if in some way I could impart the good news to the spirit of my departed comrade. I broke down yet again. It was to be two years before I could think of him, or visit his grave, without feeling the emotion of deep grief. All I knew then was that if Atalanta failed I would head for Spain.

Three days later, as I was writing a review of a wildlife book I liked (I simply would not review one I did not like), two human forms loomed outside my study window. They were Calum, the under-keeper of the estate, and Ian MacKay, a stalker with the Red Deer Commission. Concerned about the high deer mortality, the Commission had instituted a laborious foot-slogging census of all red deer in Scotland, and the two men, with walkie-talkie radios and seven others, were trying to count all the deer in the immediate hills. I groaned inwardly at the disturbance to my work but invited them in for tea. I was glad I did because they imparted some interesting information.

Calum told me that he and my neighbouring farmer had visited the fox dens below Eyrie 28 earlier in the month, had bolted a vixen and shot her. Terriers had gone down and killed two cubs but one cub had escaped. They had seen no eagles, and the eyrie had looked empty. I realised if Atalanta had been sitting tight she would have been impossible to see from below. I said nothing about finding her on eggs. Calum said the farmer had not seemed bothered about the eagles, had not even mentioned them. That was good news.

Then Ian gave me a good eagle story. His father had worked on a Perthshire estate, on which there were four eyries, for forty years, and he himself had been keeper on the same estate for twenty.

'We never had any trouble from the eagles – except for one year when we found bits of lamb below one eyrie. But maybe a fox killed the lamb first.'

I pricked up my ears at hearing that. Ian said he had once seen a fox chasing round a ewe but he had been too far away to do anything about it, so he just lay on a ridge and watched.

'The fox kept trying to entice the ewe away from the lamb, making her charge at it. Finally the ewe got far enough away, the fox darted in, killed the lamb and carried it a small distance away. But now the lamb was dead the ewe sniffed it and went away, showing no more interest in it. The fox came back but an eagle sailed down and chased the fox away by dashing at it from the air. The fox ran for almost a mile, falling into ditches and snapping back at the eagle which kept close, not trying to kill or sink its talons into the fox but just harrying it away. I waited a long time thinking the eagle would come back for the lamb but it didn't.'

I asked if they were going up near the eyries today. Ian said they had been instructed by the Commission to keep away from fox dens and eyries, so that keepers could get at the foxes if they needed to, and so that nesting eagles would not be disturbed. This too sounded good news for Atalanta.

15 · *Humiliation and Regeneration*

On April 23 I went to check Eyrie 1 and the tree nest from which the peregrines had lost their chicks to martens last year. As I climbed upwards the first cuckoo sounded its sonorous double note from a tree in the burn gorge. The eyrie was empty. It had lost most of its sticks in the winter storms. There was no sign of the falcons either, and half of that nest had been blown out too. Lower down the gorge, however, an old hooded crow's nest had been well built up with a warm lining of sheep's wool but there were no eggs or chicks in it. Maybe the martens had taken them. As I hiked down again I was rewarded by hearing the first mewing wails of the black-throated divers, back from wintering on the sea. I raked the loch surface with the binoculars but could not see them. It was good to know the water kings were here again and that night, in the hope they would nest on the nearest islet, I started the regular regime of setting out plenty of titbits to draw away the martens. If I could help fill the little blighters' bellies maybe I could stop them swimming over to the islet. This would help the common gulls too, for after losing so many eggs to the martens last season, only seventeen birds had returned.

I met up with Jeff Watson and my keeper friend Allan Peters on April 27. Jeff had searched most of Eagle Rock mountain twice already, once with Allan, who had found a new eyrie (no. 35) for Juno and her mate. We now knew of eleven eyries for this pair but none were being used this year. Jeff reckoned the heavy late snowfalls which had lasted from March 21 until April 10, could well have caused some of the higher nests to fail. I agreed, but thought a few of the younger more vigorous females could well lay one more egg in an eyrie lower down. I told them how I had seen Atalanta whitening with snow before my eyes, how she appeared to accept it as quite normal.

The two men had actually seen Juno mating. The pair had flown over last year's breeding-nest gorge to the south-east and Juno had landed on a high rock. There she had appeared to solicit the male, crouching down and twisting her tail. He had landed beside her, then had hopped on to her back, but only briefly.

'It was not a good mating,' said Jeff.

As to whether this meant the pair were not mating at all, or had tried and failed, none of us could offer an opinion. Seeing eagles actually mating is a rare event, even for professional eagle watchers. I had only seen it twice myself.

Even so, the overall eagle situation was far from bad. In my old region, most of which was now in Jeff's larger main study area containing twenty-one pairs, seven of the eight pairs were incubating eggs. Jeff had found a new eyrie (no. 36) for Pair 7, which would be ideal for observations as it was possible to look *down* into it. He would gladly help me with a hide, though we hesitated at the thought of a hard four-mile hike with a hide, camera gear, food and bed roll on each visit. If Atalanta failed, however, I might well take him up on the offer. In addition, Allan had found a new eyrie (no. 37) with eggs two miles beyond the eastern boundary I had set for myself. We agreed I might stretch my limits that far, and between us we would keep an eye on this nest too.

I could see both men were disappointed at the apparent failure of Juno and her mate, as indeed I was. The only chance now was that the pair might be nesting on the western face, maybe in the long deep gorge of the burn there. I don't know what came over me, but I found myself volunteering to search the whole north-west and western faces of the near 3,000 foot mountain.

'That would be fantastic,' Jeff said.

Next day, as I stood on the shore under sullen grey skies and both saw and felt the hunched, brooding presence of the mountain, the far side of which I now had to search, I thought I must be crazy. Hell! *I* was the one who was *not* being paid for this. I still had the miseries, no secure income and only vague notes for a new book when I had not even placed the last one. Yet maybe this hard outdoor work was the only antidote to my troubles. The challenge was there. I plodded off.

While I was climbing out of last year's nesting gorge, way past the eyrie, I noticed something odd about mountain walking. On each visit last year, the steep hike to the nest at 1,000 feet had seemed a long hard labour. Yet now my mind was on a higher target, to climb right over the mountain, cross just below its peak and search all its western face, I hardly noticed the lesser distance. I had passed the earlier hurdle as if it was not there. Trekking harsh mountain terrain is as much a matter of mind as of muscle.

Just then I saw the male eagle soaring over from the west. He saw me, wheeled north, then west, then glided past the north face of the mountain to the south-east and vanished. I climbed on, and a few minutes later saw him soaring back over the peak. He sailed to the west, circled to the north, hovered briefly as if taking a good look at me, then landed on a high green shelf. There he stayed, a black statue, watching my progress. As he seemed so concerned I thought it possible Juno might just be on a new eyrie not far away. I searched all the rockfaces up to 2,000 feet, found none, then puffed over the high north-western ridges.

As I topped one ridge a fat fox, heading my way, stopped with one foot in the air when it saw me, turned and tried to run back the way it had come, but limped and fell over twice. The rear right leg seemed to be injured.

Passing forty yards below the peak, I found a dead ewe lying on a small plateau. Her eyes had gone and a yard behind her rear lay a bloody lamb which appeared to have been still-born. The ewe, far from a shepherd's help, must have died giving birth. The two made a sad sight up there on the lonely mountainside. Seven ravens were flying along to the west, and on a rock nearby were some white splashes of eagle faeces. But the lamb had not been touched. If Juno was now on eggs, surely the male would have taken this easy carrion to the eyrie?

As I hiked south-west down to the start of the great burn gorge, white-winged ptarmigan snorting with alarm as they flew away, I found a small dead hind by a little runnel; it too was untouched. I reached the first cliffs of the gorge and tried to examine every foot through the binoculars. A third of a mile from the peak were un-mistakable signs – small white and brown feathers fluttering from the twigs of the rowans and birches which clung to the far side of the gorge: an eagle's roosting site.

My pulse rate increased, years of eagle sleuthing telling me there was likely to be an eyrie nearby. Would I have some startling news for Jeff and Allan after all? I moved even more cautiously. Then, just past the side of a jutting triangular wall, I found it – Eyrie 38. The nest was just below my level and on a superb square ledge, shielded from above by a tall concave rockface. It had some fresh greenery on it too. On my side of the gorge, only forty yards away, was a small lone rowan growing beside some fang-like rocks, an ideal place for a hide. My golly, I thought, I'll work BOTH nests this year, then pack in *all* the arduous eagle work! As I drew level and raised the glasses, however, I was doomed to disappointment. The greenery proved to be leaves of bilberry growing from the back of the nest, which certainly contained neither eggs nor chicks.

While the nest had been built in the three years since I had last checked this part of the gorge, there were no new sticks on it, so it had not been used this year. I wondered why the eagles had made this nest when they had a perfectly good site on a ledge half a mile down the gorge, and went down to check that one too. It had gone, in a great fall of rocks. I struck back up to the north-east and circled round in a wide arc to check the gully below last year's nesting gorge on the mountain's north side. On the way I found two dead deer calves and another dead ewe. If Juno had failed to lay this year, it had not been due to lack of food. Eagles do occasionally take a year off, and as she had been seen still mating in late April, it was possible she had done just that. I made an error of judgement and came out far below the second gully. I hiked back up to its head again, but before I had checked half its faces it became so dark I could not see them properly. Apart from painful bones in my feet, I had little to show for ten and a half hours of continuous trekking. On May 1 I returned and checked the rest of the gully. I found nothing. From now on it was all down to working Atalanta's nest.

Two days later I saw lights flashing on the loch shore opposite and heard a faint hooting. I boated over to find a young scientist from the Nature Conservancy Council who was conducting a survey on the Scottish wildcat and who had been writing to me on the subject. He had driven all the way from Edinburgh to get any information I could give him and was due to drive back the same day. I had bred wildcats and released nine back to the wild. I had written two books on the subject, including a 10,000 word Appendix on the biology of this rare animal, in which I also dealt with the controversial issues concerning multiple broods and the interbreeding of the species with feral domestic cats. I sold him both books for less than half price, marked down on his map the ten sightings I had enjoyed of these creatures in the wild, and pointed out that while there was a blank for a certain peninsula on the Institute of Terrestrial Ecology's distribution map of wildcats, there were at least fifty pairs there. I answered all his questions as best I could, then took him to see a wildcat's den, an otter holt, and two buzzards' nests for good measure. As I boated him back to his car I half-joked:

'I don't mind you guys coming over here and picking my brains, but I'm broke! Why doesn't the N.C.C. give *me* a grant for the work I'm doing?'

He thought it was ironical, and also wrong. He asked if I had ever actually applied for one. I had to admit I had not.

On May 8, after three days of sousing rain, I felt worried about how Atalanta would be faring at her nest. In this late season I deemed it still too early to put up a hide, but I wanted to see how she was getting along and if any chicks had hatched. It was a misty but warm day and the rain had ceased. Again I made the long hike up round the back of the 1,700-foot summit so as to come down to the eyrie from the far side and maintain the element of surprise – otherwise she would have seen me coming up her glen from a mile off, a mile of worry and alarm for her.

I had a deuce of a job to locate the ledge on which to build the hide, for now I was coming at it from the tops the terrain looked different. Three times I came out on ridges, saw the rowan at the front of the nest and had to dodge back and search again. Eventually I found it. I let myself down the small chimney beside the rocky overhang and carefully peered round.

At first the nest looked empty, then I saw the tiny white splashes over the sticks on its rim. A chick or two had certainly hatched. Just then Atalanta's head and neck appeared, craning out from the deep nest bowl and the V-shaped crevice.

She saw me at the same time as I saw her, but I acted as if I had not. I slowly looked away, moved quietly back from the eyrie crag and clambered slowly down away from her. Then I continued

153

straight down the mountainside. I kept looking out of the corner of my eye, and could see her watching me, but not flying off.

I had gone three hundred yards below the eyrie, well out of harm's way and moving in the right direction as far as she was concerned, when she launched herself and came low over my head. She banked to the east, circled to give me another good look, then sailed round the faces above Eyrie 27 much lower down. I carried on, and was just passing below that eyrie when she flew out from the cliff above it. I suppose she was waiting for me to clear the area completely before heading back to her nest.

To my surprise, however, she flapped along to the west, in the right direction, then suddenly landed on a small grassy knoll, only about a hundred yards from and above me. How odd! I fitted the long lens on to my camera and just ambled sideways, this way and that, working my way towards her. She seemed unconcerned, looked at me, looked away, frowsted up her neck feathers, then yawned twice. She appeared to be completely relaxed.

I took several photos, and she let me approach to within fifty yards – quite extraordinary – before she opened her wings and once more sailed over my head. It was in no sense a real or bluff attack for she circled right round me, presenting a massive silhouette with dangling talons, and I could hear the woofing of her mighty wings in the still air. Then she took off to the north, skirted the high cliff above Eyrie 27, and then headed back for her nest. I felt breathless, sure now that she did recognise me as the harmless individual who had hauled so many deer carcasses up into the winter hills.

My route home brought me close to Moobli's grave and again I felt overwhelmed by sadness, besieged on all sides by indifference. I still had not heard the fate of my new book, and was having to write my diaries and wildlife column by longhand as my typewriter had broken down. A replacement machine sent up from the south had been smashed in the post, yet compensation was refused. The only highlight in my immediate future was the possibility of some rewarding work with Atalanta, and possibly the divers and the peregrines at the sea cliff. I hoped so, for this would surely be my last season in Scotland.

As the sun was sinking on May 12 I heard the divers wailing again. I went out, located one and then its mate, on the far side of the loch. They paddled steadily to the east, then another pair flew in and slooshed into the water about forty yards from them. Once again they were not showing any defensive territorial behaviour in what should be their nesting time. Whether this meant neither pair had eggs I did not yet know.

One pair must have swum round the nearest islet, for a quarter of an hour later they paraded in the water only eighty yards out from my boat bay. I kept watch as the second pair also appeared, now only thirty yards away from the others, then both couples turned on their sides, showing their cream bellies. After a few minutes, all the birds righted themselves and began to steam along, much faster, to the west.

I re-made the eagle hide with new hazel poles and sewed camou-flaged canvas under plastic fencing so that it would now be water-proof for the first time, then boated out to meet Jeff Watson, whom I had promised to take on the 'killer trek' to view Atalanta's farthest eyrie. To my surprise he had a tall, willowy and attractive woman with him. He introduced Vanessa, which made me feel more lone-some than ever! I felt really ropy on the trek, especially when I discovered that Vanessa could move on the Hill almost as well as Jeff. My spirits barely lifted when we saw Atalanta's mate Melanion doing 'golden ball' display dives over the glen which contained Eyrie 18.

As I led the way up to the rowan-snag roost I was in for another surprise. It was well used, for there were eight disgorged pellets below it. Jeff took seven of them to analyse for the survey. He wondered, now that Atalanta was on Eyrie 28, if there were in fact two pairs on this terrain. I thought not, and sure enough the eyrie showed no signs of use. So why, Jeff asked, was Melanion clearly using this roost when Atalanta was on a nest three miles away? I had no idea, except that he could just be using it at nights. Besides, a three-mile flight was nothing to an eagle, which could cover that distance in three minutes if the winds were right.

While 29-year-old Jeff strode over the hills, removing saleable tusks from a few dead hinds, I chatted with Vanessa. Like myself, she had spent much time in Austria, Canada and Mexico and was now writing a thesis on Mexican forestry policy. She too was inter-ested in Spain and, what was more, she could speak Spanish. Jeff was a lucky man!

Presently he rejoined us and we climbed back down. Jeff felt sure there would be an eyrie on the south side of the glen as well. He trained his binoculars on a small face far below on the other side of the river, which could not have been more than 500 feet above sea level. I said I had checked that face in the first two years but hadn't bothered since as it seemed too low.

'There it is!' he said.

Amazed, I raised my binoculars too, and could see the great nest clearly, no more than ten feet above the steep ground below the small face. He, on new terrain, had discovered a new eyrie that I had not found on twelve previous treks to this glen. I felt shattered.

'My humiliation is now complete,' I said.

Jeff laughed, and said it was easy to miss things. Had I not found a new eyrie he had not known about on Eagle Rock mountain? I liked him for being kind. We carried on down and Jeff scrambled up to the nest. Tragedy. There were two smashed eagle eggs in it. He removed the shells and handed them to me. The slight residue of fluid in them stank, so they could not have been last year's. Jeff doubted human cause as all the vegetation round the nest was undisturbed. He thought the late snows could have wrecked the incubation period. I agreed it was possible, especially if the male had not fed the female well on the nest and she had been forced to leave it to find her own food. The eggs could then have got cold, killing the embryos. But why were the eggs smashed? Jeff said there were droppings in the nest which could have come from sheep or deer, or even wild goats. I had never seen wild goats in this area but it was just possible one of the other animals had fallen in, smashing the eggs before scrambling out again. What about crows? Jeff suggested. I said I had never known hooded crows go near eagle eyries in the nesting season, though the odd raven might, once the eggs had been deserted.

My theory was that the exact reverse of last year had taken place. Then Atalanta had lost one egg below Eyrie 28 but had laid again in Eyrie 18, and had raised the eaglet. This year, after the nest failure in what was now Eyrie 39, she had relaid, possibly only one egg, in Eyrie 28. This might also explain why Melanion was still hefted, at least at nights, to the roost in this glen. We would never know for sure. If my theory was correct, I just hoped that he was feeding Atalanta on the nest. The evidence that a chick had hatched seemed a good sign.

On the almost sheer 2,000-foot climb out of the glen Jeff forged ahead, with Vanessa not far behind. I felt gloomy, beaten, humiliated, floundering about below them, sure my heart was going to burst. I was getting too old for this hard physical stuff, and swore I would never do that trek again. At the top I caught up with Vanessa, who said Jeff always strode off from everyone like that; he had taken the short but harder route down to a lochan and over another 1,500-foot hill. He would be back at the cottage long before either of us. I said I hoped he would get the tea on. We carried on another mile and a half, came to the peaty burn that flowed into the lochan, where Vanessa deviated to the west and crossed. I said it was easier to the east, went that way and found myself in a bog with one boot full of muddy ooze. It was like a nightmare. I had trekked this ground a thousand times, yet these young things were travelling better than I was over what to them was new terrain.

As I came to the last mile of steep tussocky slopes down to the cottage, I got madder and madder at my new weakness, slowness, and what personal misery, isolation and age were doing to me. I began to run, and the faster I went the better I felt, until I seemed to be skimming over the ground, descending at great speed. My heart was in my mouth but I was careful with each step so as not to bust an ankle, the camera pack a toy on my back. I seemed back in the youthful dream, when I had run for my battalion in the Coldstream Guards. I reached the cottage, boiled water and made tea, poured red wine, cut up some cake and had bathed my upper half and changed my shirt before the other two arrived. They were amazed to find me there. I said I had cheated by going the easiest route, which they did not know. We drank and talked, but after I had boated them back over the loch and said a fond farewell, I felt lonelier than ever. Greg had his beauty, now Jeff had his. All I had left were the bloody eagles! I went up to Moobli's grave . . .

I mooched about for two days, devoid of energy. When I went out for supplies it was to learn that the newspaper which ran my wildlife column was folding up. I now had no income whatever. On May 19 I woke late with another hangover, walked blindly about feeling my life in the wilds had become a wreckage. I sat at the desk but could not work. My writings all seemed in vain anyway. My glance fell on the eagle hide, lying out on the grass by the bird table. No other real target remained. I forced down some lunch, seized the hide and started on the long trek.

It was now heavier than before and at times I thought I would expire as I weaved slowly up the steep hills. I did not care much. It

157

would be as good a way as any to go. Maybe the eagles would eat me and all that would be found would be my clothes. Somehow I got the hide up there, shoved it over the last two steep faces and into a deep dell which screened me from all but an overhead view. I stuffed its netting sides full of heather and long grasses and dragged it down to the broad shelf. The nest appeared ominously empty. The little white squirts over the nest twigs looked the same as before. Then I saw some new ones over the inner face of the granite crevice, above the nest. Or *were* they new ones? Maybe I just had not seen them before. I peered round the empty sky, the peaks of the ranges to the west. There was a tall object on one peak a good mile away. I glassed it. It was Atalanta, watching me!

I erected the tunnel hide fast, braced the insides straight with hazel wands, and left it looking just like a normal bump on the ground. I walked conspicuously away. Atalanta soared from the peak, sailed eastwards along the low ridges south of her glen, obviously watching me leave. Before I was half a mile away she turned and glided back to the eyrie. I hoped I had read the signs right.

It rained for two days — so I had got the hide up just in time for it would keep the ground below dry. On May 23 I walked to the east and checked the divers' old grassy nesting site from the shore. They were not there, but of the nine gulls I counted six seemed to be sitting on nests. Feeding the martens every night had apparently kept them off the islet. Later, I boated out to give Allan's family and Jeff a slide show at their house. I stopped along the forestry road to glass Atalanta's eyrie and was just in time to see what looked like Melanion flying over it towards the north-west. As I watched he went into a fast dive, down, down, down, then swooped up to smash through the upper leaves of some small birches on a ridge. I thought I saw a smaller dark bird flapping wildly, as if trying to escape, then both went to ground behind the trees. I was reasonably sure Melanion had caught the bird, possibly a crow.

I felt greatly cheered by the night at Allan's. We went to a pub, had a fine dinner cooked by Allan's wife, and my show was appreciated. I felt even more cheerful after boating home in moonlight for thirty-seven readers had sent me birthday cards urging me to carry on, and some had even enclosed cheques for copies of my previous books.

I was anxious to spend my fifty-fifth birthday on May 25 with the eagles. The day was dull with low cloud and mist but the air felt light, the sky brighter towards the slight western breeze. I decided to go. I checked all the photographic gear and set off. I had reached 600 feet when I saw a great curtain of grey with drooping tendrils advancing over the far peaks to the west, obliterating the rounded faces above Eyrie 27, never mind the much higher nest. I crouched in a rocky cleft with a holly tree above me affording slight shelter. Rain hit my leaky cape, my body heat faded and I was pricked all over my backside by old holly leaves that did not seem to know they were dead. It looked like the end of any eagle work today, a hellish birthday treat. But after the heavy shower, the rain stopped and I saw blue patches of sky appearing over the eyrie crag.

I marched across the burns, bogs and acres of closely spaced tussocks, keeping well to the north, and climbed over the 1,700-foot crown of the mountain. It *was* the hardest highest trek I had so far made to an eagle hide. Locating the hide ledge, I cautiously edged my way down, keeping the bulge of the overhang between myself and the nest ledge. Slowly I raised the hide's rear flap, slid in the roll of plastic foam and the camera pack, then eased myself in, inch by inch, careful not to make any noise. I straightened out the roll and peeped through the heather on the front of the hide. There was something dark in the eyrie, probably some wet vegetation. I screwed the camera on to the tripod, slowly eased the lens between the heather, then focused on the nest.

16 · The Highest Eyrie

The dark object I had taken to be a piece of wet vegetation was moving. It was in fact the rear end of Atalanta and the heavy feathers of her huge tail were pumping slowly up and down, quivering with the effort of each pull as she rended prey and fed each morsel to a chick which was behind the crevice out of my sight. My heart beat faster with excitement. Just like last year, I had managed to get into a hide while a mother eagle was on her nest without disturbing her at all.

Such had to be the position of the camera that the eyepiece was low, making it a hard, neck-straining position. I would be unable to take good feeding pictures, unless the chick came on to the front of the nest when it was older, so all I could really hope for here were flight photos. After a quarter of an hour, Atalanta stopped feeding and stood on the edge of the nest looking out, giving me two superb pictures. Then she took a step . . . *click* . . . opened her wings . . . *click* . . . flew off to the right . . . *click* . . . and was gone. In one shot her mighty wings, head and beak and dangling half-closed talons had seemed to fill the frame. If I had timed the exposures right, I had taken my best-ever flight photos of an eagle within twenty minutes of first entering a hide.

At 1.37 p.m. I looked up from easing my strained neck just in time to see her sail into the eyrie with what looked like long grasses in her talons, but I was too late on the button of the motor drive. She walked into the crevice, then sank slowly down to brood the chick, for the weather had turned dull and cold again. I now saw she had brought a great deal of dry yellow tussock grasses into the eyrie, making it the warmest, best-made nest I had ever seen, with deep sides, neat straight edges and filled with the grasses. Several times I saw her head emerge, pick up a beakful of grass and tuck it round the chick. After ten minutes she stood up and fed the chick, again with her tail towards me. When she swallowed a large hairy chunk herself, I saw what the prey was – red-deer carrion.

After the feeding, she brooded the chick until 3.29 p.m., then again posed perfectly on the edge of the nest. Suddenly she became more alert and glared to the east. I took two more photos as she floated away. Three minutes later, while I was lying down, I *heard* an eagle passing low over the hide and through a space I made in the heather saw her going down on to the eyrie. I pressed the remote-control button twice – first as she hung in the air like a huge jagged black bat, wings curved back like thick fangs, her great booted legs and talons outstretched in silhouette against the sky, then again as she landed. This time she had brought in some new prey, and as she lugged it over the nest in one set of talons and I saw its mottled grey-brown plumage, the flash of a white wing, I realised it was a ptarmigan.

This puzzled me. The nearest ptarmigan to this eyrie were on the high hills of Eagle Rock mountain, a good three miles away across the loch. Even an eagle could not travel that distance, catch a ptarmigan, then bring it back in so short a time. I presumed Atalanta had got it from Melanion, in which case he had been hunting on Juno's territory. Last year, when Atalanta had finally nested in her northernmost eyrie, I had frequently seen Juno flying and hunting near these very eyries. This year, with Juno not nesting at all, it seemed possible Atalanta and her mate had extended their hunting territory to annex some of Juno's northern hills. If this were true, it indicated that eagles would extend their territories outwards from a particular used eyrie in any one year to include some of the area of non-breeding pairs. Fascinating – if I could prove it.

Atalanta now fed the chick from the ptarmigan for a full twenty-five minutes, then lay down as if to sleep for a while. But five minutes later she was up on her feet again, preening her back and wing feathers, standing bolt upright at times, replete, happy, secure, and gazing out over her vast perspectiveless world.

The wind had switched to the north, sending cold shafts through the hide, and I began to shiver. I endured it until just after 7 p.m., then looked up to see that Atalanta was standing up and reaching down into the nest, making delicate and tender movements with her beak. She was preening and massaging the down of the chick. Twice I saw its white head and neck appear as it moved about, clearly enjoying her ministrations. I judged it to be just over two weeks old. Then Atalanta fluffed out her warm belly feathers and settled upon it and sank down to sleep.

I was so cold that I left the hide, knowing she could not see me go as all of her was now in the crevice. As I hiked round the back and top of the mountain, the sky cleared to allow some hazy sunshine, and I was so warm when I reached the boat I decided to push my birthday luck a bit further and go to check my other main target of the season, the rare black-throated divers. After losing their first egg to the marten last year, the shy but intelligent birds were not using my nearest islet, so I boated down to check the far islet where they had finally succeeded. Cutting the engine from a quarter of a mile away, I rowed quietly into the lagoon. There was a diver in the water a few yards off the islet's far shore, as if it had come off a nest. I discreetly turned and rowed back out again, slid past the islet's nearest point, then rowed into the bay on the far side of the diver. I stalked then, belly-crawling a few inches at a time, until I reached the rock round which I had built last year's hide.

To my surprise the diver was sitting on the very same nest site as last year, clearly on eggs. What luck. Having enough pictures from that position, I snaked over the island until I found a nearer site for a new screen hide beside the thick trunk of a Scots pine. Watching the diver carefully with one eye through one lens of my binoculars, so that I only moved when she was looking away, I slowly inched a dead branch to form a bridge from the ground to a stout twig three feet up the trunk of the pine, and tied it securely. From this I painstakingly erected a screen of bracken, heather and bilberry leaves which would hide my more direct approach to the spot next time. I managed to get back to the boat with the diver still completely unaware of my presence. My birthday had turned out far better than I had reckoned it might.

Early on the morning of May 27, with warm sun beating through thin cloud cover, I went to tackle the divers before the eagles. It was so calm and quiet that even when I muffled the oars in plastic they still made a noise in their rowlocks. I paddled into the island's bay and walked up the gravel as if treading on eggs, so as to avoid making crunching sounds. Now I had to tow the netting of the hide screen and its hazel poles behind me over the dry crackly old bracken stalks which made quiet progress even more difficult. I could see the diver on the nest through the green sprays of bilberry leaves and new bracken. When I reached the highest point of the route, the hide netting snagged on the branches of a fallen pine. I had to raise myself slightly to reach back and free it. As I started off again, I saw the diver was off the nest, which I could see contained only one egg, and was out in the lagoon near her mate. Damn! Had she seen me moving or just swum out to him naturally, perhaps to take a fish from his bill? I kept down and waited a few minutes, but she did not return to the nest.

I could not take the chance she had not seen me, for if she had, or was unsure, she would not return until she knew I had gone. There was only one thing to do. I showed myself, erected the vegetation-covered hide in seconds, made for the shore and walked away in full view of them. When I reached the boat I saw that one of the divers had paddled round the tip of the islet, as if to make sure I had gone. I quickly boated away.

By 2 p.m. I was in the eagle hide. I peered through the front heather but there was no adult on the eyrie. I set up the camera and contorted myself into a sleeping bag. By 3.40 p.m. the ominous silence from the nest made me fear the chick had died, been killed, or had fallen off. I was thankful to hear the chick squeaking at 3.53 p.m., but it soon stopped. I just hoped one of the adults had been passing overhead. An hour later, as I was fixing a small mirror to the hide's roof so that I could lie on my back and view the eyrie, I saw a moving shadow and heard a rush of air above the hide.

Atalanta had come in with some prey and she immediately began to feed the chick. I missed the flight shots, but was so relieved that she was back I didn't care. I ended a film on her tearing up the prey, which from the dark blue-black feathers and stout dark bill I could see was a young raven. She was right on the edge of the nest, giving me photos I had not expected to get at this eyrie. I marvelled at the power in her neck and back muscles as she rended the large bird, one of a species which is the chief mobber of the eagle in flight. I could even *hear* the thumping as the pulled-up carcass, clenched in her talons, banged back down on the nest after each upward rend. Unfortunately the chick's head was just behind the crevice so I could not see the actual transfer of food. Then the eagle turned her back to me again.

Minutes later I heard high-pitched bleatings and looked through the hide's meshes to see a ewe and her lamb grazing right below the eyrie. Atalanta peered over the rim of the nest but seemed more to be checking for danger than harbouring any predatory intent. She appeared to ignore the lamb when it would have been an easy drop on to it straight from the nest. She fed the chick until 5.05 p.m., then began looking about, blinking more slowly, as if tired. Once she peered straight up into the air, twisting her head slowly, as if seeing her mate high above. Then she picked up several small twigs in her beak, put them round the chick, now silent and well fed, stepped towards it carefully and settled down to brood it.

An hour passed. I was wondering if she had slipped off the far side of the nest. Then I saw in the mirror the dark snake of her head and neck appear from the crevice. I turned over, took two photos of her glaring to the south-west, looked away to check the shutter speed, and in that moment she was gone. I had missed two lots of flight shots this visit. I had better wake my ideas up! At 6.45 p.m. I saw her zoom past the eyrie to the west, the chick calling loud 'k'yew' cries; then eight minutes later there came a noisy rush of air by the hide. I pushed the motor drive button and got four fine shots of her coming in. She stood on the nest, just looking about, for six minutes, then took off again to the south as I took five more pictures. I waited until she would be clear of the area, packed up and slid out of the hide.

Hiking back over the top of the mountain, some three hundred yards away from and above the eyrie crag, I became aware of a presence and felt that I was being watched. I looked all around, saw nothing, then looked up. Atalanta was hanging in the sky just ahead of me, a mere hundred yards up, almost hovering on the east-north-east winds, which were now bitterly cold. She seemed to be waiting for me, maybe to see me safely off her premises. She moved at the same walking pace as I did and kept looking down and backwards so that I could see the dark orange glare of her great eyes, the light gold of her mantle against the steely clouds, which looked as if they held rain. Then she drifted slowly to the south, swept westwards over the loch with the speed of a jet and vanished behind her own eyrie ridges.

Two dull rainy days followed in which I slashed bracken and new brambles from the front pasture and trimmed Moobli's grave. The loneliness I had staved off during seventeen wilderness years began to bite harder than ever. I typed half-hearted notes for a new book, but since I had not yet heard the fate of the last one, my work seeming harder to sell than ever, there was no incentive to start anything fresh. But for the eagles, I would have given up this year for sure. There it was again – prisoner of the eagles.

May 30, Whit Monday, dawned in a cloudless sky. As rain was forecast again for the next two days, I went out early to the divers' island and slid down to the hide. I heard a loud '*kerlyee*' wail from the east end of the lagoon. The nest site was now empty. Hell! Had they deserted, had someone taken the egg? Two fishing boats and three tourist boats were out on the loch, the most I had ever seen in this area. It seemed that I had missed divers this year after all, and that for the first time ever this pair had failed.

After a few minutes I heard the softly harsh '*gowol*' note of a diver out on the lagoon, but I dared not take a look over the herbage in case I was spotted. Time passed, the sun beating down. Then I saw a diver paddle round the west end of the island, pass the nest site and swerve away from it again. A boat passed down the far side of the loch. From half a mile away I could hear the loud raucous voices of city folk. People just don't realise what an affliction noise can be in wild places. This lot did not even realise the rare birds were there.

I lay well down for several minutes, then heard the soft gull-like sounds again. Through the herbage I could see *both* divers cruising along a short distance from the nest site. They hung about offshore as if in doubt, then one went to the lagoon's centre and began washing its wings, shuffling them up and down with floppy splashing sounds, while the other remained hanging about. I kept down for a while, then at exactly midday I rose slowly and peered through the viewfinder.

The female diver was on the nest! I took a picture and then saw a movement to her right. There was a dark grey-brown chick with her on the land. The divers had hatched their single egg after all. I took some more shots as the chick walked towards her and shuffled under her left wing. Since there was no other egg to hatch, the mother diver had obviously brought the chick in for a rest on the land. Perhaps she was weaning it to the water in short stages, for it could be no more than two days old.

I had just retired for a rest when the diver suddenly shot out of the nest, propelled herself on her belly down to the water with her thick black legs, and was quickly followed by her chick. Why? Then I heard more voices. The wind had calmed down completely. Two boats and five canoes had landed on a far beach to the south, the adults in the boats calling instructions to the youngsters in the canoes. The diver had heard them long before I had. Well, humans in boats would not harm the chick now, for even at this tender age it could swim well and dive from danger. I took the camera from its tripod, poked it round the pine and took a few photos of the two divers with the chick. They had succeeded after all and my work with them was over. I removed the hide and set off for the eagles.

After the fastest climb of the year, during which I saw no eagles in the sky, I was in that hide by 1.15 p.m. I had just eaten my first lunch sandwich when I heard the chick squeaking. Moments later I saw a black blob on the nest. It proved at last to be the male, Melanion. He had come in from the far side of the nest, something Atalanta had never done so far. He looked about, his body slimmer and higher off the ground than his mate's. He made no attempt to feed the squeaking chick before taking off again. The camera clicked off four shots, the last filling the frame with the upturned pinions on the long wings, his eyes glaring, a piece of long grass clinging to his talons as he came straight towards the hide. A rabbit seeing so terrifying a vision would be paralysed out of action.

Now the chick came out on to the front of the nest. It was three and a half weeks old, black pinions sprouting from the ends of the white downy wings, dark stubs of tail feathers showing clearly. At 2.45 p.m. I heard a slight rush of air, pushed the button and got more shots of Atalanta sailing in. She looked about the nest and immediately left again. Obviously the male had come in to see what prey was needed but bringing none – and she came in with nothing to see if *he* had brought food. As he had not, off she went again, on the eternal hunt to provide the chick with food. An hour later the chick squeaked. Melanion landed on the far side of the nest, dropped something and left. The chick stood up awkwardly, made a few symbolic pecks but did not gulp any morsels. At 4.40 p.m. I heard the *wush wush wush* of powerful wings, and took more photos of Atalanta taxiing into the nest.

She fixed her talons on whatever the male had brought in and, after a struggle, pulled off two small morsels and fed them to the chick. She then stepped back, picked the object up and laid a roe-deer foreleg with precious little flesh left on it on the nest rim. She turned and again went off to hunt. At 6.30 p.m. I left and drifted easily back to the boat. As usual on eagle treks at this time of year, my leg muscles had thickened up to resemble those of a sprint cyclist, and I hardly noticed the steep descent.

I was back in the hide by 1.30 p.m. for an afternoon stay on June 5. Again the nest looked deserted, but after half an hour I saw a long white wing with longer, darker flight feathers flap right across the nest: the chick was fine. I took photos of Melanion soaring in with a twig in his beak. He stayed only a few seconds then took off to the south, still holding the twig. As I was changing films, he returned from the east, soared upwards on the north-westerly breeze, then made a spectacular dive down beside the eyrie with his talons out. Needless to say, I had not quite fixed the new film into the camera. Inside half a minute he was back on the far side of the nest. As he tramped into the bowl, I had a brief glimpse of two voles held in one set of talons. One of these, the five-week-old chick, now sprouting dark feathers all over his wings, back and chest, managed to gulp down whole as the male took off again.

Next I saw an eagle flying towards me, then pass right overhead as the chick called loudly. It was Atalanta. Some way behind the hide she turned and came in, looked at the vole, felt no need to proffer it to the chick herself, and left again as I took more pictures. Two more hours passed before Melanion came labouring in, flapping heavily, from my side of the nest. He had a light greyish lump in his talons. I got some fine shots of him on the very edge of the nest. He kept looking at the chick with paternal anxiety, a soft caring look, then down at what he had brought in and back at the chick again. Twice he tapped the eaglet gently on the tip of its bill with his great hook, as if trying to say: 'Here you are, eat it up. Use this − your beak.'

As he left again, his legs cleared from my view of the prey, and I saw it was the hind section of a lamb. I could not tell at that distance if there were signs that he had actually killed the lamb, but by this time of year lambs do not die as often from natural causes as in their first few days of life, though they can certainly get stuck in rock crevices. I would have to record this one as 'doubtful'. The eaglet was pecking at the lamb from a lying position when I left at 7 p.m.

The following day I boated out in gorgeous cloudless weather to check the islets. I counted nineteen common gulls on the nearest one, and they had five nests with three eggs each, three nests with one egg each, and four empty nests. My ruse to keep the martens away from the colony by stuffing them with bread and raspberry jam every night, had worked this year. As I stalked over the divers' island, I was rewarded by the sight of both birds and their healthy chick swimming between them. I came back to find an orange tip butterfly flitting among the rare checkered skippers in my front pasture, the first I had seen at Wildernesse.

On June 8 I drove down to see if the peregrine falcons were nesting on the cliff near the sea again this year. I had not gone earlier as they nested above a small public road and I had not wanted to risk putting the female off any eggs. Besides, the landowner and two estate keepers had proved their interest and pride in the falcons and, as they lived nearby, were able to do more than I could to discourage potential intruders. All I needed to do was to check the breeding success, or failure, for the N.C.C. As before, I parked half a mile away, then sneaked up the back of the heathered hill so as not to be seen from the road. Whereupon it began to drizzle.

I sat in the deep heather, afflicted by midge bites, but the ledge opposite, where they had nested last year, looked deserted. The night roost in the overhang above it, however, was still being used, for the rock below it was splashed with new white droppings. At last I heard an adult peregrine making harsh rasping calls, '*raich raich raich*'. A young couple walking along the road below did not look up, despite the racket. Then I located the falcon as it flew to a projecting rock to the right of and just above the two ravens' nests. From its dark blue-black wings and deeply barred chest plumage I judged it to be the male.

Presently he flew off to the west, rapidly flapping his scythe-like wings, then making long glides. As he passed along the cliff face I was sure I heard some higher-pitched rasping calls, '*rehk, rehk, rehk*', coming from somewhere to the left of the ravens' nests, surely made by falcon chicks on seeing their parent flying by. Although I raked the area and the whole cliff with binoculars, in the reduced visibility I could not locate an actual nest ledge. Defeated by the rain, I left after an hour.

South-westerly gales and frequent rainstorms prevented me going back to the eagles until June 13, when the winds lessened and the sky brightened enough to make me feel the rains would hold off. It was to be a day of extraordinary experiences.

17 · Amazing Aerobatics

To lop half a mile off the usual trek, I set off in the boat, with the wind still strong enough to biff waves into the prow. As I bounced along, I saw a hooded crow, one of a pair that had a nest in a birch tree high up, land on a ridge above. It was probably the male, keeping guard while his mate tended to the youngsters.

Suddenly it shot up and flew with rapid and panicky beats towards the east. With the wind it was really shifting along. A large hawk-like form heading towards it looked like a female buzzard. As it went past a gap in the ridges, I saw its outline against the sky — it was the male eagle, Melanion. With no apparent effort, just jet-gliding along, he soon gained on the speeding crow and went straight for it with his talons out. This was very odd behaviour. Usually the smaller bird tries to mob the larger off its nesting territory, but this time it seemed Melanion had become angry at the sight of the crow on what was *his* territory too. The crow spiralled and dived, flapping madly, looking as tiny as a swallow against the eagle's immense form. Melanion made it swerve about some more then soared away to his right, airily wheeling back to the west as if he had just been having fun.

Now he kept pace with the boat, drifting against the wind, wings half back and sort of falling along, sailing past the ridges. Then suddenly he performed a complete sideways somersault. I had seen eagles turn on their sides to slash at a mobbing raven or crow, turn on their backs to touch their mate's talons, but had never witnessed

169

a complete somersault before. It was as if he was making a victory roll, or perhaps he was just showing off to Atalanta, whom I saw soaring ahead on the far side of the ridges. He must have left her side to chase the crow. By now he had overtaken the boat and I watched him wheel northwards over the ridges, make a couple of folded wing dives and upward loops, before disappearing in the direction of the eyrie.

I landed and set off up the first steep tussocky ground, the bog myrtle bushes giving off a strong fox-like scent. When I reached the last dipping valley before the final ascent round the back of the mountain, the wind blowing more strongly at this height, Melanion came heading back over the eyrie summit. He treated me to three more 'golden ball' dives, dropping straight down with wings tucked back, pulling out just when it seemed he would hit the ground, and soaring up again on opened wings. Then he vanished behind a ridge to my left.

I climbed on, buffeted by the wind, as a huge black eagle, Atalanta, appeared from my left, circled above me, once, twice, coming even nearer, until I could see the glare of her dark orange-gold eye, which took in the sight of me before dismissing me as a threat, then wheeled away to the north. It was good to see both eagles together so near the eyrie, for it surely meant that, despite the gales and rainstorms, the chick was still all right. Once a nest fails, eagles are rarely seen near it again during that season. The next thing I knew Atalanta was again heading over the eyrie cliff and then *she* performed two 'golden ball' dives, the first time I had seen them made by a female. I made sure there were no eagles in the sky as I began the last descent.

Fortunately the hide was fine, only a sprig or two of heather having blown away from its front. I slid in, replaced the sprigs from inside, set up the camera, then pulled a back muscle getting into the sleeping bag. I was glad I had brought it, for the winds were blasting through the hide. I had also carried up a cassette tape recorder into which I described all the happenings on the trek, and this I set up to catch any action and sounds from the nest.

After half an hour I heard the familiar squeak, then silence, and after a wait of ten minutes a few more squeaks. One of the adults was passing by. At 4 p.m. the chick called again and in came Atalanta with a ptarmigan from which she fed the chick. It staggered comically about in the high wind. The great eagle's feathers were blown inside out at times in the blasts, forming rosettes all over her wing and body, and once her twelve broad tail feathers were blown right over her back. Yet she stood rock-solid, talons securely gripping the woven twigs and small branches of the nest. After five minutes she turned and slid easily away into the gale.

Shortly after six, as I was lying down, hands frozen, wind now blasting rain on to the hide, I heard the eaglet squeak once more. Atalanta was in again, this time with half a rabbit which she must have brought all the way from Eagle Rock mountain in the rain, unless she had got it from Melanion at a nearer spot. Her feathers were now all spiky from the wet. She fed the eaglet fifty-seven slivers then settled down to brood it, probably needing a rest herself. I left, shivering, and staggered back down the mountain to the boat, my trews soaked through. But it had been another grand day, for yet again I had learned something new about eagles.

The next few days were filled with little wildlife incidents, quite separate from those with the eagles. A pair of sandpipers which had hatched three of their four eggs in a ground nest in my east wood were teaching their young to forage on the shore, usually near the boat bay. Every time I went down, and the chicks ran about like tiny ostriches to hide behind rocks, the two adults treacled over the wet stones bobbing their tails, their legs moving so fast they were invisible to the eye. All the while they issued plaintive *'wee peep'* alarm calls, loud enough for me to capture well on my little cassette recorder. Then I heard the scolding, ticking notes of wrens coming from the west wood, so I squelched over the boggy path to seek the source.

There, perched high in a larch, calmly ignoring the din of two wrens which were agitatedly flitting through the twigs near her broad head, was Crowdy, the last of three tawny owls I had looked after in my cottage and whom I had released to the wild three years earlier. At first she seemed alarmed as I took photos, glaring from one tree to another as if about to fly off. But as I talked soothingly to her with the old phrases she had known, she relaxed, her eyes went small and sleepy again, and I felt sure that even after all this time she recognised me, for she stayed where she was. Delighted to know she was still alive, by the sense of continuance of life round Wildernesse that seeing her gave my spirits, I headed on through the upper edge of the wood, then saw what looked like nest mosses protruding from a hole at the top of a leaning dead tree snag twenty feet above my head. Wondering if it was a great tit's nest, I tapped lightly on the bole. Out flew, not a great tit but a spotted flycatcher. It perched bolt upright on a nearby larch twig, looked briefly down at me with its unusually large black eyes, looped up after a flying insect and as I turned away flew back to the nest with it.

Next day, the sun at last trying to peer through the watery clouds, I trekked through the eastern lochside woods to check two buzzards' nests, for I wanted to work with these 'woodland eagles' again this year if I could. As I came into a clearing above the first great cliffs I saw a disturbance in the grasses ahead. Four browny-orange velvety northern eggar moths were all trying to mate with one huge fat-bodied female, who looked so ponderous as she clung to one stem it seemed impossible that she could fly. One smart male had beaten them to it and was already mating with her, clinging tenaciously to the underside of her furry torpedo body. While the two copulated blissfully, the other four crawled over them, wings flickering, bodies shivering, antennae vibrating, tufted legs everywhere; all consumed by unquenchable ardour, sexual desire and serious intent, uncaring of my presence. As I watched a second male also got his rear parts into those of the female! There was no doubt at all that her eggs would be fertile.

I carried on through the steep oak and birch woods, and had just located my twentieth badgers' sett below the tangled branches of a fallen tree, when I saw something reddish ahead. It was a sprightly little roebuck, superb in his summer coat, all lit up by dappled light in a green dell. I looked away, slowly removed my pack, fitted lens on to camera and darn it if he did not wait while I clicked off three fine photos before he galloped upwards to the north-east like a great red hare. Both buzzard nests, however, were unused and empty. That evening, in fading light at 10.20 p.m., I had just come into the study with a steaming plate of supper, when I saw a large dark shape on my mossy bird table complex just outside the window. My heart skipped a beat.

It was Mickey, the male pine marten I had been feeding during the harsher seasons since first discovering him in the woods three years ago. I had not seen him for weeks and had thought he would not return in midsummer – if these rain-filled days could be called summer. I gave the usual 'grub up' whistles, swiftly set out his favourite titbits of bread and jam and he was soon back, grabbing several bits at once in his jaws then dropping to the ground to eat them. His return also did much to raise my flagging spirits.

At last a really fine sunny day dawned on June 18. Before returning to the eagles I tramped through the front hay pasture from which, over the years, I had scythed away the once engulfing bracken. I had never seen so many butterflies. Pearl-bordered, small pearl-bordered and large gaudy dark-green fritillaries flitted and glided among the white tops of pignut, the golds, yellows and oranges of ragwort, tormentil, bog asphodel, bird's foot trefoil, creeping buttercup, golden rod, and the dark-blue chips of milk-wort flowers and pale mauves of late violets. But among them all, hard to see with their jerky, wispy flight were hosts of scarce checkered skippers, a butterfly so rare it is given special protection under the Wildlife and Countryside Act of 1981. Over the years I had planted and encouraged their food plants, and now I was reaping a full reward. One landed on a late bluebell before me, holding its forewings, with their delicate patterns of yellow-gold plates, stiffly upwards, its rear wings dropped in true skipper fashion. Farther on, I saw for the first time two pairs actually mating at the ends of long grasses and finally got some photos of this rare sight.

On the eagle trek later in the morning I again carried up the tape recorder. The blustery winds on the mountain top last time had all but obliterated my spoken commentary and I needed to re-record the business of getting down to and into the hide, as well as any new exciting action at the eyrie. With the extra weight I decided to cut a corner off the climb by slogging up the steeps of the long wood on a more direct route. The shade of the oaks and larches took some of the heat from the broiling sun during that first, hard 500-foot climb. I had just clawed my way up and over a nearly sheer rockface when I saw something reddish ahead, a queer rounded shape.

It was a fox, a vixen, and as it turned its head it looked just like Aspen, one of several young injured foxes I had looked after in my cottage years before. Aspen had escaped back into the wild and had raised four families of cubs with the dominant dog fox of the region, but I was sure she had been dead these past two years. This was surely one of her cubs, for she was of a similar auburn colour and also had a white tip to her tail. For a few seconds she just stayed still, looking back at my immobile form, orange eyes glaring, nostrils quivering, black-tipped ears pointing forward, one foreleg raised, her brush curling up in a gentle curve. Then she took off through the trees, before I could extract the camera from the pack. Ideally, you should carry your camera ready for action at all times in the wild, but on such terrain it was not possible – you need your hands for climbing up and down the sheer parts.

Her scent came back to me strongly, so I took out the camera and tracked her like a dog for a while, before coming on to a definite fox ground trail. I followed it up and up the sloping land, still getting scent where the fox had leaped off rocks or over fallen trees as they lay too low over the trail. Then I lost it at the last burn before the open land of the eagles' corrie. I did not see the vixen again. How I missed Moobli's nose, but not nearly as much as I missed my only companion in the Highland wilds. Grief welled up again as memories of him flooded back. I disciplined myself by seizing the tape recorder and describing into it all the phenomena I saw on what proved to be the hottest trek of the year – the carrion carcasses of winter dead deer, the warning '*hoff!*' barks of suddenly startled hinds, the butterflies, dragonflies, flowers, the sound of drinking from the last burn before the hide, even the sight of Atalanta coasting along the northern ranges of the mountains. I decided to send the tapes to the B.B.C. Natural History Unit in Bristol. Surely such adventurous treks amid Britain's most spectacular wildlife would make a good 'Nature Trail' type of radio programme for them, a change at least from those on such urban species as blue tits, blackbirds, grass snakes, frogs, toads and hedgehogs – especially if I could record more of the eaglet calling out and dramatic action at the eyrie.

That action was not long in coming, for no sooner had my boots disappeared into the hide than Atalanta swooped up on to the nest, having come in from the front, hidden from the hide by the edge of the long ledge on which it was built. The eaglet had been pulling at a rabbit carcass but now it gave some soliciting squeaks, then promptly mantled its wings over the rabbit and turned its back on its mother. Atalanta seemed to look on approvingly, as if saying, 'That's right. Protect it. Don't let even me get at it!' I waited until her head was in the crevice then set up the recorder and camera. As I did so I saw that in the usual struggle to wriggle into the hide the camera's back had been pulled open. I had to tie it shut with cord. Clearly I had fogged some pictures, including those of the mating skippers. (In fact I lost ten.)

Atalanta did not stay long. She watched the eaglet feeding, then dropped off the far side of the nest. At just over six weeks old the eaglet now had all its browny-black back feathers, the wing primaries and secondaries were well grown though still short, and brown flecks dotted its white chest, neck and head. Up until this age a well-cared-for eaglet has a fine time; all the world is new and it is fascinated by every little occurrence in its confined environment, even watching the crawling buzzing flies with interest. But now it was entering the 'bored' stage, when its parents would come in far less frequently, just dumping prey and flying off again. Any day now I reckoned Atalanta would be off on the female eagle's usual 'vacation'. Having done most of the egg incubation, the brooding and all the feeding of the chick in its early stages, the female often takes a few days off and for that time leaves all the food collecting to the less-hard-worked male. Where these females go on such 'holidays' I have no idea, but often one does not see them on their territory at all. On the right wind an eagle can 'jet glide' at well over 100 m.p.h., so could conceivably be taking a break along the coasts of even Norway in four and a half hours.

After feeding, the eaglet slumped down and sunbathed for a while, holding its wings out over the nest. Often it wiped midges and flies from its head by violent sideways and downward movements, using the heather or leaf sprays brought in by the adults as both wipers and scratchers. Two hours later it called out, glaring straight up into the sky as one of its parents checked the eyrie from the sky. Just before 5 p.m. it began calling again. I looked up to see Melanion glide in from the far side, swoop up and land. The eaglet grabbed what looked like a vole from his feet and gulped it down in one.

Suddenly, as if he had dropped something, Melanion shot off the nest, dived down by the eyrie cliff at great speed, then treated me to the sort of amazing aerobatics one would not believe a bird as big as an eagle was capable. He straightened out to the south, wheeled back in a very tight circle, then dived down with closed wings below the hide ledge. Had he brought in two voles, one still alive, and was now chasing it as it sought a hiding place? Voles can shift when they have to. The chick, fascinated by all this, was craning its neck over the edge of the nest and glaring at him. Now there was a loud whoosh of wings right by the hide ledge and for about two seconds my vision was filled with the broad wings, head craned down, of a hunting eagle, merely twelve feet away. It blotted out the sky. I had not a hope of getting the camera, fixed on its tripod, on to him and focused in so short a time. Nor did I dare attempt any such thing. Any panning movement of the big telephoto lens seen by the eagle would have blown my cover, and he would not be back for the rest of the day, even two. Now he dived down again, below the ledge.

A few minutes later the chick squeaked and once more Melanion came in from the far side, this time with half a rabbit in his talons. Evidently this was what he had dropped. He had had to chase it as it rolled and bounced down the steep hill below the eyrie. He looked briefly at the chick mantling over the rabbit, then stepped across the nest towards me. He had his great beak open, panting with the heat, and I took two photos of him glaring past me, his red throat and tongue showing clearly. Then he jumped into the now windless air, lifted his wings . . . *click* . . . beat away with dangling talons, beak still open . . . *click* . . . then sailed past the hide . . . *click* . . . for a perfect sideways shot. These proved to be the finest pictures I had ever taken, or probably ever would take, of a flying wild eagle.

A quarter of an hour later there was a rush of air above the hide and Atalanta taxied into the eyrie. For a few moments she stayed on the edge, looking around, blinking her orange eyes slowly, as if needing a rest. Then she looked at the chick with great affection, tramped towards it and fed it seventy-one slivers from the half-rabbit. At nearly 6 p.m. I looked up again to see her standing erect on the front edge of the nest – with the foreleg of a red-deer calf in her beak. She was about to clear it from the nest. I took one photo as she posed there, another as she leaped up, and a third as she soared away with it.

Shortly after that I left, feeling exultant. Not only had I taken the best-ever flight pictures, I had also captured the whole trek and the incidents and sounds at the eyrie. Two days later I posted both tapes to a leading producer at B.B.C. Bristol. I said I realised that the quality might not be good enough for a radio programme, but would he listen to the *content*. If he liked the idea itself, I would buy better equipment and do it all again. I could also produce tapes on the red-deer calving and rut, rare black-throated divers, pine martens and other Highland species.

Back came the reply that the technical quality of my tapes was very poor and unsuitable for transmission. He said I could best

above: Although the eaglet was eight weeks old and capable of rending prey, the mother eagle still came in to feed it.

below: By July 12 the eaglet had all its brown plumage and was ready to fly.

Atalanta circled round me, a massive silhouette with dangling talons.

below: The buzzard's yellow toes showed as the eaglet picked up its carcass. Almost ready to fly, it called up into the sky.

After feeding her chick for twenty minutes, Atalanta left the nest.

below: Keeping the nest clean as usual, Atalanta leaped away with a red deer calf's foreleg in her beak.

The cliff containing Atalanta's farthest eyrie.

contribute by going out with one of their own presenters on a radio 'Nature Trail', and that I might be able to arrange for *them* to have access to difficult subjects like wildcats, pine martens and golden eagles. He added that broadcasting was a highly competitive and increasingly specialised art, difficult to break into.

I replied to the effect that I would help all I could with any of their work in the Highlands, that I would be happy to do such a 'Nature Trail', and that in one day I could probably take them to hides near eagles, divers, peregrines and buzzards, as well as show them and talk about otters and seals mating in the sea.

I heard no more. Their radio programmes would continue to feature tits, robins, blackbirds, frogs, toads, grass snakes, bats, hedgehogs and the like, I guessed.

On Midsummer Day, June 21, the sky like a hot yellow cauldron, I hiked back to the eagles. It was my worst visit yet. As I had suspected, Atalanta seemed to be away on 'vacation' and in a nine-hour stay Melanion only came in once, to quickly drop off a young stoat. During two dark, dull days, loneliness setting in again, I half-heartedly tapped out notes for a new book. But as I still had not heard from Cape about my best one, I felt I was wasting my time. After the two and a half month wait, I feared a letter that began, 'We finally regret to say we cannot . . .' and having to start the search all over again. I now had no income, was living on savings. The fact was I could not *afford* to move out and live a normal life, even in a £20 a week bed-sitter. I had paid for my lease when I had had some money; now about all the cottage cost me was less than £10 a year for rates and a little paint. I had lived for seventeen years amid wild mountains, not to beat them or just climb to their tops, but to learn all their rare wildlife secrets and by imparting those to others in an enjoyable form, in books, earn enough to carry on. I had *wanted* the wilderness life. I had had the wilderness life. Now I was trapped by it. And my dear companion Moobli was dead.

As I sat lethargically at my desk on the second afternoon, the sky lightened and I thought to hell with this. Get out on the Hill, kid. I boated out and drove down to the long oak woods where I had watched nesting buzzards last year, hoping to find their new nest. On the climb up, secretive willow warblers gave out their soft '*deeu*' notes after breeding, a great spotted woodpecker went '*kik*' as it jerked up the huge dark trunks, and I saw a young grazing red-deer stag, antlers thick with velvet, lifting one rear hoof and delicately scratching one ear, careful not to touch the sensitive blood-carrying velvet. At the top of the wood I zig-zagged up and down between the oaks for a quarter of a mile before locating a perfect buzzards' nest containing a fat, healthy, two-week-old downy grey chick. From a big square rock, ideal for obscuring a hide, I could easily see right down into the nest. Keeper Allan Peters was delighted at the news; we would have a hide up there in a few days and I would start to work the nest. Allan, always helpful, then told me of a certain lochan away to the west where he had seen several pairs of short-eared owls hunting in daylight. He was sure I would get good photos there.

Next day, sunny again, I decided to have a crack at both the peregrines on the sea cliff *and* the owls. Even as I climbed out of my van half a mile away I could hear one of the falcons screaming. Maybe someone was walking along the road below their cliff. It certainly sounded as if they did have chicks again this year. The bird would not make such a fuss otherwise.

As I climbed the deep heathered hill, wading through the midge-filled herbage until I was overlooking the sheer face, the falcon kept quiet. Had it gone? But as I took out the camera and tape recorder, it began to scream again. Determined to stay until I found the nest this time, I began to rake the cliff systematically with the binoculars. Suddenly I saw something small and white move. I shifted the glasses back and there, clear to my gaze at last, was the new nest.

It was on a small curved shallow shelf, not under the kind of sheltering overhang that peregrines prefer, but out in the open. It was some twenty yards to the right of last year's nest ledge. One plump all-white chick was sitting bolt upright in the bright light, a second was lying down but what I thought to be a third was just a white piece of dead stick on the right of the ledge. Peregrines usually lay four reddish-brown mottled eggs, sometimes five, in mid to late April and they take just four weeks to hatch. Yet here we were on June 24 and these chicks were not more than two and a half weeks old. Possibly the birds lay a little later in northern climes. It appeared two chicks would survive this year, the same as last, but as the survival rate has been estimated at between 2 and 2·19 per breeding nest over the United Kingdom as a whole in recent years, this seemed normal enough.

I recorded the falcon's occasional '*raich raich*' calls which were coming from somewhere about thirty yards to the right and slightly above the nest ledge, but I could not locate her by sight even with the powerful binoculars and the aid of her calls. I waited for nearly three hours but she just would not shift. Was she waiting for the male to return with prey? Many small birds were singing and flitting among the small trees and bushes which grew all over the large expanse of rough cliff, yet she chased after none of them. Certainly the chicks appeared to have full crops. I climbed back down and went over the road to the foot of the cliff. She shifted then and began to soar and circle not far above my head while I recorded her better on tape and film. She even accompanied me in the air for a little way as I walked back to my van. Again I thought what foolish behaviour this was for so magnificent a bird. If peregrines did not kick up such a fuss at human closeness, their bare rocky nest sites would be almost impossible to locate. Illegal robberies of eggs or chicks is the biggest problem peregrines have to face now that the use of persistent organochlorine pesticides in agriculture, which brought the birds to their lowest ebb twenty-five years ago, has been severely curtailed. Indeed, during this very season, the R.S.P.B. were to find that out of some 730 British peregrine eyries occupied by pairs, no less than seventy-two were robbed. It was the worst year on record for robberies and could have meant a loss to the wild of 280 peregrines, taken either as eggs or chicks.

With plenty of light left, I then drove to a forestry road and hiked half a mile to the lochan where Allan had seen the owls hunting in daylight. At first I saw nothing, just large expanses of deep bulldozed furrows on the tops of which grew small conifers in irregular profusion. I stumbled through and over the ankle-wrenching trenches, camera at the ready, but had to look as much where I was putting my feet as for birds. Allan must have had a lucky day, I thought.

After another quarter of a mile I saw what looked like a light brown gull floating over the little conifers two hundred yards to my right. The wings were blunter with brown markings, the chest a creamy buff and then I saw the broad-dished face with two wide-apart dark eyes. It was a short-eared owl questing along after its favourite food – field voles. These young forestry plantations provide ideal habitat for voles and when plagues of these chunky little rodents erupt, the owls soon find out and move in from a wide area.

The owl flapped slowly, glided a little and hovered often, its rear wing 'flaps' moving farther up and down with each beat than the front of the wings, rather like the backstroke swimming motions of a human. Often it flew along, made a rapid turn and performed what looked like a suicidal 'header' into the heather and grasses but not once did it come up with a vole, or even beetle. Clearly, they miss far more than they hit. I took a few photos although it was really too far away, and a sideways view of one that floated over a knoll, then I saw no more. I found no nests and as the light was fading I walked out and drove the thirty-five miles back to my boat, arriving home in the near dark. I did not go back because the very next day Allan and I put a hide up overlooking the buzzards' nest and I started intensive work from it.

18 · Surprising Prey

Tired after an overnight watch on the buzzards, I was plodding along above the west wood on June 27 when I heard two common gulls shrieking faintly high up over the northern ridges. Before them, taking no notice of their wild mobbing dives, floated an immature eagle. Through the binoculars I could see its creamy white wing and tail patches clearly. It appeared to be the eaglet Atalanta had reared in her farthest eyrie, no. 18. If so it was fascinating that it should still be on the eastern end of its parents' territory the following summer. It was the latest I had known that.

I did not get back to the eagle hide until June 30 and it proved to be the most fruitless visit of the year. I was just squeezing through a narrow corridor between the last giant gnarled rocks before going down to the hide, when I saw Melanion labouring through the hot still air from Eagle Rock mountain across the loch. He was flapping really hard and had something large and dark in his talons. I ducked back so he would not see me and felt acute disappointment. Once he dumped that prey on the nest it was unlikely he would be back until the next day, unless I was very lucky.

So it proved. In a 7½-hour watch neither adult came in again. It seemed Atalanta was still on 'holiday'. The eaglet was now almost fully grown, with just a few light flecks on its chest, its white head filled with small sprouting brown feathers, and its tail long. It could fly now if it had to. Although it pulled morsels off what its father had brought to the nest, it did not lift it high enough for me to

181

identify it clearly. It *looked* like the rear leg of a large lamb, but it had much brown and black wool or hair on it. It looked more like the leg of a young goat. I would have to also record this item as 'doubtful', for there was no way I could get up to that high nest in the sheer crag. I felt weary on the descent home, at times just shuffling along with very short steps under the weight of the camera gear and unused recorder. I did not really want to go back again but I would have to so that I could report the final success of the eaglet's rearing to the N.C.C. and take the hide away.

When it was not raining now I went to work with the buzzards. What puzzled me there was that after the first hide visit I never saw the female buzzard again. The doughty little male was having to work twice as hard as normal, bringing in lizards, frogs, voles, mice, even eels. At first he seemed perplexed because the chick was not feeding but he soon learned to rend morsels and tender them to the youngster, a job normally performed by the female. This was the first time I actually saw a male buzzard deliberately feed the chick. I wondered what had happened to the mother bird.

On July 5 I boated out for supplies and then drove to the post office. I took my mail into a nearby tea room and morosely thumbed through it. There was only one letter from London, a brown envelope with a second-class stamp. It looked like a bill. I opened it – and startled the other diners with my triumphant thump on the table. It was from Jonathan Cape, the publishers, and they *did* want *A Last Wild Place*! An editor at Cape who loved the book had written a detailed critique which indicated he understood exactly what my work was all about. If I agreed to some cuts, they would make me an offer. Even a likely publication date was mentioned. I left the cup of tea undrunk and raced to a kiosk to telephone my agreement. They also thought it was essential to include some of my precious colour photos in the book and wanted to discuss my *future* works. I said I would drive down in two or three weeks for final discussions and to agree a contract. They were somewhat flummoxed when I explained that I could not leave just yet as I had to see an eaglet safely out of its nest.

As I drove back to the boat a lovely warm feeling swept over me, one that had little to do with the temporary financial security the acceptance of my book now promised. The nightmare weeks, months, of lonely depression since Moobli's death now began to lift. And now I would be able to do what had been at the back of my mind for a year – buy a professional 16 mm movie camera and start actually filming the rare wild life around my home.

Two hot, muggy and windless days later, I set out on what was surely the last trek to this year's eagle hide. The loch was like heavy grey treacle, with surface swirls of yellow pollen everywhere. I climbed slowly, sweating profusely even though for the first time ever I was stripped to the waist. Every blade of grass, bracken frond and slab of granite beat heat back at me. On the last steep slog, just as I crossed the last burn, Atalanta came soaring over from the direction of the eyrie face like a great flying blackboard. She glided along . . . two beats . . . another long glide . . . two more beats . . . It was good to know she was back and I was sure she had just been into the eyrie.

I had not been set up long in the hide when a great beak and head emerged from the crevice. The eaglet then stood up, flapped its wings twice – heck, it was huge, clearly a female. She squirted what looked like half a pint of faeces clear of the nest edge, beat her giant wings again then flumped down for a sleep. Two hours later she came to the front of the nest and I took photos of her calling up into the sky, yawning, grabbing rowan sprays in her beak and trying to weave them into other twigs, and of two wonderful balletic exercises where she stood on one leg then slowly stretched the far wing and other leg right out to the side as far as they would go without losing balance. Sometimes she glared out over the void, at the blue haze of the distant mountains, and crouched down a little with slightly uplifted wings, as if she really wanted to go. But she was not quite brave enough or ready yet. There were still a few white flecks on the back of her neck and head. I reckoned she would be away in just under a week.

After a long sleep, she got up at 6 p.m. and several times half-lifted something dark-brown and big with her beak. It looked like the flattened carcass of a grouse yet oddly larger. Once I saw a foot but could not discern its texture or colour. Well, the photos should show that. A few minutes later she began to tug the carcass round the nest with the talons of one foot, then plucked out some long brown feathers before tearing off and swallowing snippets of meat. When the light began to fade, I left the hide. I went slowly to the last burn then put on some speed through the tussocks. All of a sudden I felt weak, my legs went all wobbly, as if all the strength had suddenly drained out of me, and I very soon slowed down.

Not until I had all my photos developed in London later was the astounding truth about that last carcass revealed. Showing clearly in one was the yellow foot and dark talons of a buzzard. Whether it was the same missing female from the oak-wood nest I had been observing I had no way of knowing but it seemed likely. Between us over the years, Allan Peters, Greg Hunter, Jeff Watson and myself had now amassed evidence that proved that eagles are capable of predating upon every other species of daytime raptor that exists in the Highlands. There was only one exception so far – the hen harrier.

On July 12 I went to check the peregrines. Again the falcon started to scream as I climbed the opposite hill. I soon located her this time, perched on a protruding rock below and to the right of the nest ledge. She was holding her wings drooped down and outwards as if to keep them cool, and after her first bout of harsh calling she gave several big yawns, rather like a chicken with the 'gapes'. To my surprise, the nest ledge was empty. Had the chicks been stolen after all? Surely they could not have fledged fully in the eighteen days since I had seen them, when they had still seemed to be mainly clad in white down.

Finally I heard two higher-pitched voices farther up the bushy cliff and through the glasses I located the youngsters. Both were perched on thick twigs and clinging hard with their talons. Fluffier looking than their mother, they were clearly fledged well enough to flit from ledge to ledge and twig to twig. I was relieved. They would be all right now. As I left I met the two estate keepers who told me that every time they passed by they checked the rare birds were not being disturbed. Good lads, these.

On the way back to my boat I visited the buzzards' nest. That chick too had flown and I found it perched on a fallen tree higher up the slope. The plucky little male *had* reared it on his own and as I stood looking he came over the trees with ringing 'kee-oo' calls, and the chick flew away through the oaks quite professionally, following his father's flight path. I removed the hide.

All my thoughts now were on dashing down to London to tie up the book contract, select all its photos, have this year's films professionally developed, buy a movie camera and a host of other urgent business. Before leaving, however, I had to check Atalanta's nest once more. Surely the huge eaglet would have flown by now.

I set out on July 14, a dull day with occasional light showers of misty drizzle. It was not too bad at first but as I reached the 1,000-foot level, the drizzle fell more strongly, the mist thickened and by the time I was up to 1,700 feet and heading over the tops to come down again to the hide, I could hardly see more than eight yards ahead. But I had gone too far by then to turn back. I could only find my way by memorising every slab of wet granite, every cluster of rocks, as they came into view.

At the hide the mist was swirling round the crags like eddies of smoke and I could not see the eyrie at all. I tore the heather and other herbage from the hide's meshes, pulled out all the bracing wands and stakes and rolled the whole caboodle up into a neatly tied hefty bundle to carry away. When I looked up at the eyrie again the mist had cleared temporarily.

The eaglet was still in the nest, sitting down on the edge, her huge form, head and shoulders showing distinctly, illumined against the white backdrop of the sky. I took one picture, just saw her head move, a side view of the great beak as she looked towards me, then once more the mist obliterated her from view. But I had seen enough. She was in superb shape and would be away with her parents, learning to hunt, any day now. Atalanta had succeeded yet again.

The trek out was tougher than the trek in for I could not see where I was going, and with the hide tucked under one arm, I had to use the other hand to feel my way down and along the cliff bottoms below Eyrie 27, until I reached the first burn. I almost missed it. Then after 800 feet of descent the mist ran out and I could see the way ahead. The rain increased, every tussock crown was soaked with gleaming wet crystals, every bramble frond and bracken fern loaded with water, and I was soaked through to the skin. All were fully grown now and bent or fallen over so that I could see none of the path I had made (along with sheep and deer) on all the earlier treks. With the bracken seven feet high in places, it was like fighting one's way through a tropical jungle. Frequently the long bulky hide got stuck and sent me off-balance. My boots were wet and slippery inside, new insoles adrift. Despite all my experience, I reached the boat with sore feet.

I looked back at the mist-shrouded mountain, at the wild domain of the eagles, and swore aloud:

'That is *it*! My last eagle season. Never again!'

It was only as I loaded the hide and pack into the boat that the realisation struck me. If I *did* get a movie camera I could not possibly make a film about the rare wildlife of the Highlands without showing the bird kings at their eyrie. Well, maybe I would do one more season after all. There it was again – prisoner of the eagles.

I dashed about in London, signed a contract with Jonathan Cape to publish *A Last Wild Place* and collected the developed flight pictures I had taken of the eagles, knowing I need hardly bother to photograph them in the normal way again. From now on I would concentrate on filming. I blew all the first part of the book's royalty advance on a secondhand 16 mm Arriflex ST movie camera and an assortment of lenses, batteries and other gear. It took two weeks to assemble this lot and have it all checked by experts. Running costs were horrendous: to buy a roll of film lasting only three minutes and have it developed came to more than £20.00. I did not realise then that I had entered, foolishly without training, a hard professional world. When I boated home in mid-August, the pair of black-throated divers greeted me with a salvo of strident, weirdly metallic calls. It seemed a good omen.

On August 21 I saw Atalanta flying over the northern ridges. She made one soaring circle then set off in a glide to the east. Suddenly I heard faint 'k'yew' calls and there, following a quarter of a mile behind and trying to catch her up, was the eaglet. By the time I had rushed inside for the movie gear they had vanished. For the first few days, when not re-writing parts of my book, I tried to familiarise myself with the complicated operation of the film camera. I would now have to carry a minimum of 45 lbs on the Hill – three times the weight of normal camera gear. And that was without a tripod. I reckoned I could keep the long lenses still enough by resting them on the tops of rocks and boulders. I trained for this by hurrying round my hilly acreage every day with a 70 lb pack of books and tools on my back.

A week later I set off up to Eyrie 28 and before I had climbed 600 feet I felt I had probably gone crazy. No wonder film-makers use a whole *team* of technicians. I weaved slowly upwards, and just as I came in sight of the eyrie peak, right on cue, Atalanta came sailing over it. She headed for me, circled, went back over it, reappeared and came towards me in a long glide. It seemed to take ages to get the camera out of the pack and make all the connections. When I finally got it resting on a rock I found I could not focus on her at all. With the movie camera the lens is offset from the viewfinder and one cannot sight along the barrel as with a normal camera. Three more times she appeared on that trek. By a fluke, I eventually got on to her and filmed her flight for over forty seconds. Then she went into a jet glide, sailed across the loch and right over Eagle Rock mountain – Juno's territory – followed by the eaglet. I slogged on up to the eyrie, filmed that, a panning sequence over the hills and into the nest, to show her terrain, then packed up the gear. Long before I got back to the boat every little bone in my feet seemed to have developed its own ache or pain, from carrying the extra weight over such rough terrain. Even so, I felt happy. It was not every wildlife cameraman who filmed eagles on his very first day out!

19 · *Wingtip to Wingtip*

After writing my yearly report on the black-throated divers, peregrines and eagles for the Nature Conservancy Council, and a full
report on the prey brought into the eagles' eyrie for Jeff Watson, for
which I duly received another £100 cheque, I set out to capture more
sequences for my projected film of Highland wildlife.

When the red-deer rut began in the high hills in mid-September I
made over a dozen treks, stalking the roaring stags and their harems
of hinds. On some days, after labouring for miles, I got nothing; on
others I felt I had garnered some good material. Filming was
decidely more difficult than still camera work. If, for instance, a
dark rain cloud was suddenly replaced by a path of brilliantly sunny
sky, one could not reach out and close down the aperture without
shaking the camera in the middle of the sequence. Yet this was a
simple operation when just taking single individual photos. The
other trouble was there did not seem to be the usual number of stags
about this year.

The weather was mainly wet and windy. When I next met Allan
Peters, an expert stalker, he said it was the worst rut he had ever
known in the area. Still, I plugged on when the weather would
allow. I filmed Mickey the marten running about the bird-table
complex, even coming through the window to take titbits by the
light of a paraffin lamp and two torches. I filmed flying buzzards,
swimming divers – any sequence I felt would illustrate Highland
wildlife through all four seasons.

In late October, feeling a little desperate, I lugged the gear to high above Eyrie 28, to what were usually the highest and most prolific rutting grounds. Plod about though I may, there was not a damn stag in sight! I heard one roar – from across the loch. I hung about up there for a cold hour, then packed everything up and set off for home. I was almost a mile beyond the eyrie peak at the 900-foot level, trudging through fallen bracken which snagged my ankles, when I noticed a dark shape in the sky to my right.

It was Atalanta, only two hundred yards above me. She headed slowly westwards to above the eyrie peak. Out came the camera again but I could not get on to her, and the heavy 500 mm lens kept twisting the stiff turret mount of the camera out of position. Suddenly two more eagles, one as big as she which I was sure was Juno, came over from Eagle Rock mountain. Atalanta went to join them and they began wafting about each other. Next a fourth eagle came from the north-east, a smaller male and doubtless Melanion, and he too flew to join them. There were now *four* eagles drifting close together, no animosity shown, and although I was now using a rock as a pivot, I could not get on to them at all. They sailed around like that for almost five minutes – hovering, stalling, almost wingtip to wingtip round each other, as if each was taking a good look at the individual faces of the other eagles. This was the seventh time I had seen this multiple flying of eagles in autumn, when two or more families meet and soar round each other. It was as if they were exchanging information about the season just passed, or working out winter territories, but perhaps this is rather foolish human speculation.

I wove the barrel of the long heavy lens all over the sky beside them, trying to capture this rare sight. I focused on the land peak below them, then panned upwards, but still I could not find them through the viewfinder. Exasperated, furious, I could only watch them drift out of sight to the west. No sooner had I covered a farther two hundred yards over the tussocks than the eaglet came right over my head from the east, calmly heading towards the others. I did not bother to get the equipment out again. It was clear now I would have to save up for a heavy and costly tripod. How I would carry that up the mountains too I had no idea. As I came within sight of the cottage, a tiny dot below, it began to pour with rain. It was the worst and most abortive trek ever.

Back at the cottage, I saw that all the grasses on Moobli's grave were five times as dense and thick as anywhere else, where no doubt their roots were eating into his dear body. After all the terrible effort, frightful luck, I could have wept with frustration, rage, and bitter loneliness.

During the first dark dank days of early November I made two more dreary stag treks. Once I saw Melanion make a playful dive on Atalanta, and she made a quarter-turn to the side to acknowledge his pair-bond gesture. She now had two secondary feathers missing from her right wing, and one from her left, while her mate appeared to have moulted none. The eaglet was still with them, wheeling high in the sky half a mile in their wake. This time I got on to them but too briefly. At least it was good to know the family were all still together.

Two days later I set off south to deliver the revised manuscript and photos for *A Last Wild Place* and to have my first 800 feet of film developed. On the way I met Jeff Watson in Edinburgh. We exchanged notes, and I gave him a few pellets for analysis. He told me that out of the twenty-one pairs in his main west Highland study region (which included much of my old area) only four eaglets flew this year. This was half the number that had flown last year, and this 50 per cent drop was also reflected over Scotland as a whole, with only 10 to 20 per cent of pairs being successful in much of his study region and up in Wester Ross.

Jeff felt that most of the failures had been caused by the prolonged cold spell, when much snow fell, between March 21 and April. Food had not been short. Indeed, as we had both found, carrion had been super-abundant. However, at this stage Jeff was not sure that carrion had much to do with breeding success. I pointed out that during my nine years of study, snow in April had been a normal phenomenon, and I again described how I had seen Atalanta whitening with snow before my eyes as she incubated her eggs. As for carrion, I felt that a good supply of sheep and deer carcasses in winter must help large birds like eagles lay strong-shelled fertile eggs. Jeff then reminded me of the exceptionally mild late winter. He thought this caused many eagles to nest in their highest eyries, which then failed when the unusually heavy late snows came in early spring. I agreed this was possible.

The final results for my old 300-square-mile area were as follows: Pair 1 (Atalanta) raised one eaglet. Pair 2 (Juno) did not breed. Pair 3 raised one eaglet. Pair 4 laid eggs but did not hatch them, probably due to human interference. Pair 5 laid two eggs late but the nest failed. Pair 6 laid eggs but the nest failed, again probably due to human interference. Pair 7 laid eggs late and raised one eaglet that did not fly until after August 15. Pair 8 laid in a new eyrie but failed to hatch them. The pair that Allan found two miles east of my old boundary and which were also not included in Jeff's study area, also raised one eaglet. For my old slightly 'stretched' area, therefore, four eaglets had flown successfully, so it was not too bad.

Before I left him Jeff told me his personal good news – he and Vanessa were to be married in December.

Among my mail a few weeks later was the winter issue of the R.S.P.B.'s excellent magazine *Birds*, which is only issued to members. It contained excellent news regarding Britain's golden eagles. In my first eagle book, I had estimated the population at 270 breeding pairs, plus fifty to sixty immatures and unmated adults in Scotland, as well as the two pairs in England's Lake District. I suspected, however, as I had written earlier to Jeff Watson, there were a good many more eagles in Scotland than this. I just had not felt it wise to express that view.

In the magazine now was a report compiled and written by Roy Dennis, giving a preliminary analysis of the results of the full-scale survey made by the Society and the N.C.C. the previous year, when every known eagle territory was covered.

Roy's report revealed that just over 400 pairs of eagles were occupying home ranges, and in half of the remaining 200 areas which were known to have once held pairs, at least one bird was present. While birds were absent from many of the grouse-moor areas in the east of Scotland, in some parts of the central and west Highlands, 75 per cent of home ranges were occupied. At least 182 pairs were successful that year, rearing over 209 young. This meant an overall productivity of 0·52 young reared per occupied home range – enough to maintain a stable population.

While these figures indicated the birds had recovered from their reduced breeding success, caused by pesticides like dieldrin (banned in 1974) during the early 1960s, I felt they were as much due to far more efficient survey techniques than a rapid rise in numbers. As I had stated in my book, and Roy now also pointed out, Scotland's eagles are still very rare birds, and represent a quarter of western Europe's total populations. They still suffer from innocent disturbance, direct persecution by illegal poisoning and the theft of eggs and chicks, and in some areas blanket afforestation, which reduces their hunting areas.

Roy's report added, 'We also need to take note of greater human pressures due to new hill roads and increased tourist facilities in wild country. In fact, the next step must be to formulate a new management plan for the golden eagle to ensure it always has a future in our country.'

When I first saw the movie films which had cost me so much hard labour, I felt excited and quite pleased. A long time later I showed them to a professional wildlife cameraman, a man who was tops in his craft, although he had not worked in the Highland mountains with wild golden eagles. He was blunt.

'Most of it is far too shaky,' he said. 'You obviously have a great ability to get close to rare wildlife, but what you have got from it so far, technically, is almost criminal.'

'I've seen shakier films than that on television,' I protested.

'Very seldom,' he replied. 'If you get a reputation for that kind of stuff you'll put yourself out of business before you start.'

It was harsh advice, and I was put out at the time, but I eventually realised he was right. I threw most of that year's footage away. The bungling prisoner of the eagles would virtually have to start again, from scratch.

That winter I spent three months in Spain pursuing eagles, rare vultures and lynx in the wild mountains there. I even succeeded in filming a female brown bear and her three yearling cubs roughhousing in the snow. It was a costly trip and as I had also had some hefty bills to pay, I returned to Wildernesse in mid-April armed with only 800 feet of film for the new, and last, season. I still could not afford the £1,000 heavy tripod and fluid head I really needed, so compromised with a fairly stout pan-and-tilt model, designed for ordinary camera use, which I bought secondhand from a friend. I resolved to concentrate on only key wildlife sequences; most landscape and habitat material could be shot later.

After carrying up the first of many heavy loads, I went round the cottage and everything seemed fine. Despite the gales and heavy snows, which had made the high road out to the nearest village impassable for many weeks, the roof and all the windows were intact. Then I saw some scuff marks on the inside of the kitchen window, and an awful possibility dawned on me. Last year I had arrived back a few days earlier and found that the owl Crowdy had come down the chimney. She had been thin but still alive, and after feeding her some meat I had released her. Although I had regarded it as a freak occurrence, before leaving I had put two crosswires over the chimney top and some wire netting over them. I looked up now – the netting had blown away. I went close and peered through the window.

There she was, on the deer skins in front of the hearth, her face tipped downwards into the thick hairs, one wing bent oddly back. In those agonising seconds I could not see if she was breathing. I burst into the cottage – she was dead. She could not have been dead for more than three days because her eyes had not begun to sink in and there was no smell at all. As I sadly held her body, its plumage still so bright and perfect, her head fell back against my hand and it seemed she was looking at me with her usual smiling half-closed eyes. Then came another tragic find – she had laid one white round egg in a deep fold of the deerskins. Had she come into the cottage, her old home, in order to try and nest herself? If I had returned just a few days earlier I could have saved her life.

As I carried her up the hill and saw again the grasses growing over Moobli's grave, I broke down. Blinded by tears, I buried her next to him. How much I had loved him, and her too, the two of them, and in many ways how I had failed them. Everything dies here, I thought, and the spirits wait for me also. The sad desolate hills await with inexhaustible patience to suck me into them too, just as they had sucked Moobli, and now Crowdy.

After carrying up ten more loads of gear and supplies and rescuing the boat from the reach of the loch, now seething in sudden gales, I walked round the east wood. I could not understand why Crowdy had made such a determined effort to get back into the cottage, for she must have had to force herself past the two crosswires which were still in place. Then I found a clue, another of her eggs, broken, lying on the ground below the nearest rhododendron bush. There were droppings there too, from where she had been perched low, maybe sheltering from a storm. Perhaps feeling the eggs inside her, looking for a place to nest but having no experience or mate to help her, she had lost the first one here, then had decided to go 'home' to lay the other. Maybe some innate instinct had made her feel her old guardian would return in time to help her. But he had not – and she had died of starvation. I saw that plaster had been torn from the windowsill where she had made desperate attempts to get out again. I could not remember a sadder homecoming. In case she had been impregnated by a male, although I heard no hootings during the following days, I set the remaining egg in an incubator, hoping I might at least carry on her line. But it did not hatch.

I left the eagles alone until the first sunny spell, so I could glass the eyries from a distance in the bright light, and so not put any sitting bird off its eggs, which should now be near to hatching. On April 22, in the cool brisk sunlight only late April can bestow (though it rarely does) I set off in the boat to check the nearest eyries. No sooner had I launched it than I saw a big eagle fly from a ridge to the west, circle towards me then set off eastwards. Moments later I saw a smaller darker eagle beating along behind the first. Up with the glasses. The front one was last year's eaglet, *still* on the territory, and her huge white wing and tail patches made her look a bird of dark-brown and cream. The rear one appeared to be Melanion. His flight had a definite pursuing aspect, as if he were chasing the eaglet away and this indeed seemed to be the case for as soon as she reached the far eastern boundary he airily circled back then went into a fast glide towards Eyries 27 and 28. This behaviour gave me great hopes. Two days earlier I had seen an eagle suddenly turn behind the cottage and vanish over the peaks towards Eyrie 1, though it was not possible to see that eyrie from my garden. At any rate, it appeared one of the closest eyries was being used.

I climbed first to Eyrie 33 but it was empty. I checked last year's breeding nest, no. 28, from both sides of the high crag but, as I expected, it was not occupied. Surely, they must be using no. 27. I climbed down again and approached the long ledge with cautious suppressed excitement. This was the eyrie where I had taken the best photos for my first eagle book, and its cover picture of Melanion flying in with a headless ptarmigan. It would be ideal for filming. To my chagrin, it too was stark and devoid of life, with not a single new stick added. Damn!

After boating home, I still felt good, my legs strong from the big treks in Spain and their recent rest, so I stormed up to Eyrie 1. I felt certain that at last this nearest eyrie was now being used. Before I entered the dark burn gorge and negotiated the wet slippery rocks, so that I could come up to the best rocky hide site unseen from the cliff, I saw two silver dots soaring above the peak. Were the peregrines which had lost their young to pine martens two years ago now back? Maybe I would find their nest ledge as well. I came out at the rocks and peered through a gap between them. Eyrie 1 was not only empty but almost all the nest sticks had been blown away. Hell. That was the end of any hope of filming eagles at any of the closest eyries.

As I lay there in disappointment I heard some weak high-pitched '*kri kri kri*' calls above me. Then sailing into the eyrie was not an eagle, not a peregrine, but a common little kestrel! It was a bright copper-coloured female. She landed on a dead rowan sprig, then hopped down on to the rough woody chips, all that was left on the ledge. She walked and looked around for a few seconds before flying off again to join her mate in the air as I took a few photos. Oh well, it looked as if I could do some work with nesting kestrels this year; I had never bothered with these small common falcons before. As I staggered back down, I realised I had found no dead red deer on the entire twelve-mile trek. Other hikes round the woods had revealed only two dead hinds and one dead calf. The carrion supply was so far a thirteenth of what it had been last year. The very cold snowy winter had been good for the deer but not for carrion-eating species like eagles.

On a supply trip I dropped in to see Allan Peters. He too had found it a poor carrion year. He listened with interest to my tales of Spain, then said:

'Now, what can we tell you about the *real* mountains! Er, you remember me pointing out that low eyrie in those gorges and cliff faces to the left of the big gully last year when we were on the Beinn [Eagle Rock mountain]?'

'Yes,' I said. 'Eyrie 34. I've never actually been up to the nest though. You said in all the years you'd known it that it had never been used.'

'That's right,' said Allan. 'But I reckon you'll find her in it now. I was up there twice in the past month, herding deer out of the compartment with two other forestry lads, and each time she sat tight until we were quite close before coming out over our heads. She seemed little bothered by us and each time flew back into the same cliff. I didn't actually go up to the nest, mind, but I reckon that's where she is this year.'

By 'she' Allan meant Juno, the eagle which had given me the most intimate observations ever two years earlier. I felt excited at the possibility of actually filming her and her mate at the nest. I thanked him profusely for his kind information.

'Aye, I reckon it'll do no harm to go up there in a few days, but choose the right weather, mind. There is a good cliff opposite and you should be able to see down into the nest from it.'

Driving back, I was horrified to see smoke puthering up in a wide swathe near Eyries 27 and 28. Someone was setting light to the Hill deliberately, for I could see many separate fires. I watched for a while but could see they were burning a few hundred yards west of the eyries, and that the slight breeze was not going to blow the flames actually on to the nests. In fact they remained unharmed.

A few days later I met the neighbouring farmer at a local store and told him about the fires.

'Yes, I'm the guilty one,' he said with an affable smile. 'It was getting very overgrown up there and needed clearing.'

Such 'muirburn' is practised by some Highland sheep farmers, to burn off long heather, brambles, bracken and other herbage so new grass can grow and provide a 'green bite' for the sheep in spring. When such fires go out of control they cause great damage to the natural vegetation and on steep slopes contribute to soil erosion. Luckily this fire had not. It soon transpired the farmer *knew* the eyries were not occupied this season and so had felt this year as good as any in which to burn off that particular hill.

On a hot April 26 I boated over to Eagle Rock mountain, ignored some little faces at about 600 feet and began slogging upwards, zig-zagging over the steep terrain so that I could examine all the long cliffs and outcrops above the gorge. Most were fringed with birches coming into leaf. I had to go close below each one in order to examine them individually for a nest. It was hard going, with deep forestry drainage trenches covered in tussocks everywhere. Perspiration poured off me. Face after face I searched without luck. In the end I climbed right up to Eyrie 30, which Juno had used two years earlier. I leaned over the yawning drop into the gorge, holding on to an inadequate rowan and peered in. As expected, the eyrie was empty and unused.

I then struck out in long quarter-mile zig-zags, examining all the ridges and eyebrows of cliffs, climbing and re-climbing high deer fences, but still had no luck. I was back down to the 700-foot level when I saw a huge steep rounded buttress of land to my right. May as well check round its far side, I thought. I struggled in and out of the trenches, through small scratchy sitka spruces, over a sheer drop, and was just thinking I was probably not going to film eagles this year after all, when there she was.

Juno was floating eastwards at eye level only twenty yards away, soaring along on mighty dark mottled wings. What a sight! I took out the camera and got two photos of her as she circled, then sailed off and landed on a bare rock less than half a mile away. She was keeping a close watch on me all right. She *must* have come off a nest. I went a few more yards through deep heather and looked up to my right.

There was the nest, resting on a projecting ten-foot crag which was screened from the gorge by two large birches. I climbed up a steep patch of lush great wood-rush then saw wisps of white down clinging to the outer nest twigs. That was all I needed to know. Trying to pretend I had not even seen the nest, I turned away, headed up then down a deep gully and came to the foot of the opposite cliff which Allan had said overlooked the eyrie. To my delight, there was a natural rocky staircase all the way up it. I climbed this and came out on to a level area ideally covered in deep heather. I turned and could see down into the nest and the back of a downy white chick about a week old. Near it lay the carcass of a hooded crow. This was almost as good a site for a hide as two years ago.

To allow Juno to go back to her nest I left immediately, and in full sight of her headed down the steep tussocky slopes until I was lost in the trees lining the burn at the bottom of the gorge. I was still half a mile from the boat when I saw Juno fly back and land above the eyrie, half-screened from my view by the tops of the birches. She stayed there a minute then through the binoculars I saw her launch out again, sink down through the air in two tight circles, and glide back into the eyrie. Triumph! I would let the chick grow at least a week older before setting up the hide.

20 · Under Attack

On the way home I puttered over to the lagoon beside the islet where the water kings nested last year. It was now time to start checking the rare black-throated divers. I was delighted to find that both birds were back there but the water level was now too high for them to nest on the same site. I left quietly.

Four days later Allan and I were checking the mainland woods near the islet when we found a wildcats' den. On the pine-needle carpet beside a cairn of rocks, the holes of which were littered with bones of a winter-dead hind, was a pile of thick, corded wildcat scats. They had been systematically laid across each other. I had seen this behaviour among the wildcats I had reared years before and knew it to be something to do with the pair bond. Whether the cats were in the den now we could not know, but there were fresh four-toed tracks in a patch of sand between the woods and the loch.

Later I baited the area with meat and set up the movie camera on a bluff above the den, but had no glimpse of either animal during two watches of several hours. If they were still about, I hoped they would not swim over to the islet and go for the nesting divers. Two days later I saw both black-throats paddling past my nearest islet, to which only five common gulls had returned this season. I thought this odd, for surely the pair should be nesting by now.

Although I began working intensively with the eagles in early May, I feel it best to recount first the complete sequence of the divers' breeding adventures, just as they happened.

On May 13 I boated down to their islet, having to pass the kayaks of the new adventure centre which were drawn up on the beach by the wood containing the wildcats' den. Towing a hide-screen behind me, I slid through the heather, new bracken and fallen trees down to last year's site. There was no sign of the divers. I examined the shore and came upon tragedy. Thirty yards east of last year's nest scrape was a new one, close to where I would have put the hide. Lying beside it, all scrimped up into tiny fragments, was the broken shell of a new diver's egg. Nearby in the mud was a tell-tale four-toed print. My fears had come true − a wildcat had come upon the egg, probably after seeing the bird on the nest, and had chewed it up there and then. A pine marten would have carried it away. I puttered over to the eagles' mountain and saw a diver floating off shore. It had a sad look to it.

On May 16, after two days in the eagle hide, I saw one of the divers close to my nearest islet at dusk. Were they trying to re-lay there?

Next day, returning from a visit to the peregrine falcons' sea cliff, I decided to go and check this islet, and turning the engine off I quietly floated into its eastern bay. There was not a diver in sight. Well, I could at least see if the five common gulls which had returned this year had managed to lay any eggs. I had been feeding the marten nightly on the bird-table complex for weeks now, and recently he had arrived with a mate. Naturally, hoping to film them together, I had been putting out more food than usual, which should surely have kept them off the islet. There was no need for either of them to make that cold water swim now they had a plentiful source of food.

While four of the gulls flew overhead with muted '*keeya*' calls (they knew me of old), I walked carefully through the tussocks and found first one nest and then another, each containing three eggs. Good. I went on, along the islet's far southern shore, sure that I would find no more, when a more surprising sight met my eyes.

Lying neatly together in a shallow natural bowl the size of a large dinner plate and ringed by stones, were two huge, fat, olive-brown, freckled black-throated diver's eggs! Sure they would be cold, I felt them. They were warm. I searched the waters and there she was, the female diver. She was floating high in the placid water like a white and blue-grey goose, looking back anxiously at what I was going to do.

I backed away and frantically searched with my eyes for a good hide sight but there wasn't one. The only natural place seemed to be beside a small alder tree growing in a rocky dell some twenty five yards from the nest. The old hide site, up among the heather below the dwarf pines, would be useless because a small rocky ridge hid the nest from its view. This new situation was really going to tax my brains, for I dare not alarm the divers into deserting their nest. With no helper to take my boat away each time, I would probably have to set up the hide with the movie gear in it, then swim to the islet on each visit, out of sight of the sitting bird, in my wet suit, and sit for hours wearing it. I did not exactly relish that idea. Quietly I boated away, then from my shore watched the diver paddle back to her eggs. That night I put out luxury foods for the martens, including two eggs which they galloped away with first. I had certainly to keep them off the islet now.

Last year, after the martens took their first egg on this islet, the divers had flown to the far one, laid another egg and had succeeded in raising a youngster. It was astonishing that this year, after the wildcat had eaten their first egg on the far islet, they had returned to this one and laid two more. Such determination and intelligence deserved its reward.

While I was in the garden on May 21, putting the finishing touches to a special hide for filming the divers, I heard a great hulla-baloo coming from the islet. I grabbed my binoculars and ran to the shore. There were six gulls in the air now and three of them were screaming and diving down by the west edge of the islet, just swerving up again in time to avoid hitting the water. I kept looking – and almost dropped the glasses.

A huge otter emerged from the loch, shook its big head and whiskers then its whole grey submarine body clear of water, and lolloped slowly over the little gully where I was going to put the hide. Up the rocks it went and over the far side – straight towards the site of the divers' nest! Now what should I do? If I dashed over with boat and engine, the otter would hear me coming and elude me. If it was after eggs, it would have taken the lot anyway by the time I rowed over quietly. Surely an otter would not take birds' eggs? I had never seen these listed as being among this animal's food diet. I gulped down breakfast – a mere cup of tea – and carried the hide and camera down to the boat. Then I saw the diver, floating well away from the islet and keeping low in the water.

I rowed quietly to the north side, sneaked over the rocks and heather and peered through. There was no sign of the otter, and three gulls had landed back on the rocky ridges. Well, the diver had probably just been scared off the nest by the otter's sudden appearance. I had better put up the hide, now or never. First, I went to check her nest.

Both eggs had gone! And so had three eggs from the gull nests. Hell! I almost wept with rage and frustration. Not so much because I could not film the birds at the nest but because after all their efforts the poor divers had finally failed. There were no bits of shell near the nest, so it seemed likely the otter had carried them into the water to eat, and the shell fragments had sunk.

Partly I blamed myself. If only I had set up the hide when I had first found the nest, it and my scent might have kept the otter away from that area. I now found the otter had been using the islet regularly. There were two wet lie-out places in the moss below the pines, several spreints and large greenish scats filled with fish and frog bones, and the burrows used by the marten last year had been enlarged. I was sure the divers would come back to check again that their eggs had really gone. I set the hide up in the heather under the pines and settled down to wait.

Two hours passed, then I saw the female diver swimming back, just off the southern shore. Sure enough, nearer she came and started marking time in the water, turning her dagger-beaked head this way and that as she checked and re-checked that her nest site really was empty. She looked indescribably sad and forlorn. Soon her mate joined her, and I filmed them bouncing along through the radiant paths between the wavelets on the blue waters. They came into the bay below the hide, and when their heads were frontal to my view, they had the look and grace of cobras. They drifted away to the left, keeping close together, as if comforting one another in some silent language, their whole mien one of desolation and bereavement. Often they put their heads back under their wings, as if to snatch a brief sleep that would blot out the awful reality of what had happened. When they went out of sight behind the second islet, I left.

On May 23, I spent eight hours in the islet hide but the divers did not return. The otter had been back for now the other gulls' nest was empty but I did not see the otter. The gulls shrieked often and appeared to relieve their feelings by harrying a sandpiper, whose mate had a nest of eggs on the smaller islet, and chasing off a newly arrived pair of oyster-catchers.

As for the divers, they spent the rest of the summer drifting aimlessly about the loch, seldom together, as if the loss of their eggs on two far-apart nests had broken up the breeding pair bond. It was as though one bird was blaming the other in some way for the double tragedy. Although a diver's dagger beak must be a formidable weapon, the bird is clumsy and ungainly on land and it would have been a poor defence against a determined wildcat or otter. It seemed ironic that these rare birds' failure should have been caused by two uncommon and also legally protected mammals.

Now let us return to what had been happening meantime with the eagles and peregrines. After finding Juno's nest with her young chick in late April, the eagle work began in earnest on May 6 when Jeff Watson's van arrived on the forestry track opposite. Vanessa, now his wife, was with him and so was their young Labrador pup, which went by the name of Doran. Jeff had checked Juno's eyrie the day before; the chick was fine and there had been a big fat grouse on the nest. Both now wanted to go on their favourite hike – the killer trek! As I too wanted to see if Atalanta was nesting in one of her two farthest eyries, we set off at once. On the high tops before the last near 2,000-foot plunge, Doran disappeared. Vanessa said she would try to find him; if we missed her on the way back, she would head home for the cottage.

On the steep climb up to the roost site and Eyrie 18, Jeff well ahead, I was about to tell him to hold on when out from the cliff shot an eagle. It was Atalanta, still with a feather missing from each wing. I caught up and asked Jeff if she had come off the roost but he had not seen her at all. It seemed likely she had heard our clumping boots on the still air and had taken off from the nest. Certainly it seemed well built up as we passed below it.

We climbed up to the rock the eagles used for dismembering prey and were disappointed to find the remains of three lambs. One, judging by the unformed hooves, had been still-born. One remnant was clean, indicating it had been found dead. But the third, a rear leg, was well bloodied and I had to admit the eagles must have killed it. As I looked across to the eyrie I was sure I saw the white head of a chick emerge momentarily. Braving the sheer heights in a way I would never have done, Jeff climbed up high enough to see into the nest. It contained just the one chick but that was good news enough; Atalanta had never failed in this eyrie yet.

We discussed the lambs. On our treks we had both found deer and sheep carrion in exceptionally low supply and there seemed to be a shortage of normal wild prey too. Rabbits were down, grouse were scarcer than ever and we had not seen a single golden plover on our hike today. It appeared the eagles were being forced to take a lamb or two more than usual, in order to survive at all.

Jeff pointed out that this eyrie, with the long open glen yawning below it, would be ideal for filming. I gave a bitter laugh and said there was no way I could tackle this awful trek with the heavy movie equipment *and* a hide; I had never contemplated working this eyrie even with normal camera gear, although I was now carrying that. After the usual near sleepless night in a hide, I would never get the heavy cine gear back up the almost sheer 2,000-foot wall. I did promise, however, to complete the killer for yet another 'last time', to check the eaglet had fledged successfully.

Later, as we were eating lunch on a knoll a quarter of a mile south of the eyrie, we saw Melanion drifting over the ridges to the north. Suddenly back went his wings and he went into a powerful dive, racing across the arch of sky like a meteor. Down, down, down he dived as I took photos, then chased one of two hooded crows. He matched the twists and turns of the aerobatic crow with amazing agility for so large a bird, while the other fruitlessly tried to dive-bomb him from above. The first crow eventually sideslipped and escaped into a tree, then Melanion soared up, circling higher and higher until he vanished into the hazy clouds. We hiked on to the bottom of the great wall and then looked back, to see both eagles rocketing out into the blue from behind the eyrie buttress, as if making sure we were heading away. Atalanta's mantle gleamed almost grey in the sun and although she was as vast as ever, her tattered wings made her look really old.

I prefer not to recall much of the trek back. Jeff more than had my measure this time. He stomped up the killer steeps like some tireless machine, while I heaved my camera pack up slowly, feeling my heart would burst any second. He waited for me on the crest for a brief rest before setting off south-westwards towards another deep glen, to look for Vanessa and the errant Doran. Even so, I felt I was really moving well on the longer but easier route and after a mile was sure that I was well ahead. To my surprise, as if in a nightmare, I kept seeing Jeff's ghostly form appear on ridges a quarter of a mile ahead, wait a while, then vanish again. I could not catch him up and at fifty-six had to admit that age had caught up with me. He waited on the last bluff above the cottage while I took a breather, then shot away again. This time I managed to stay with him and we arrived at the cottage together. When Vanessa, who had found Doran already there, saw our red, sweating and panting faces she burst into laughter, but I left her in no doubt as to the truth.

'Your husband', I said, 'could have left me by half a mile or more had he so chosen.'

We enjoyed some wine and good eagle talk, and thought we had solved one puzzle of the territoriality of eagles. Two years ago, when I had seen Juno often flying over Atalanta's Eyries 27 and 28, Atalanta had been nesting in her northernmost eyrie; thus Juno had felt able to trespass on the southern fringes of the older bird's range. Last year when Atalanta had nested in Eyrie 28, and Juno had not bred at all, Atalanta and Melanion had been able to hunt the nearest slopes of Eagle Rock mountain without hindrance. This year it seemed likely Juno would again be able to utilise some of Atalanta's southern range. (Later, this proved to be true.) Before they left, Jeff said he would help me set up my new hide on Juno's nest in two days' time, if Allan, who was busy with deer counts, could not do so.

The day came, Jeff arrived, and at 10 a.m., in bright sunny weather, we were on our way. Although it was a trek of less than a mile and only up to 700 feet, it was hellish terrain. Jeff carried the hide and normal camera gear, while I packed up the hefty movie equipment and the tripod. We toiled over deep drainage trenches, tussocks, marshes, rocky beds of burns, nearly sheer bluffs, miniature canyons and many fallen trees on the steeps. We wove heather all over the hide's netting, tugged it up to the site and had it finished in less than an hour. Jeff checked the prey in the nest – a greyhen, a grouse and a piece of lamb carrion. The chick, nearly three weeks old, had a full crop. Jeff saw me into the hide and then left. With all that prey in the nest I did not think Juno would be in for a good while, and so it proved.

I filmed the chick staggering about, ejecting faeces and flumping down for a sleep. There was no more action until 7 p.m. when the chick began to squeak. I shot up to the viewfinder, hearing a rush of wings, but was only just in time to see the dark male leaving the nest. He had dumped a wood pigeon but I had missed him. Damn.

A few minutes later I was lying on my back for a neck rest when I heard what sounded like three small gusts of wind and saw the top of the hide sag, very gently. About two minutes went by before I heard another faint swish and the top of the hide moved up into its normal position again. Odd. I waited until after 9 p.m., then slid out of the back of the hide into a natural tunnel in the deep heather. The sky was empty. I lifted my head and looked at the top of the hide. On it was the unmistakable orange and white belly feather of an eagle! The sagging of the roof had clearly been caused by one of the eagles, probably the male, landing on it. Thank heaven I had had the sense not to move or make a sound. Well, it proved the hide was a good one. I hiked back down to the boat with aching thighs, carrying both packs of gear (over 60 lbs), still without filming the adults despite an eight-hour stay.

When I climbed back to the hide on May 11, there was a ptarmigan in the nest, which had had so many sprays of heather and rowan dropped on to it I could not see the chick. Had it been taken? I had seen tent campers on the nearest shore the previous day. After twenty minutes I saw its white head come up and go down again. At 5.20 p.m. it clambered to its feet and shot a squirt out of the nest, so it was being fed all right. Almost two hours later I happened to have my eye to the viewer and saw a tawny form glide up as the dark-faced male landed on the nest. The chick did not move or call out, nor did the male appear to hear the whirring of the movie camera as I took my first footage of an eagle on its nest. He looked down at the chick, his beak half open in the heat, peered round the nest as if assessing the food situation, then turned and left.

At 7.40 p.m. I heard the familiar rush of air and pushed the lever just in time to film Juno landing, walking forward then standing dead still. I saw again the large, broad, almost cowled head, the large light-orange eye. The chick squeaked and shuffled out and under her legs, hoping to be fed. But Juno stayed there, alert, listening. Could *she* hear the movie camera at forty yards? At any rate she did not feed the chick and after a minute she too turned and left. Damn. When the light faded I packed up and slid out of the hide.

On May 13 I staggered up with an even bigger load, carrying also a foam mattress, sleeping bag, food for a twenty-five-hour stay, plus a wool and leather 'blimp' for the camera that would drown out the sound of its motor. I could not see the chick for its favourite lying place was behind a sliver of dead wood which projected from the left of the nest, but there was the hind section of a rabbit lying over the sticks. Not until 9.20 p.m. and in poorish light did Juno come in. She had no prey, and did not feed the chick, which got to its feet without squeaking and flapped its wings, on which were sprouting tiny dark feathers. Juno just stayed beside it, blinking slowly, and I thought she would brood it for the night as it was now becoming cold. Twenty minutes later, however, she beat away again and did not return. I was worried that she had not fed the youngster and intended to leave it alone through the cold night. Two years ago she had been overly protective of her chick; perhaps that had been her first. I dozed fitfully, blasts of cold air hitting eyes, ears and the back of my neck, but the bag kept feet and body warm.

At 5.42 a.m. next morning I heard the double thump of wings breaking the air, and in came Juno with a huge spray of birch she, or the male, had torn off, its shredded bark still hanging. Again she just stood very close to the chick, for six minutes, but left without feeding it.

At 9 a.m. I was glad to see the chick get up, trying hard to re-gurgitate something big, banging its head forward and shaking it hard. Finally it did – a huge pellet. Then it flopped down behind the wood sliver. How it survived alone on a night when a human would have suffered from exposure I do not know. At just over three weeks old it was learning you need to be tough to stay alive in the wild. Twenty minutes later Juno swept in, with a beakful of long white tussock grasses. She dropped most of them round the chick, stood awhile then once more left without feeding it. There *was* a shortage of live prey this year but Allan had shot a deer and left it on the hill less than a mile away, just for the eagles. Why did they not bring back carrion?

Through the afternoon the eaglet got up twice and preened its tail and back. It *seemed* all right.

In early evening, after the long cramp-filled, neck- and back-aching, muscle-tiring hours, I packed up and left. It was raining steadily but when I had stumbled down a quarter-mile of the drenched tussocks and trenches, Juno came flapping round the hill, saw me, sailed to the side without apparent alarm, circled, then soared towards the eyrie crag. By the time I had boated home I was soaked to the skin, shivering with cold. Above all I was worried about the chick. After thirty-nine hours in the hide I still had not seen, or filmed, it being fed by its mother.

21 · *Filming the Impossible*

After shopping for much-needed gas canisters and food supplies three days later, I went to the peregrines' sea cliff. As I climbed up the tiercel flew out over my head, soared and circled on his stiff sharp wings, then landed near the ravens' nests. No sooner had I settled into position than I heard the harsh rasping cries of the falcon. I soon located her through the glasses, perched on a crag at 11 o'clock from the ravens' nests. After a few minutes, as I kept dead still, she stopped calling, flapped out briefly and went down on to a grassy ledge that obviously contained her nest. She fluffed out her belly plumage then settled very firmly on what must have been eggs, though at that distance and angle I could not see them through the glasses. I left quickly.

On May 18 I had an easier hike up over the short but awful terrain to the eagle hide, for by now I had found the best route. Near the top I saw Juno sitting bolt upright on a conical rock above the eyrie face. She looked so big that at first I thought it was a human standing there. I sneaked between small spruces, then crawled to some jagged rocks atop a knoll and poked the long movie lens over. I was just in time to film her flying off. She wheeled to west and south, beat up to a higher ridge and made a perfect, gentle landing, talons extended like landing wheels, her wings back like those of a giant bat. I had my first good footage of a flying eagle. I waited until she flew again and vanished over the far south-west ridges, and then quickly wriggled into the hide.

After leaving half a rabbit, Melanion jumped into the windless air and lifted his wings. He beat away with dangling talons, his beak open in the heat, and swept sideways past the hide.

A hill fire, started by a farmer, blazed near two of Atalanta's eyries.

below: The tawny owl, Crowdy, had come down the chimney and starv
to death in the kitchen before I returned.

A peregrine nest on the high cliff contained two downy chicks.

below: Tragedy for the black-throated divers. Their first egg had been eaten by a wildcat.

I would have to make the 'killer trek' yet again. Was this to be for the very last time?

below: On June 17 Juno's chick had most of her brown plumage, but still a white face.

The chick, bigger now, seemed in fine shape, but there was a bloodied chunk of black-footed lamb on the nest. Oh dear, she had probably killed this one. I filmed the eaglet tottering about and flapping its brown-flecked stubby wings, and at dusk Juno came in. She stood with her back to me, looked out, yawned a few times, then turned to look at the eaglet. Slowly she arched her neck in a perfect bow regarding the youngster with what seemed great affection, then settled down right beside it. Although she did not actually brood the chick she was certainly keeping the wind off, so it remained warm in the lee of her great body.

Before dawn I could see she was still there, a large, boat-shaped mass against the granite wall. I filmed her asleep with her head behind a wing, looking down at the chick, drowsing with her grey-white eyelids slowly opening and closing, and grooming the chick's down with her beak. When the light improved she tramped carefully across the nest and fed the youngster, not from the lamb but from a young raven. Annoyingly, she kept her back to me but I waited, neck aching with strain, until she turned sideways and I could film the tender beak-to-beak transfer of morsels. After the eaglet flopped down for a sleep, Juno turned and left the nest.

It was a long wait after that. I endured the torture of heather roots digging into my body by reading a book. At 4.20 p.m. the eaglet cheeped. I looked across but Juno was already back in the nest, with a ptarmigan she must have brought in. Now she began feeding the eaglet in perfect sideways pose, its white head darting back and forth as it snatched the snippets of flesh she ripped off in her beak. I had only filmed a few feet when a mist came over, causing droplets to form on the lens and the picture to haze. The mist cleared briefly, then fell so thickly that I could hardly see the birds or the cliff at all, just the moving white down of the eaglet. Damn! Was this why chicks were white, so parents could locate them on dark misty cliffs with innumerable ledges? Juno flew off into the mist. I waited a good while more, but after this twenty-six-hour stay I had had enough, so I packed up and left.

On May 24 I reached the eagles' hide by late afternoon, but had to be content with just filming the eaglet staggering about and flapping its stubby wings. I could see no prey on the nest.

After another almost sleepless night, I spent the morning of my birthday with the eaglet, for neither adult came in. At midday Allan arrived for an afternoon watch. I told him, half-joking, that he could expect Juno to come in at about 4 p.m. (Allan told me later that he was amazed when Juno came shortly after 4 p.m. with a fat ptarmigan in her talons! More, she fed the eaglet for a full twenty-five minutes, in good light and facing him all the time. After all my stays, I still had not filmed this.)

'What was most fascinating', he enthused, 'was that she often held a bit of meat near the chick, then put her beak back down to the prey. As the chick pecked at what she was holding, it also pulled pieces off the prey. I think in that way she was teaching the chick how to pull bits off the carcass for itself.'

On May 27 I spent an excellent day at the peregrines. The falcon floated in the air with rasping cries, then landed on a rock near the new nest ledge, where I could just make out the tops of two white chicks' heads. The full-grown grasses made a clear view impossible. The bird seemed to have got my measure now, and knew I was harmless, for she half-closed her yellow eyelids and regarded me superciliously. The constant heatwaves shimmering up made her go in and out of focus through the glasses. I watched her preening her breast feathers, stretching one dark wing and one foot down towards the ground and lifting both bent wings high above her head in 'Hottentot' stretches.

What a superb creature she was, smart black and blue-grey wings, the lovely soft plumage of her cream and navy-blue-barred chest looking pinkish in the direct sunlight, great hunter face so solemn with its dark moustaches, all her movements wonderful. Like the eagle, here was a creature beyond man living in her own world, resting and flying when she felt like it, killing when she was hungry or needed to feed her young; no attitudes, no intellectual pretension, glorying only in being *alive*.

A gull flew overhead and she showed no reaction, but when a raven croaked to the north, off she went. She soared high above it, then chased the raven off by whooshing down beside it, making no attempt to strike. The raven is a nest raider, so it seemed she was protecting her young.

On May 29 I spent nine hours in the eagle hide. The eaglet, wing feathers now three inches long, pecked a few morsels off the denuded carcass of a hooded crow. Two hours later it squeaked and in shot the little dark male with a young raven. He looked out and upwards, seemed alarmed, and shot off the nest. Immediately in swept Juno, who stood there with a proprietorial air, glaring, as if she had told the male to get off the nest as she was still doing the feeding. She stamped on the raven, plucked off a few feathers and then began to feed the eaglet. Yet again she kept her back and tail towards me. I whistled and gave a couple of deer barks, hoping she would turn round. She just looked up, appeared to decide the sounds were normal, and carried on as before! What awful luck I was having, but I did manage to film some of the beak-to-beak transfers before she turned and flapped away. I left at 8.30 p.m. As I was going down the second gorge Juno came over the top. She saw me, turned as I gave my usual gentle eaglet whistle, came right over my head, dipped her left wing, then sailed over the crest behind me.

I checked the eaglet was fine on June 2, though I could see no prey on the nest, then set up the cine camera behind the jagged rocks on the knoll, hoping to film the adults flying. After two hours it began to rain and that was the end of that. I was soaked to the skin again.

On June 4 I spent eight hours in the hide. At 5 p.m. the eaglet called and the male came in without any prey, looked about briefly, then left again. At 6.30 p.m. I saw Juno gliding towards the front of the hide. The eaglet called loudly as she passed the nest, but she just wheeled gently and flew back the way she had come. The eaglet ate nothing during my stay but preened and leaped about, exercising its wings. By now I was also filming two nesting buzzard families from separate hides so did not return to the eagles until June 15, when I put in a further ten hours in the hide.

A fine misty drizzle began to fall on the climb up, and the full-grown bracken, bog-myrtle bushes and long molinia grasses soaked my legs. I did not set up until the rain stopped. The eaglet was huge now, surely a female, with most of her wing, chest and back plumage, though her head was still white with just a few brown flecks. I filmed her feeding from another raven carcass. At 7 p.m. she gave some breathy squeaks and in shot the male with some bird prey. He looked about briefly and flew off again. Although the eaglet soon jumped on to the new item and tugged it about, it was low in the nest and I could not see clearly what it was, except that it appeared to have powder-blue wings with dark tips, a white and light-bluish chest and a light-grey tail with indistinct grey-brown bands. Any thoughts that it *might* be a wood pigeon were dismissed when I saw slender yellow legs ending with dark talons. The nearest identification I could make was that it was a cock hen harrier. If so, this was an exciting discovery for it would be final proof that Highland eagles are capable of taking *all* the species of other diurnal raptors. I hoped my film would show it clearly. (Unfortunately it did not.)

On the following day my friend wildlife writer Jim Crumley walked in. Because he wanted to see a big eaglet in its eyrie and I wanted to identify definitely the mysterious bird prey, I took him up to the eyrie crag. I climbed above the nest and took some still pictures of the eaglet, which calmed down visibly as I talked soothingly to it. The odd 'cock harrier' prey was nowhere to be seen. There was just a fresh ptarmigan in the nest. We refurbished the hide with fresh heather, then left. On neither of the last two visits had I seen Juno anywhere in the sky. I felt that she too was taking the female's 'vacation' now that the eaglet was as capable as any adult of feeding itself, leaving the male to bring in food.

I had only ten feet of film left. When I saw Allan's forestry boat pulled up on the nearest shore to the eagles on June 20 I guessed that he and Jeff Watson had gone to ring the eaglet and so did not go there myself. Later Allan told me they had not only ringed the eaglet but Jeff had put palatial wing tags on it too. We still know little of how far eaglets travel when looking for territories of their own. These tags, which last about five years, enable the birds to be identified in flight from the ground. They had found a hooded crow on the nest and a fledged cuckoo below it, which they threw back for the eaglet to eat. As bad weather set in, I took advantage of it to get some new films. After frantic phone calls, I finally arranged to have another 800 feet of film sent up to a Glasgow photo shop from Manchester by Red Star express, and on June 25 I drove down to pick them up. Twenty-four minutes of film, much of which has to be thrown away, cost me a further £112 34p. Development costs would be double this. Phew!

On June 28 I spent eleven hours in the hide, which was wet and cold. Just as I neared the top I heard the eaglet calling. Juno was hanging in the sky high above the peak of the mountain. It had seen her. As I watched, just as she had done two years earlier, Juno went into a jet glide to the north, crossed over two other eagle territories, and vanished over the peak of the highest mountain eight miles away. Possibly she was still on this strange 'holiday'.

I filmed the eaglet preening her back, wings and tail, walking about the nest with frequent yawns, and then she started tugging at something deep in the bowl. She clamped her talons on it, reached down with her beak and tugged hard. I caught a glimpse of a sharp, red-brown predatory animal head before she let it go again. Once more she tried, hauled up the wide head but still could not seem to make any impression on it. Finally she lifted the whole animal. It was a stoat! She jerked it about until its head was in her beak then with many backward gulps as my camera whirred, she swallowed the entire animal whole! I watched in amazement as the rear legs and then the black-tipped tail were the last to go down her throat. She made several sideways wrenchings of her neck to ease it down, held her head high, blinking her dark brown eyes owlishly as it slid down her gullet, and that was the end of that. I had never seen anything like it; nor had several hardened wildlife cameramen who gasped with surprise when I later showed the unique piece of film to them.

After a long sleep the eaglet began tugging at something with white and black wool or fur with her talons. When she then picked it up in her beak with ease, I saw it was the whole skeleton of a large lamb with not much flesh left on it. There was no way of telling if the lamb had actually been killed by the eagles, but it seemed likely. If this was disappointing, so was the size of the wing tags on the eaglet. With their huge black numbers they were both unsightly and unnatural.

I do not go along with too much scientific interference in the lives of such large rare birds, and would certainly be against radio tagging them. What real use were these wing tags when there would be so few observers in the hills to follow the eaglet's course over the next five years? It must be borne in mind what happened when in 1978 the population of the rare California condor was found to have dwindled to between thirty and forty birds, and scientists invaded their wilderness to start a captive recovery programme. Teams of spotters were sent into the mountains, eggs and chicks were taken from the wild to be reared in captivity, while other chicks were sexed, weighed and measured; one even died from this handling alone. Over the years too, all known wild adults were baited to carcasses, had cannon nets fired over them and were sexed (by a surgical incision), examined, weighed and measured. Most had radio transmitters fixed to their wings before being released. The trauma all this must have caused to a prehistoric species acutely sensitive to human disturbance can only be imagined. In 1985 the last condor egg to be laid in the wild was snatched by scientists because they saw ravens harassing the adults and 'eyeing the egg hungrily'. Ravens have been harassing condors and eyeing their eggs hungrily for thousands of years, before even the Red Indians held sway over the mountains and plains. But then they were not helped by over-eager, inexperienced and ignorant observers scaring the birds away from their nests.

At the time of writing the wild California condor population was down to five birds, with only one breeding pair left, and there were just seventeen which had been reared in captivity. My fear is that the scientists' hope of releasing these captive birds, which have lost a true sense of wildness, which have not been naturally trained by free-flying parents to scavenge efficiently, to become a viable wild population, will prove to be a pitiful delusion. In my view what the scientists will have achieved is to *hasten* the condor to extinction. It would have been far better to protect the birds' habitat rigorously, stamp down on all human persecution, shooting and poisoning, and help feed the condors with judiciously placed surplus dead deer and a few carcasses of stock animals that would otherwise have gone for pet meat. This policy has certainly worked with rare vultures in Spain.

During my stay in the eagle hide the male twice flew near the eyrie, just checking it from the air. Although the eaglet called loudly he did not come in. When I next met Allan I estimated the eaglet would fly between July 5 and 9.

In hot sunshine I set off on the killer trek for the last time on June 30. If I did not go now I would never know if Atalanta had raised the chick in her farthest eyrie, for it would have flown. I knew it was crazy to tackle the 12,000 feet of ups and downs with the heavy cine gear, but I cut it down as much as I could and took not a tripod but a monopod, which I could also use as a walking stick to help me up the steeps. Even so the pack weighed 48 lbs. I resolved that if I felt weak under its weight I would just turn back. I plodded up through tussocks, bracken and bogs to 800 feet, levelled out on to the edge of the big corrie, hiked steadily upwards to 1,600 feet, down 700 then up another 1,000 until I was on the near 2,000-foot ridges of Guardian mountain. There was no way I could tackle the descent of that steep wall with such weight, so I struck off to the north-east and emerged with the valley floor far below and the eagles' glen and eyrie buttress a mile away to the north-west. I went down the wall sideways, traversing the nearly sheer turfy ledges and gorges with care. One fall here and I would be away to a bouncing death. Yet my knees were feeling fine, despite the weight. I reached the valley floor, drank from the river, and forced my way out and up again, boots now pinching my feet. I traversed the great buttress, having to walk on the right-hand edge of my feet, making them even more sore on the twisty ground.

Somehow I misjudged direction and came too high, above a cliff almost level with the eyrie crag. Higher again, the same thing happened twice more. In the end I just had to work my way over a short sheer face over a thirty-foot drop, but on to ground so steep I would not stop tumbling until I was all the way down. I got over it, trembling, heart pounding, and sank down for a short rest. Then I had to work my way *down* to the 1,000-foot level until I came to the roost site. The dead rowan snag was still being used, a good sign, and I pocketed four pellets for Jeff Watson's survey. As I walked under the eyrie, the grey sticks of the nest looked old and abandoned. Had the chick flown already, or been killed? I slogged up the hill until I reached the 'kill' or dismembering rock, which was itself perched over a ravine, then turned to look down at the eyrie.

There was a black blob in a fissure away to the left of the nest. After assembling the gear I found I could rest the camera on the flat rock in such a way that it held steady and looked directly into the nest. I peeked through the viewfinder. The dark blob was the eaglet, huge and fully fledged, in fact ready to fly. It had probably heard me walk past and had stepped into the crevice to hide. Intelligent youngster, this.

I lay curled up on the bumpy slope, perched above the ravine, with my camouflaged pack hiding me from the eaglet's view.

Soon it lost interest, stepped out on to the nest and acted as if I were not there. I filmed it looking down at the flies on the red-deer calf and the remains of the golden plover. When it picked up the plover in its beak there was an odd noise from the camera. The re-wind button was stuck. Damn! I removed three feet of tangled film, joined the ends up again with sellotape, and this time it worked fine. The eaglet performed royally, preened its chin feathers by bending its neck so sharply I thought it would snap, then made a superb wing and talon stretch. Standing on its right leg, it flirted the full metre of one wing right across the nest, then extended its left leg to full stretch before bunching its talons into a fist, swelling out its belly feathers and lifting the foot up into their warmth, so it could doze on one leg.

After an intriguing hour of filming I could see a vast white shawl looming up from the north-west, about to obscure the sun, and a cold breeze blew through the thin shirt under my camouflage jacket. Was this the rain that had been forecast, twenty-four hours late? It *would* come now, when I was at the end of the longest trek, above this dark, yawning, brooding glen. I filmed the eaglet sitting down, yawning, then lying down flat so that unless you had strong binoculars you could look straight at the nest and be sure there was nothing in it.

The clouds shut out the sun and suddenly it was dark and cold, like winter, and I saw thick mist sweeping over the ridges of the great wall. A dangerous situation, for now it seemed I would get trapped in that mist up on these tops. I packed up and set off, almost yelping with pain as my rested sore feet once more took the weight. Up and down endlessly, round and over the cliffs of the buttress again, then down through the thick snagging tussocks to the river, where I drank again. Then I started the awful, weary climb up the nearly sheer 2,000 feet. The pack seemed heavier and heavier, my shoulders ached, and I had to use the monopod with both hands to help my tired thighs and calves. Eventually I struggled over the tops, where I was indeed enveloped in swirling eddies of mist.

I must have gone too far to the east, for after an hour I found myself above the river, of which even the estuary was still two miles from my home. I struck south-west, still at 1,600 feet, and then the thickest part of the mist engulfed me. I plodded on and on, then found myself back above the glen east of the eagles' eyrie. My heart sank. Again I struck south, or tried to. As I tramped, mist swirling, I could recognise no landmarks and felt momentary panic. I could not even trust the wind as an indicator because its direction was so distorted among the constant gullies and peat hags. I went faster and faster, heart pounding, legs aching, the pack as heavy as a tombstone. Then I found myself back on the slopes of Guardian mountain, the mist clearing just long enough for me to see the intermediate glen I always tried to avoid stretching out below. Hell!

I rested a while, trying to figure out the best route. It began to rain. I was exhausted, but still had over three miles to go. I cut back down to the south-east, hoping to find the upper reaches of my own burn, which straggled through the big corrie, and switched my mind on to mental 'Automatic', only caring about one step at a time. It was impossible to achieve any kind of rhythm. The steeps were like a harsh staircase where every step was unlike the one before, each twisting to right or left or forward, and each capable of breaking an ankle under such a weight when one was tired. Finally I reached the burn. If the mist thickened any more at least I could get home – if only my legs would keep going.

Now a few golden plovers landed on rocks nearby, uttering mournful '*klooee*' notes, the very epitome of upland loneliness. I found a bright eggshell, fawn with superb black markings, showing that one nest had succeeded anyway. The sight cheered me a little. Plod, plod, plod – trying to conserve my remaining strength yet not be caught by oncoming darkness, slowly the mist receded behind me and suddenly I was looking down the last steeps above the cottage. These were now the worst of all, each step such agony on my sore feet that I slid down every slope I could on my backside. I felt as if my heels had parted from their covering flesh. The last half-mile was torture. After trekking fifteen hard mountain miles up and down some 12,000 feet with 48 lbs on my back, I reached home in the gathering dusk. As I washed my painful feet, I was amazed to find no blisters at all; they were just inflamed and sore on all their edges.

Never again, I swore to myself, yet the relief I felt that the fearsome trek was over was now matched by my joy that yet again Atalanta had succeeded in rearing her eaglet.

A final check of the peregrine falcons' nest revealed both fully fledged youngsters, perched on trees near their ledge. As I watched, one flew off making high breathy calls. Then the second chased after it and made as if to sink its talons into the other's back before both landed again on separate ledges. It seemed a playful gesture, as if the rear one was just practising. Both had softer plumage, rosier in the sunlight and with fluffier chests than the adults. It was good to know the peregrines had again raised two youngsters to flying stage.

After a restful day at my desk, I climbed up to Juno's eyrie on July 3 and sneaked a look through the heather near the hide. The eaglet was standing bolt upright on the edge of the nest beside a dead grouse, her wing tags showing up like blazer badges. She was ready to fly. Not wanting to risk scaring her off prematurely, I did not go into the hide.

On July 7 Juno's nest looked empty. To make sure the eaglet was not just lying down I climbed carefully above the eyrie and looked down into the nest. There were raven remains and a ptarmigan's wing below it, but, thank heaven, the eaglet had flown just when I predicted it would. I filmed some panning sequences to and from the nest, took down the hide and by towing it behind from a rope round my waist, brought it down to the boat and then home.

So yet another season of recording the breeding successes and failures of three of our rarest and most magnificent birds drew to a close. I was sure it would be my last, for every time I recalled that horrendous killer trek I could not suppress an involuntary shudder. I had been lucky to reach home that day.

22 · *The English Eagles*

Just when I felt sure it was time to hang up my eagle boots, I received an intriguing letter from nineteen-year-old Nick Robinson, who lived in North Wales. He told me that he had spent the season as a volunteer with the R.S.P.B., which has wardened and monitored the breeding success of the only two pairs of golden eagles to nest in England for a century, since the first pair had begun nesting in the Lake District in 1969. So keen was his interest that even when the breeding season was over, he still journeyed to the Lakes at least once a month from his Welsh home, hoping for distant glimpses of the great birds flying. He said he had read my *Golden Eagle Years* and thought it the best of all the eagle books he had been able to find. He now wanted to meet me, and said if I would share my years of eagle lore and show him how to photograph the birds well, without disturbing them, he would show me the Lakeland eagles.

I had not received such a positive and enthusiastic letter for years. I wanted to help him to avoid the kind of mistakes which inexperience makes inevitable. I had toyed with the idea of finding the English eagles for myself, but knowing that no licence would ever be issued to photograph them at the nest, I had never done so. This seemed too fascinating a chance to miss. I checked Nick's credentials with the R.S.P.B., wrote an encouraging letter in reply giving him some basic advice, and on my next trip south in late September contacted him by phone. We agreed to rendezvous in a

219

certain car park, not far from the eagles' valley, on a night in early October.

It was already dark as I drove along the narrow winding lane to the lakeside car park. The drizzle which accompanied me all the way up from the south had been replaced by lashing rainstorms. Trees crashed their crowns in the high winds and bunches of wet twigs and leaves flopped to the ground around me. As the headlights stabbed through the rods of rain, it was clear Nick Robinson's car was not in the car park, nor was any other vehicle either. Well, we could hardly go looking for eagles in this weather. I turned back and camped in a pull-off between cliffs, so that the van would not be buffeted all night by the storms.

I was relaxing with a glass of wine, my stew bubbling on the van's stove, when a car pulled up beside me. A slim young man wound down the window. It was not Nick but thirty-year-old Dave Walker, who had come to tell me that Nick's car had broken down with a damaged cylinder head, and that he would try to get here on the morrow. I soon learned that Dave himself had completed seven seasons as an R.S.P.B. summer warden on the eagle protection project. He had even bought a house nearby, so as to be able to study the eagles not just in their breeding season but every week of the year. I observed the fit form, the steady gaze and clear blue eyes of the hill walker, the self-effacing manner, and knew him to be a true eagle man. I invited him into the van for a drink.

When two eagle enthusiasts get together they always have much to talk about. By the time he left in the early hours, I realised that Dave probably knew as much about England's eagles as any man alive. If Nick did not arrive next day, he had said, he would take me round the eagle valley himself. What luck, I thought, as I slid into bed. That would cut out much laborious work, and what better guide could I have?

I woke to a gorgeous sunny day, the sky that deep aquamarine blue that seems only to come in October. I had a splitting headache! Somehow, we had managed to consume three litres of red wine and a liberal amount of Scotch. Damn fool, I upbraided myself, and was glad we had agreed to make a late start, to allow the sun to warm the land and develop the thermal air currents on which eagles prefer to soar. I gulped down two large mugs of tea, washed up the summer dishes and had the van tidy when Dave arrived at 11 a.m.

It turned out he could not take me today after all but said that, if Nick did not show up, he would come with me round the valley tomorrow. I was feeling none too spry, but I had no intention of just sitting in my van on a superb day like this.

'Well,' I said, 'I've come all this way. I might as well plod about on my own and see what I can find. Where *is* the eagle valley?'

To my surprise Dave pointed across the arm of the lake to a huge mile-long shoulder of a ridge.

'It starts over the far side of that ridge and heads on up for over two miles. There is an eyrie at the top of the valley. The best route to take is along below the ridge to its end, then double back and walk on up the valley bottom.'

After he left, I drove to the car park, noting with some alarm that it was filling up, nearly all the cars containing keen hikers! Were they all looking for the eagles? Cautiously, I chatted to a few of them and discovered that they were all going on a well-known walking route along the high ridges of the valley's horseshoe and seemed to know nothing of any eagles. I did not mention them either. I packed the normal camera gear, not the heavy cine equipment, and set off round the end of the lake along the low muddy path Dave had indicated. I passed several walkers in the first half-mile before deciding not to hike right round below the end of the ridge. It was becoming too low for there to be any eyries on its far side. Instead I turned and climbed straight up the steep side of the ridge to about 800 feet. At the top, I found myself overlooking a sheer cliff and a long drop. I worked my way down round it, and then began heading up along the north side of the great shoulder to the 1,500-foot level.

As the full extent of the valley opened before me I was surprised by its grandeur. Some of the jagged peaks on the skyline were over 2,500 feet high, and below them were many cliff faces, both bare and half-wooded, where there could be eyries. It certainly ranked with some of the hardest glens I had covered for years in Scotland. After half a mile I came to a partly wooded area where the trees made it difficult to keep glassing every face and crag. Suddenly I saw a small dark platform higher up ahead. I stepped back down a few yards, where I could see it clearly, just above a small fallen tree.

It was certainly an eagle's eyrie, but broken down, with blackish stick and twig debris all over it. I guessed it had not been used for some years, but here was Eyrie 1 already! As I lowered the glasses, I saw a large animal ahead, all lit up by the sun where it was standing on a small ridge. I raised them again. It was a red-deer stag, lighter reddish-brown than Highland stags, but not much of a beast. Since I was now having to use my hands as well as my feet to climb, I did not bother to photograph him. He watched me for a while as I scrambled towards him. Then he turned away and joined a few hinds, and they all ran and vanished over the crests ahead.

The sun shone down though I was in cool shade, for which I was grateful, since the terrain at this height was very difficult and I was already drenched with sweat. The steep slopes were covered with long falls of great tangled boulders which had to be negotiated carefully, for one slip could break a leg. I found this Lakeland stone, covered with a thin green veneer of tiny lichen, very slippery under my boots, even when dry. Heaven knows what it would be like in the rain – impassable, I would think, without crampons. My fingers grew sore from the constant clinging, but at least my exertions kept me warm. Between these jagged rockfalls were slopes of scree, millions of small stones that shifted unnervingly underfoot, threatening to send me downhill in a slide of rubble. It was a dangerous and strenuous route that I had chosen, but the pounding heart soon cleared the alcohol poison from my head and I began to feel better.

After another half-mile, the small trees became sparser. I saw a huge flat overhanging rock projecting like a fang above a small face only four feet high, some 300 feet higher than my route. Knowing that eagles rarely nest in a ground cleft, I made my way up to it. Yes, there was the foundation of a nest, just a few twigs and small branches, under the overhanging rock. Perhaps it represented the nesting attempt of a pair of immatures. Here definitely was Eyrie 2. If they did not know about it already, it would be worthwhile for the R.S.P.B. to keep an eye on it in future.

I clambered down to my original route and glassed all the ridges and faces at the end of the valley, still almost a mile away. Within minutes I located Eyrie 3 in a cleft on a smooth dark rockface! Finding three eyries in so short a space of time was a record for me; how odd it should happen in England. I began to feel I was in some wonderful dream. Sunshine was coming through a dip in the mountains, making the nest look browny-orange in colour. It was a good 1,600 feet high, ranking with the highest eyrie I had watched in Scotland.

I struggled on across the ridges, but always there were more ahead, and the eyrie seemed no nearer. The rockfalls and scree were even worse towards the end. I had to move sloth-slow over the slippery stone, careful not to imprison a foot. By now I had found four old ewe carcasses, white bones scattered amid the rocky tombs, where the sheep had perished in winter. Sheep carrion must be a good source of eagle food in this valley. As I scrambled upwards, I realised the sun was sinking behind the hills. I had just taken two telephoto shots of the eyrie, before the light left it, when a male eagle came over a shallow gully high ahead, circled twice before I could get on to him, and then went back again.

Climbing higher, so that I could come down to the eyrie from far above it, I saw the male eagle flying over again. This time he kept going and beat past me like a great buzzard, just sixty yards from my head. I got the camera out and took two pictures of him, one showing his outer pinions spread like fingers, as he went over the ridges below which I was climbing. Wonderful! He seemed quite a small male, dark against the sky, until the sun's rays struck him as he soared over the peaks, showing him to be a light glowing golden beige.

I descended the steep shoulder opposite the eyrie and found two perfect places for hides, from which I could see right down into the nest. What a place, better than any I had known in Scotland! But it was no use indulging in such fanciful notions. While it would be easy enough to work here without disturbing the eagles, especially when any chick was three weeks old and the adults were away hunting, I would never get a licence for what were, after all, England's rarest breeding birds.

As I stood there, large ravens kept wafting out from behind the ridges above me, each one momentarily looking like a small eagle before my eye focus became exact. The skyline here contained several sharp isolated rocks that at first looked like perched eagles watching me. I had just photographed the eyrie cliff with the standard lens (a picture I would never publish because I would not want to give away the exact site to hikers) when I heard a sudden scuttering sound ahead. A large fox with a white tip to its tail, which had probably just picked up my scent, shot from behind a boulder and bounded slowly upwards, working its way along the top of the sheer cliffs above the eyrie. I just had time to focus and click off a shot before it disappeared over the top.

The descent down from the nest towards the valley floor was tough and steep, slippery green turf making it almost as exhausting as parts of the killer trek. Finally the ground levelled out and I began to plod back, keeping high enough to avoid the marshes and bogs lining the beck that wound through the valley to the lake. Human heads and figures with bright red, orange or blue backpacks kept appearing and disappearing on the ridges of the great horseshoe round the valley, like non-precious gems on a giant brooch. To nest inside such a popular walking route, these eagles had to be fairly tolerant of human presence.

It soon became clear there were no eyries in the fewer smooth high rockfaces on the far side of the valley, which were still being lit up by the sun. Even though my eyes began to ache from the hours of intense scrutiny through the binoculars, I kept glassing all the ridges and faces under which I had walked earlier, despite the diminishing light. A mile farther along, I suddenly spotted Eyrie 4!

It was a huge grey nest, five feet across or more, on a jutting crag, with a small tree growing in front of it, rather like Atalanta's Eyrie 28. It was a good 1,800 feet up, and the great cliffs all around it were sheer. I would not like to have to work that one. Yet the excitement I was now feeling took me back to the first days of trekking after eagles in Scotland, when every mountain was new and ahead lay only challenge and discovery. Almost forgotten now were those recent tiring and tedious treks over the same old hills, for the same old eagles. It was all in the mind, I realised, for here I was in new country and far from tired. Despite the hangover, I was feeling inspired.

After a farther hundred yards I had even more reason to be so, for I saw a huge dark eagle fly through a high gully ahead and land in a small tree on the summit of the ridge. I struggled with the pack knots as it launched out again and sailed towards me, but far higher up, gliding along like an avenging shadow past all the cliff faces. It was the female all right, and she looked as big and dark as Atalanta. On she came as I finally managed to extract the camera. I took two photos of her, then one more as she winged out into the blue before vanishing over the shallow gap where the male had first appeared.

I moved on, once more cutting out the long low walk round the edge of the ridge by powering up over the top and down the far side. I tramped back towards my van. Dave Walker had told me that when the first pair of eagles had returned to England, they had nested in a low crag not far from the car park in 1969, but had failed to raise an eaglet. I now glassed a series of grey faces less than half a mile away, and in minutes had located Eyrie 5. It was on a low shelf, so easily accessible that anyone reasonably fit could climb up to it.

Lowering the glasses, I reflected on what a fantastic day it had been. In only five and a half hours I had seen a stag with its hinds, a wild fox, had photographed both male and female eagles, and had located five eyries with no help from anyone. I had never achieved that in Scotland.

I drove back to the camp spot and was brewing tea when a car sped past, screeched to a stop, and reversed to park beside my van. Out climbed young Nick Robinson, with profuse apologies for being late. He had borrowed his father's car to drive up from Wales. He was amazed when I told him I had found five eyries in one afternoon; he knew only of the one I called Eyrie 3, in the far crag. As I cooked supper, he plied me with questions which I tried to answer, for I admired his enterprise and was grateful that he had alerted me to try to find the Lakeland eagles.

Next day – brisk, cold but cloudless again – the three of us set off for the eagle valley with Dave Walker leading the way along his long low route below and round the ridge. This time I carried the full 60 lbs of movie equipment, yesterday's experiences having turned me overnight into an optimist. Dave relieved me of the weight of the tripod and fluid head for half a mile and even Nick, plodding doggedly behind under his own load of small tripod, camera, 500 mm lens and telescope, bore it a farther 300 yards. But we were travelling such an easy route that I took it from him and carried the lot to the far end of the valley and, later, all the way out.

Dave suggested that we should set up near the two dismantled R.S.P.B. hut hides which had been left amid the rocks of an old sheep fold down near the beck. I was surprised when I saw these hides; they had been covered with thick plastic, held down by rocks. I said that if I was in charge of the operation I would have had them completely covered with turf, for they were an eyesore and could easily be seen by the eagles. Dave said he had made this suggestion himself, but he had left the actual nest monitoring operation in late April this year and was now just doing his own studies. The R.S.P.B. method was to erect one hut where the two now stood, to oversee the far crag nest, Eyrie 3, and the other hut farther back to oversee Eyrie 4. Dave confirmed that the broken-down site, Eyrie 1, had been used by the eagles in 1971, when they had raised one eaglet, but not since then. So my surmise there had been correct.

He told me that in recent years this pair had used only Eyries 3 and 4. In 1981 the watching voluntary wardens thought they had seen food brought in and a chick being fed in Eyrie 4, but when they had climbed up a week later, they found nothing in the nest. The eagles failed that year. In 1982 they raised one eaglet in Eyrie 3, and again one in 1983 in Eyrie 4. In 1984 they returned to raise one eaglet in Eyrie 3, and nested there again in 1985 when the eggs failed to hatch. With Dave acting as sherpa and rope man, N.C.C. bird-ringer Jeff Horne, the brilliant observer who had first discovered the return of the Lakeland eagles in the early 1960s, had abseiled down to the nest on May 20 and removed the eggs for analysis, which revealed two two-week-old embryos in the eggs. Bad weather and much late snow, it was believed, had forced the incubating eagle off the nest and the eggs had chilled.

When the two men told me that during their wardening hours they frequently had to call away hikers who were passing too close to Eyrie 3, I said it was just possible that human disturbance had been the true cause of the failure, and added that while the two huts were necessary for preventing hikers from going too close to the breeding nests, they were too far away for the wardens to make exact identification of prey brought in to the nest, and surely this was also important. It might be a good idea, I suggested, to put up my type of invisible observation hide nearer to a breeding nest for this purpose, up high where no humans would find it. Such a hide would also be useful for getting hikers who *were* going close to an eyrie away faster than was possible from the more distant huts on the valley floor. Dave had only known the eagles to use the same eyrie two years running on three occasions, and they had always failed in the second year. We agreed that, as this pair had used Eyrie 3 in 1984 and failed in it this year, they would be likely to use Eyrie 4 next season. If that was so, I said, then these huts should be moved to the overseeing site below Eyrie 4 right *now*, and completely camouflaged with turfs. If the R.S.P.B. wardens waited until Eyrie 4 was actually occupied, moving the huts would cause considerable disturbance to the eagles at a crucial time. Both men thought I should present all my ideas to the officials in charge of the R.S.P.B. project. I did so, a month later. (In 1986 the eagles indeed used

Eyrie 4, and raised one eaglet. One hut was shifted before nesting began and the other was moved at a non-crucial time, one being set near the start of the valley to prevent hikers going too far up it.

It was bitterly cold in the shade of the valley, for not once had the sun appeared over the ridges to the south. The fingers of my left hand had gone white and lost feeling. So had some of Dave's. I was sure the eagles would not appear until the same time as the female had done so yesterday – between 3.20 and 4 p.m. I decided to sit in the sun on the higher land across the beck. Dave reckoned I could be right, but he was sure that the eagles were hunting a grouse moor on a fell three miles away and that they would appear first over the ridges to the north. I leaped the beck and was thawing out a quarter of an hour later when the other two joined me. Dave gave me more information.

Since 1969 this pair had raised ten eaglets in all, while the second, more secret pair, which began nesting in the Lake District in 1975, had raised four. In that time five eagles had been found dead, one in the valley of Pair 1, one in the valley of Pair 2, two were picked up near the motorway, and the fifth was found on a grouse moor. Most were just bones and feathers, but it was believed that two had been shot. This pair often brought stoats into the eyries, and the male seemed to specialise in ring-ousel nestlings. Each year he found four or five nests and brought the nestlings in one by one. Once a badger cub was brought to the nest, but mostly the prey consisted of mice, voles, rabbits and lambs and ewe carrion. Yes, several times Dave had actually seen eagles kill lambs. Once he had been with the farmer who grazed his sheep on this land in a hut hide when they had witnessed such an attack. The farmer had just shrugged his shoulders and taken it philosophically. I said the farmer deserved a medal in that case, and if I were in charge of the operation I would make sure he received some reward for his forbearance.

Half-joking, I said at 3.20 p.m. that the eagles would appear any minute now, and headed back to my movie camera. Dave and Nick followed. We became rather anxious waiting there, and once Dave jumped at the sight of a distant raven. I even briefly mistook a pair of buzzards for the eagles. But fifteen minutes later, as I was staring over the northern ridges, the male eagle came sailing over them.

'There he is!'

The two men turned, saw the eagle, and Nick leaped for his

camera, while Dave had his telescope up in a trice. As we focused our various instruments on the eagle, Dave said:

'It came just at the time you said it would.'

'And right over the ridge *you* said it would,' I rejoined. 'We would make a great team!'

We all laughed and got down to business. The male eagle landed below the skyline and was hard to see, so I did not press the button. Then along came the female and I filmed her landing on a high rock with super back sweepings of her long dark wings. She stood there, pantalooned legs straddled wide, glaring down at us, a glowing bronze statue all lit up by the sinking sun. I stopped filming as it seemed she would wait there a fair while, but then she launched herself to the west. I missed her first two wing beats but got the last two and then filmed her soaring along below the ridges, out into the blue sky, past some more crests gleaming orange in the sunlight, into the blue again. Then I cut the camera as she landed in the dark shadowed gloom at the end of the valley on what Dave called her ledge perch.

'Oh! The male's away now,' Dave cried.

I swivelled back, got on to him and filmed him sailing along the precise route the female had taken, until he appeared to vanish behind the peaks at the valley's end. Dave, watching through his powerful telescope, said he had landed near the female. I could see neither bird through the frosted glass of the movie camera's viewer, but I let the film whir on for a few more feet in case the lens could capture what I could not see, then stopped filming.

'That ranks with some of the best days I've ever had in Scotland,' I said. 'Thank you both very much.'

Sure that I could take no more usable film in the fading light, I packed up the cine gear and tramped out, while the two men stayed on a while longer. Forty minutes after I reached my camp site they joined me saying that indeed no more photos had been possible, for the eagles had stayed where they were, and seemed settled for the night. We talked about the eagles some more and I promised to return. Then Nick drove Dave home and carried on back to Wales.

Later, as I set off towards my home in Scotland, I knew I had enjoyed a fantastic two days with England's eagles. Dave wrote to me at the end of the month to say that my sightings during those two days had been the most anyone had experienced in the valley for the whole of October. I had been extremely lucky. One thing the whole marvellous experience taught me was that, at fifty-seven, I was not quite finished yet. It gave me a great spiritual uplift and new hope for the future.

My feelings of joy were marred when, because I had no electricity, I saw the films I had taken earlier in the year on a projector at Allan Peters's house. I realised then that I would be forced after all to complete one more eagle season at Wildernesse. The light on Juno's north-facing eyrie had been too dim for the really clear sequences I needed for a first-class film. I also wanted smoother and longer footage of the birds flying to and from the nest. Well, dammit, I would attempt one last season. What was more, I would even try to film the king of birds at a deer carcass in the snow, which, as far as I could find out, had never been achieved in Scotland.

I could not help a rueful, ironic, smile. I had to face it – I was still indeed the Prisoner of the Eagles.

Postscript

In the autumn I wrote my report for the Nature Conservancy Council on the visits paid to nests and the breeding success of the eagles, divers and peregrines. I also produced the usual full report on the prey brought into eagles' nests for Jeff Watson and the eagle survey. As I went through my diaries I was surprised to find I had clocked up 840 hours in eagle hides, and about five times as many miles on foot-treks over the years, just to study the king of birds. Jeff again put in for £100 to cover my travel costs and I was grateful to receive the sum, small though it was.

I did not feel too guilty about accepting the £300 I had received over the last three years when I later read the N.C.C. annual reports which covered those years. They revealed that the survey, which also included a study of the impact of land-use changes in the Highlands on other predatory birds, and was conducted in the field by Jeff Watson and Stuart Rae under the aegis of Dr Derek Langslow of the Chief Scientists' Team, had cost a considerable sum. In Year One the research allocation had been £7,974. In Year Two it grew to £20,197, and in Year Three it amounted to £23,220. There was now talk that the survey would be extended for a further year. For conducting the eagle census, when every potential nesting area was visited, the R.S.P.B. had been allocated £3,000 in Year One by the N.C.C., and £2,000 in Year Two. Nine contract wardens were recruited to augment staff visiting the areas, so the R.S.P.B. also had to dig deeply into their own funds to meet the total cost.

In November I met up with Jeff Watson to hand over pellets and exchange notes. In his west Highland study area, only 5 young fledged this year from the 21 pairs, one better than last year but fewer than the year before when 8 had fledged. He reckoned in a very good year 10 to 12 chicks from the 21 pairs would be the best we could hope for. In the large part of my old area he was studying, Pair 3 raised 1 eaglet, Pair 4 laid eggs but failed, Pairs 5, 6 and 7 did not lay, Pair 8 laid but failed. Although 'my' eagles, Pair 1 (Atalanta) and Pair 2 (Juno) had both raised eaglets this still meant only three had flown successfully from my old ground. Jeff said he was coming to the belief that the reason for the high density of eagles in my region was the large number of sheep on the hills, which provided much winter carrion. I frowned at this, and said that in all the years I had watched eagles at the nest, deer carrion had been a far more frequent item. I had found very little carrion from either sheep or deer this year; but then I had not this year covered the huge amount of terrain that Jeff had done south of my home.

As for peregrines in his study area, Jeff said numbers had risen from 5 pairs in Year One to 11 pairs this year. Other raptors had also done quite well this year, with 5 merlin falcon nests fledging a total of 19 young; and 4 hen-harrier nests had succeeded, with 10 young fledged. One harrier nest had been found by Allan Peters, but too late in the season for me to get a licence. A photo of the female proved that she had been ringed in Orkney ten years earlier and had bred there regularly until three years ago. Now, at ten years old, she had turned up breeding successfully in 'our patch'!

At the end of the year, *British Birds* published a paper entitled 'The Status of the Golden Eagle in Britain', prepared by Roy Dennis, Peter Ellis and Roger Broad of the R.S.P.B. and Dr Derek Langslow of the N.C.C. It is a fascinating document detailing the 1982 census, as well as further field work in a few areas in 1983.

It revealed that a total of 598 home ranges were identified. Of these 511 (85·4 per cent) were occupied by golden eagles; 424 home ranges (70·9 per cent) were occupied by a pair and 87 (14·5 per cent) by single eagles. Other important findings of the census are presented in the Appendix. The British population forms an important part (nearly 20 per cent) of the west and central European population, and nearly 50 per cent of the EEC countries' population (excluding Spain and Portugal, where the eagles belong to the North African race).

The paper identifies the most serious threats to eagles as the continued degradation of the environment and extensive monoculture of exotic conifers. (While the latter may be true in some areas of the Highlands, I must point out, for reasons stated in this book, that the Forestry Commission plantations in my area of the west Highlands have given as much help as hindrance to the eagles.)

The paper concluded, 'An integrated land-use policy for the uplands encompassing agriculture, forestry, nature conservation, hunting and leisure is urgently required.' To which I can only add – hear, hear! Surely, no sensible person today can dispute that so rare and majestic a species as the golden eagle has as much right to exist unmolested in the historical lands of its birthright as any humans or human endeavour.

Eagle Appendix

1 'Eagle Mountain Year' – a new 125-minute VHS video tape

I spent the last four of my years in the Scottish Highlands making a film, *Eagle Mountain Year*, which tells the story of a magical Highland mountain through all four seasons. It shows golden eagles at the nest, their beautiful 'air dances', an eaglet swallowing a complete stoat, and a female eagle hauling a whole deer uphill on her own. Nesting black-throated divers are also caught in sequences never filmed before. The comic, and tragic, sibling rivalry at buzzard nests is included, as well as nesting peregrine falcons and ospreys, pine martens coming in my study window to take food from my hand, stag fights in the autumn rut, even a hunting wildcat. While stocks last, you can get a copy by writing to the address given on the back cover of this book.

2 Eagles' Range, Distribution and Breeding Success

The first two subjects were dealt with fully in my book *Golden Eagle Years*. However, it is necessary for some facts to be recalled, and others up-dated. In Wales the golden eagle survived as a breeding species until the late 1800s – one was found on Snowdon in 1880. There are none breeding in Wales today, although a few sightings have been claimed in mountainous regions. In Ireland eagles ceased to breed after 1912. A single pair returned to nest on the Antrim coast of Northern Ireland from 1953 to 1960, then disappeared.

In England eagles had become extinct as a breeding species by the early 1800s. In the early 1960s, rare sightings of eagles occurred in the hill areas of north-west England. The first pair to reach the Lake District nested in 1969 but failed to raise an eaglet. Since then, up to and including 1993, they have raised seventeen eaglets to flying stage. A second pair began nesting in the Lake District in 1975, in a location kept strictly secret by the R.S.P.B., and raised four eaglets to flying stage before the female died in 1982. A third more secret pair further north raised a chick too in 1992, but they seem to have gone back across the Scottish border. That gives a total of 22 eaglets reared in England since the first nesting attempt in 1969. In that time five eagles have been found dead, and some of the young eagles must have died before reaching breeding age, their mortality rate being up to 70 per cent.

Until the 1982–3 R.S.P.B./N.C.C. Census, Britain's population was estimated at close to 300 pairs. Or, as I put it in my book, 270 pairs plus some 50 or 60 immatures and unattached young adults. The Census revealed that there were 598 home ranges in Britain, all but the two English pairs being in Scotland, and mainly in the Highlands. 511 of these were occupied, 424 by pairs and 87 by single eagles. In 1982 alone, before further field work in 1983, 402 pairs were found to be occupying home ranges. Of these at least 260 pairs laid eggs, and non-breeding by pairs in different regions ranged from 10 per cent to as much as 41 per cent. At least 199 pairs hatched eggs, and 182 of these raised young to fledgeling stage (210 young in all). Mean brood size was 1·15, and production was 0·52 young per home range occupied by a pair. It is interesting that the highest success rate of raising fledged young (63·3 per cent) was in the eastern Highlands, where there is more wild prey available. The lowest (18·2 per cent) was in the northern moors, north of the Moray Firth and east of Loch Eriboll, though the single pair in Orkney managed to raise two young. The success rate in my west Highlands region was 41·3 per cent.

The authors of the Census paper suggest that as there are still suitable areas where eagles do not currently breed in unmolested conditions the Scottish population could reach 600 pairs.

In 1992 the government conducted a second Census, ten years after the first. It proved to be one of the worst eagle breeding seasons in fifteen years, but while the data is still being processed (at time of writing) it is expected that there will be little change from the 1982 total of 424 pairs, although breeding success will have gone down. Disturbance, and occasional deliberate persecution by man, remain the golden eagles' biggest problem, followed by increased afforestation.

3 Prey Brought into West Highland Eyries

(Observed over eight breeding seasons, late April to mid-July.)

SEASON ONE:	Short tailed vole (2)	Red-deer carrion
Hooded crow	Rabbit	Black-headed gull
Hooded crow	Hooded crow	nestling
Rabbit	Red-deer-calf carrion	Fox
Hooded crow	Rabbit	Heron nestling
Raven	Hooded crow	Water vole (7)

SEASON TWO:
Hooded crow
Lamb carrion
Rabbit
Rabbit
Kestrel nestling
Hooded-crow
  nestling
Rabbit
Woodmouse
Red-deer carrion
Hooded crow
Water vole
Red grouse, young
Hooded crow
Rabbit
Red-deer-calf
  carrion
Rabbit
Curlew, young

SEASON THREE:
Lamb
Hooded crow
Rabbit
Red grouse
Lamb carrion
Rabbit
Rabbit, young
Rabbit, young
Golden plover
Rabbit, young
Ptarmigan
Rabbit
Rabbit
Hooded crow
Curlew, young
Red grouse
Wood pigeon
Ptarmigan, young
Rabbit
Short-tailed vole (2)
Red grouse

SEASON FOUR:
Cormorant, young
Red grouse
Ptarmigan
Red-deer-calf carrion
Lamb carrion
Hooded crow
Herring gull
Rabbit
Rabbit
Rabbit
Red-deer-calf carrion
Rabbit
Red grouse
Mallard, young
Ptarmigan
Red-deer-calf carrion
Curlew, young
Red grouse
Short-tailed vole
Red-breasted
  merganser, young
Cormorant, young
Wader, unidentified
Red grouse, young
Sheep carrion

SEASON FIVE:
Rabbit
Rabbit
Hooded crow
Curlew
Red grouse, young
Red grouse, hen
Ptarmigan, young
Rabbit, young
Ptarmigan
Curlew, young (2)
Red grouse
Ptarmigan
Mallard
Curlew
Fox cub

Lamb carrion
Fox cub
Mallard, young
Red grouse
Lamb
Red grouse
Rabbit
Raven

SEASON SIX:
Licences came too
  late for close nest
  observations.

SEASON SEVEN:
Sheep carrion
Deer carrion
Sheep carrion
Heron, adult
Greyhen
Ptarmigan
Hooded crow
Hooded crow
Ptarmigan
Rabbit
Stoat
Greyhen
Red grouse
Wood pigeon
Raven
Lamb (4 legs)
  (doubtful)
Red grouse
Red-deer carrion
Lamb carrion
  (still-born)
Fox cub
Fox
Red grouse
Roe-deer fawn
Red-breasted
  merganser
Raven, young

Red grouse, hen
Roe-deer fawn
Rabbit, young
Roe-buck carrion
Fox cub
Red grouse, young
Lamb, rear leg
  (doubtful)
Raven, young
Rabbit
Red-deer-calf carrion
Red-deer calf, leg
Rabbit
Ptarmigan, young
Ptarmigan (used by
  adults to teach
  eaglet to hunt)
Peregrine*
Kestrel*
Merlin*
Herring gull (4)

SEASON EIGHT:
Red-deer-calf carrion
Red-deer carrion
Hooded crow
Red-deer carrion

Ptarmigan
Raven, young
Roe deer, foreleg
Short-tailed vole
  (2)
Lamb, hind section
  (doubtful)
Ptarmigan
Rabbit
Rabbit, young
Short-tailed vole
Rabbit
Red-deer calf
Stoat, young
Lamb (or young
  goat) leg (doubtful)
Buzzard

SEASON NINE:
Hooded crow
Red grouse
Lamb carrion
  (still-born)
Lamb carrion
Lamb, leg
Greyhen
Red grouse

Lamb carrion
Wood pigeon
Ptarmigan
Rabbit
Lamb
Raven, young
Ptarmigan
Ptarmigan
Hooded crow
Raven, young
Raven
Large bird,
  unidentified
  (looked like
  cock hen
  harrier)
Ptarmigan
Hooded crow
Cuckoo (fledged)
Stoat
Lamb, skeleton
  (doubtful)
Golden plover
Red-deer calf
Red grouse, hen
Raven
Ptarmigan

Discussion: the term 'lamb' is used when it seems certain the eagles actually killed the lamb; the term 'lamb carrion' when they found it already dead; and the term 'doubtful' when there is no clear evidence either way.

It will be noted that in eight years of watching 8 breeding pairs, plus visits to other nests, representing 840 hours of close observations throughout each rearing season, only 4 lambs were definitely killed by the eagles. If, for the sake of hypothesis, we assume 60 per cent of the 'doubtful' cases were also actually killed by the eagles, we have a figure of 3 more = 7 lambs (Bear in mind that 17 per cent or more of all lambs born on Scottish hills die within 24 hours, due mainly to poor ewe nutrition in the winter months, so most lambs taken by eagles are already dead.) Against this highest possible predation of 7 lambs, during some 90 weeks of eagles feeding eaglets, we can set the fact that the eagles also took a total of 6

* Unusual prey recorded by Greg Hunter and Jeff Watson at Pair 3's eyrie near the sea.

foxes. If the sheep farmers' estimate that in Lochaber one fox family kills an average of 8 lambs per season is correct, and these 6 foxes had each raised just two families in its lifetime, the eagles indirectly 'saved' the lives of 96 future lambs. And if only 10 per cent of the cubs from these families also went on to raise families of their own, the figures become even more interesting. Against this highest possible predation figure of 7 lambs must also be weighed the fact that in the eight years the eagles also accounted for 19 hooded crows, 10 ravens, 32 rabbits, 2 herons, 2 red-breasted mergansers, 2 cormorants, 3 roe deer and 3 stoats – all classed as 'vermin' pests depending upon whether one is a sheep farmer, fish farmer, forester or poultry-keeping crofter.

Note: the English eagles do not have the 'normal' food or prey supply of their Scottish counterparts, and take a higher proportion of sheep carrion and lambs. They have been known to take young ring ouzels and even the occasional badger cub, neither of which I have recorded in west Scotland.

4   Heights of West Highland Eyries

Analysis of the figures for 40 eyries reveals an average height of 1,166 feet. Highest nest is at 1,650 feet. I have disregarded two nests at 200 and 300 feet. Both were built by young birds on sea cliffs and are completely non-typical.

Note: average height of the five English eyries is approximately 1,700 feet.

5   Direction Eyries Face

It is popularly believed that eagles nest mainly on north-facing sites, largely to protect their young from direct sunlight. There is not much of that in the Highlands. Analysis of 40 eyries reveals 19 with northerly aspects, 17 with southerly aspects, with 2 facing due east and 2 facing due west.

Note: the English eyries all have northerly aspects.

6   Greenery Used to Freshen Eyries

I can only add one plant to my list in *Golden Eagle Years* – birch.

7 Breeding Success of Ten Pairs of Golden Eagles over 320 square miles of the West Highlands across ten recent years.

Years:	1	2	3	4	5	6	7	8	9	10
Pair 1 (Eyries 1, 18, 19, 27, 28, 33, 39)	E	E	E	E	E2	E	E	F/E	E	E
Pair 2 (Eyries 2, 3, 8, 9, 11, 17, 30, 31, 32, 34, 35, 38)	NB	E	F	PNS	NB	NB	E	NB	E	Fh
Pair 3 (Eyries 10, 13)	E	Fh	E2	E	E	NB	E2	E	E	E
Pair 4 (Eyries 12, 23)	E	E	E	E	Fh	F	Fh	F	F	Fh
Pair 5 (Eyries 4, 5, 16, 20, 29)	Fh	E	E	E	E	NB	E	F	NB	E
Pair 6 (Eyries 6, 7, 40)	F	NB	NB	NB	U	U	F	Fh	NB	Fh
Pair 7 (Eyries 21, 22, 36)	U	U	NB	Fh	U	PNS	Fh	E	NB	E
Pair 8 (Eyries 15, 25, 26)	E	E	PNS	NB	E	U	E	F	F	E
Pair 9 (Eyrie 24)	U	U	U	U	U	U	E	U	U	E
Pair 10 (Eyrie 37)	U	U	U	U	U	U	U	E	NB	PNS

Pair 11?
(Eyrie 14)   ?   E   (This eaglet could have been raised from a
                             new egg laid by Pair 3 after losing their first two
                             eggs after a hill fire. No new pair has been seen since
                             in this area and the eyrie has fallen into disuse.)

E = Eaglet flew; E2 = Twin eaglets flew; F = Failed; Fh = Failed (human cause); U = Unrecorded; PNS = Pair not seen (on territory); NB = Non-breeding.

Note: eyries are numbered in order of their finding but four have been re-numbered since the text of *Golden Eagle Years*. For these, I have used the numbers of eyries then known outside this study area, for the sake of convenience; so that the eyrie numbers cover 1 to 40 in this Appendix.

Summary

(100 nesting seasons). Out of 62 known nesting attempts by 10 pairs of west Highland eagles through ten successive recent years, 42 succeeded in raising a total of 45 eaglets to flying stage. Only 3 pairs raised twin eaglets successfully, one pair (3) achieving this twice. Of the 20 known nesting failures, at least 10 were suspected of human cause. There were 15 known instances of non-breeding recorded among the 10 pairs during the 10 year period. In addition, there were 4 instances where eyries were not used on known home ranges during the period but this has not been attributed to non-breeding because pairs were not seen on the territories during these particular seasons. (Eagles can lose their mates in harsh winters, which is one significant cause.) There were 21 instances of no records being made, due mainly to some home ranges and their eyries not being found until the later years .

Twenty Wilderness Years in the
Scottish Highlands, told in the books of
MIKE TOMKIES

Between Earth and Paradise

The beginning of his extraordinary Scottish odyssey,
revised and with a new introduction (1991). 'There is a
kind of Defoe quality to Mr Tomkies' writing.'
Ian Niall, *Country Life*

A Last Wild Place

His bestseller, commended by the Duke of Edinburgh. 'A
beautiful book about a beautiful place, written with grace
and humility.' *Sunday Times*

Wildcat Haven

'When Mr Tomkies declares his love for this terrifically
bloody-minded feline, I thought it a moment of true
sublimity.' Jan Morris, *The Times*

Out of the Wild

'His empathy with birds and animals is altogether exceptional. Duff Hart-Davis, *Sunday Telegraph*

Golden Eagle Years

'Each observation is as celebration of nature, almost a
mystical experience . . .' Brian Jackman, *Sunday Times*

Moobli

The story of his Alsatian dog. 'By far his best book,
written from the heart by a man who remains true to his
ideals against the odds.' Brian Jackman, *Country Living*

Last Wild Years

'Will remain in the troubled and consoled minds of his
readers.' *The Times Literary Supplement*